Simon Gray

PLAYS TWO

Simon Gray was born in 1936. He began his writing
c̲   ̲ with *Colmain* (1963), the first of five novels, all
̲ ̲ed by Faber. He was the author of many plays for
̲ ̲ radio, also films, including the 1987 adaptation
̲ ̲ Carr's *A Month in the Country*, and TV films
including *Running Late*, *After Pilkington* (winner of the
P̲ ̲ ̲alia) and the Emmy Award-winning *Unnatural
̲ ̲ts*. He wrote more than thirty stage plays, among
̲ ̲ *Butley* and *Otherwise Engaged* (which both
̲ ̲ed *Evening Standard* Awards for Best Play), *Close
̲ ̲y*, *The Rear Column*, *Quartermaine's Terms*, *The
̲ ̲mon Pursuit*, *Hidden Laughter*, *The Late Middle
C̲ ̲es* (winner of the Barclay's Best Play Award), *Japes*,
̲ ̲ *Old Masters* (his ninth play to be directed by
̲ ̲ld Pinter) and *Little Nell*, which premiered at the
The̲tre Royal Bath in 2007, directed by Peter Hall.
̲ ̲ *Nell* was first broadcast on BBC Radio 4 in 2006,
and *Missing Dates* in 2008. In 1991 he was made BAFTA
Writer of the Year. His acclaimed works of non-fiction
are *An Unnatural Pursuit*, *How's That for Telling 'Em,
̲ ̲?*, *Fat Chance*, *Enter a Fox*, *The Smoking
̲ ̲rit̲s*, *The Year of the Jouncer*, *The Last Cigarette* and
Coda. With Hugh Whitemore he adapted his *Smoking
Diaries* for the stage: *The Last Cigarette* was directed by
Richard Eyre in 2009. Simon Gray was appointed CBE
in the 2005 New Year's Honours for his services to
Drama and Literature. He died in August 2008.

For more information please visit
̲ ̲ ̲ ̲ ̲ ̲ ̲ ̲

SIMON GRAY

Plays Two

Otherwise Engaged

Dog Days

Molly

Pig in a Poke

Man in a Side-Car

Plaintiffs and Defendants

Two Sundays

Simply Disconnected

faber and faber

This collection first published in 2010
by Faber and Faber Limited
74–77 Great Russell Street, London WC1B 3DA

Typeset by Country Setting, Kingsdown, Kent CT14 8ES
Printed in England by CPI Bookmarque, Croydon, Surrey

Otherwise Engaged, Two Sundays and *Plaintiffs and Defendants*
first published in *Otherwise Engaged and Other Plays* by
Methuen and Co. Ltd, 1975. *Otherwise Engaged* was also included
in Simon Gray, *Key Plays*, published by Faber and Faber Ltd, 2002

Dog Days first published by Eyre Methuen Ltd, 1976

Molly and *Man in a Side-Car* first published in
The Rear Column and Other Plays by Eyre Methuen Ltd, 1978

Pig in a Poke first published in *Close of Play and Pig in a Poke*
by Eyre Methuen Ltd, 1978

Simply Disconnected first published by Faber and Faber Ltd, 1996

All the plays in this volume except *Simply Disconnected* were also included
in *The Definitive Simon Gray 2*, published by Faber and Faber Ltd, 1992

The right of Simon Gray to be identified as author of this
collection and the works in it has been asserted in accordance
with Section 77 of the Copyright, Designs and Patents Act 1988

A CIP record for this book is available from the British Library

978-0-571-25487-3

2 4 6 8 10 9 7 5 3 1

Contents

OTHERWISE ENGAGED

For Harold
Two summers, 1971 and 1975

Introduction

In the five years after *Butley*, I was working on three stage plays and two television plays, and had completed none of them when I wrote, very quickly, *Otherwise Engaged*. This, as I've hinted elsewhere, was probably written as a briskly snubbing answer to the problems I hadn't yet been able to formulate properly in *Dog Days*. While the hero of *Dog Days* is unable to stop talking, the hero of *Otherwise Engaged* only prefers brevity when he can't have complete silence – or rather a silence filled with music. Everything in the play flows from that simple fact, which can be confusing on the page unless the reader remembers that, though not uttering, the hero would be visible – highly visible, I like to think, on the stage. This treacherous relationship between stage presence and page absence was illustrated by the response of the play's first producer who nearly rejected it on the grounds that there was no main part. What lines the hero had I pared down in rehearsal, then to the bone during our week in Oxford. In previews in London I chipped away at the bone, until we were left with what I fondly assumed was the merest, if not the purest, marrow.

It was suspected in some quarters by the way that as I'd given the hero my Christian name, I'd based his character on my own. The truth is that out of a combination of laziness and a desire to get on with the writing I stuck down the first name that came into my head, with the intention of changing it when I got to the last draft. The reason I didn't finally change it was that, by the end of the writing, Simon Hench seemed to me to have as much right to his name as I to mine.

Now, as to whether *Otherwise Engaged*, or any play I've written, come to that, is any good – there's a passage in my diary *The Year of the Jouncer* that says pretty well all I have to say on the subject:

> There have been a few occasions when I've finished a play – there's been a sort of click that goes right through me, a click of everything, with the last line written, falling into place, of everything being absolutely right, no, perfect is the word, of the play being perfect – it's not a question of it therefore being perfect for other people, audiences and critics might in fact hate it when it's put before them in its perfection, but that isn't the point, whether it's liked or not, the point is that there it is, inviolable, intact, unchangeable, quite distinctly itself and quite distinctly apart from me. I've had this clicking experience four times – with all the other plays I've sometimes had the echo of a click, which is really, I suppose, merely the memory of the experience, and which signifies that though it isn't perfect I can no longer make it any better, time to let go before I begin to make it worse, knowing that I'll always be attached to it in an un-happy sort of way, it'll have the status and future of a partial orphan.

Otherwise Engaged is one of the four plays that clicked. And what still clicks for me is the memory of that first production, thirty years ago. Five years earlier, Michael Codron had produced, Harold Pinter had directed, Alan Bates had starred in my play *Butley*, and here the four of us were again, all of us an age — somewhere between our mid-thirties and our early forties – and no doubt in our prime though we all probably assumed that our prime was really just around the corner, there for the taking when the time was right. From the beginning everything went well, the casting was done in no time, and the rehearsals in London,

4

in the hall of the Chelsea Old Church, were only threatened by the sometimes too much pleasure we all took from them. For instance, there was a moment in the first act which Alan, Nigel Hawthorne and Julian Glover seemed unable to get past without collapsing with laughter; Harold and I and the four other actors, Jacky Pearce, Mary Miller, Benjamin Whitrow, Ian Charleson (straight from drama school, I think) and everyone else in the room joining in – actually hanging on to each other, shrieking and shaking, as if we were in our teens and back at school. Eventually this moment – it was a sentence spoken by Nigel, responded to by Julian – became a genuine obstacle, seemingly insurmountable. Harold became anxious at so much time lost, then impatient, then commanding, then ferocious. The three actors, jittery as the moment approached, kept straining for gravity. One of them, usually Alan or Nigel, would break, the other two would go off, first imploding and then exploding, and then the rest of us, one after the other. It really became quite unbearable for a day or so but, of course, being professionals etc, they finally managed to play the scene with the complete seriousness that might make it funny to an audience, indeed came to forget all about their collapses until the first night at Oxford, when the audience behaved as they themselves had once behaved in the rehearsal room – but now, on stage, locked in their parts and concentrating on each other, they stood in increasingly stiff bewilderment, waiting for the audience to control themselves, for God's sake! so that they could get on with their proper business of being at each other's throats.

At Oxford, for the try-out, Alan's wife, Victoria, came down for a week with the twins, Ben and Tristan, who were about three or four, hyperactive and good-natured, an unusual combination, I think. Antonia Fraser came for part of the second week, and she and Harold made their first public appearance as a couple – they were in the process of leaving their marriages – at a party given by I can't remember which member of the cast, who arranged two large chairs for them in the centre of the room. They had to sit in them for a time out of politeness, looking rather like royals in exile, to be viewed rather than mingled with, until dancing broke out, and Harold began to sing Irish songs in a menacing, gravelly voice. I remember, among many delightful things, the presence of a famous young actress who arrived bra-less in a see-through blouse, and talked, boldly – rather like Davina in the play – on serious political subjects that I couldn't keep my eyes on. There were also lots of people there that evening who had come from London for the night, agents, actors, writers, backers, hangers-on, and, as it turned out, gossip columnists who'd just got wind of the Harold–Antonia situation. There were small, impromptu parties most nights, rehearsals in the mornings, afternoons on punts or swimming in the river, and best and most importantly, full and responsive houses in the evenings. It seems to me now rather like the sort of picnic described somewhere in Scott Fitzgerald, full of the promise of happiness that you subsequently realise is happiness itself.

From Oxford we went to Richmond for a week. All I really remember of it is standing on the balcony of the theatre bar in the evenings and watching the cricket on the green, when I should have been in the theatre, watching the actors and listening to my text. It really was that sort of summer, for me the summer of summers, when nothing could go wrong – although they did, in fact, go slightly wrong when we moved to the Queen's Theatre in London and gave three previews, none of which Harold could attend as he and Antonia were now front-page news, and were being hounded and harried by the press. At the dress rehearsal we stumbled across photographers crouching behind the seats, or lurking behind pillars in the circle, hoping, I suppose, to take snaps of some impossible image – of Harold with Antonia on his lap, directing a half-naked actress in the seduction scene with Alan Bates. Harold realised that if we wanted the play to take centre stage, he'd have to quit the production for a while, so he slipped away after a dress rehearsal to a secret address in the country, where Antonia joined him. In due course the press stopped hiding in the theatre and following the actors, although a man from one of the tabloids turned up at my home in Highgate; he was small and middle-aged, and he had a club foot, possibly fake, which he shoved between the door and the jamb, refusing to move it until I'd given him a paragraph or so of nonsense about Harold's whereabouts. I took on directorial duties for the previews – mainly a matter of reminding the cast of Harold's notes – and we proceeded comparatively unmolested to the opening. At the first-night party I phoned Harold and told him that, as far as I could judge, the performance had gone very well. He told me that Antonia had cooked a stew for their supper, the first stew she'd ever cooked, and it was good. That was on the night of 30 July 1975.

On the night of 1 July last year, *The Old Masters* opened at the Comedy Theatre in London. At the first-night party a producer I knew, Mark Rubinstein, came up to me, and discussed the possibility of a revival of *Otherwise Engaged* – this revival, in fact. As we began to consider casting, I felt an odd blurring sensation – of the original cast of seven Alan is dead, Ian Charleson is dead, Nigel Hawthorne is dead; furthermore Alan's wife Victoria is dead, and one of his twins, Tristan, is dead and furthermore . . . furthermore I suddenly find myself thinking, as I write this, that for the playwright, much more than a play is revived, when one of his older plays is revived.

From a programme note for the revival of *Otherwise Engaged* at the Criterion Theatre, London, 2005.

Otherwise Engaged was first presented by Michael Codron on 30 July 1975, at the Queen's Theatre, London. The cast was as follows:

Simon Alan Bates
Dave Ian Charleson
Stephen Nigel Hawthorne
Jeff Julian Glover
Davina Jacqueline Pearce
Wood Benjamin Whitrow
Beth Mary Miller

Director Harold Pinter
Designer Eileen Diss
Lighting Leonard Tucker

Characters

Simon

Dave

Stephen

Jeff

Davina

Wood

Beth

Act One

The living room of the Henchs' house in London. It is both elegant and comfortable, but not large. Two sofas, two armchairs, a coffee table, a telephone with an answering machine, an extremely expensive and elaborate hi-fi set, and around the walls shelves to accommodate a great range of books (which are evidently cherished) and an extensive collection of records, in which Wagner and other opera sets can be distinguished. Stage left is a door that leads on to a small hall, at one end of which is the front door, and at the other a door which, in its turn, when opened, reveals a passage that goes on to stairs going down to the basement. More stairs lead up from the hall to another section of the house. The house has, in fact, recently been divided into two, so that there is a top flat. Stage right has a door that leads to the kitchen, and, as becomes evident, there is a door that opens from the kitchen into the garden. When the curtain goes up, Simon is unwrapping a new record. He takes it out with the air of a man who is deeply looking forward to listening to it – there are several records, in fact – the complete Parsifal. *He goes to the hi-fi, puts the first record on, listens, adjusts the level, then goes to the sofa and settles himself in it. The opening chords of* Parsifal *fill the theatre. The door opens, left. Dave enters. Simon turns, looks at him, concealing his irritation as Dave wanders into the kitchen, returns, and sits restlessly in the armchair. A pause in the music.*

Dave What's that, then?

Simon gets up and switches off the record.

Simon Wagner. Do you like him?

Dave (*standing up*) No, well, I mean, he was anti-Semitic, wasn't he. Sort of early fascist, egomanic type.

Simon What about his music, do you like that?

Dave Well, I mean, I'm not likely to like his music if I don't like his type, am I?

Simon (*concealing his impatience*) Everything all right? In the flat, that is. No complaints or other urgencies?

Dave No, no, that's all right. Oh, you mean about the rent?

Simon Good God no, I wasn't thinking about the rent.

Dave It's all right if it waits a bit then, is it?

Simon Good God yes, pay us this week's when you pay us last week's – next week, or whenever.

Dave OK. I'm a bit short, you know how it is. Your wife out again, then?

Simon Yes, she's gone to . . . (*thinks*) Salisbury. She left last night.

Dave That girl in the first year came round last night for something to eat. I dropped down to borrow a chop or something, fish fingers would have done.

Simon Would they really?

Dave But she wasn't here, your wife.

Simon No, she wouldn't have been, as she was either in, or on her way to, Salisbury.

Dave So I had to take her out for a kebab and some wine. Then I had to get her to come back.

Simon Ah, she stayed the night, then? Good for you!

Dave No, she didn't.

Simon Oh. You managed to get rid of her, then, instead, well done!

Dave She just left by herself.

Simon Before you had a chance to get rid of her, oh dear, why?

Dave Said she didn't fancy me.

Simon Good God, why ever not?

Dave I don't know. I mean, I asked her if she'd like a screw and she said no. Then I asked her why not, and she said she didn't fancy me, that was why not.

Simon Still, she's left the door open for a platonic relationship.

Dave Yeah, well, then she went off to see something on television with some friend. I haven't got a television.

Simon Well, I'm afraid I can't help you there, nor have we.

Dave Anyway she said she might be going to that Marxist bookshop down the road today.

Simon What time?

Dave About lunchtime, she said.

Simon But good God, lunch will soon be on you, hadn't you better get going? It would be tragic to miss her.

Dave Yeah, well that's it, you see. I'm a bit short, like I said. I mean we can't do anything –

 Pause.

Simon Can I lend you some?

Dave What?

Simon Can I lend you some money?

Dave Yeah, OK.

Simon (*giving him a fiver*) Is that enough?

Dave Yeah. Right. (*Takes it.*) That's five.

Simon Well, I'll get back to my music while you're making your own.

Stephen (*enters, through the kitchen door*) Hello. Oh, hello.

Simon (*concealing his dismay*) Oh, Stephen. This is Dave, who's taken over the upstairs flat. Dave, my brother Stephen.

Stephen Oh yes, you're at the poly, aren't you?

Dave That's right.

Stephen What are you studying?

Dave Sociology.

Stephen That must be jolly interesting. What aspect?

Dave What?

Stephen Of sociology.

Dave Oh, the usual stuff.

Stephen Psychology, statistics, politics, philosophy, I suppose.

Dave We're sitting in at the moment.

Stephen Really? Why?

Dave Oh, usual sort of thing. Well – (*Goes towards the door and out.*)

Stephen What is the usual sort of thing?

Simon No idea.

Stephen (*after a pause*) Well, I must say!

Simon Oh, he's not as thick as he seems.

Stephen Isn't he? He certainly seems quite thick. (*Sits down.*) I'm surprised a student could afford that flat, what do you charge him?

Simon Two pounds a week, I think.

Stephen But you could get, good heavens, even through the rent tribunal, ten times that.

Simon Oh, we're not out to make money from it.

Stephen Well, *he* seems rather an odd choice for your charity, with so many others in real need. Beth's not here, then?

Simon No, she's taken some of her foreign students to Canterbury.

Stephen Did she go with that teacher she was telling Teresa about?

Simon Chap called Ned?

Stephen Yes.

Simon Yes.

Stephen What do you think of him?

Simon Oh, rather a wry, sad little fellow. Bit of a failure, I'd say, from what I've seen of him.

Stephen A failure? In what way?

Simon Oh, you know, teaching English to foreigners.

Stephen So does Beth.

Simon True, but Beth isn't a middle-aged man with ginger hair, a pigeon-toed gait, a depressed-looking wife and four children to boot.

Stephen You know, sometimes I can't help wondering how people describe me. A middle-aged public school teacher with five children to boot. A bit of a failure too, eh? Anyhow, that's how I feel today.

Simon Why, what's the matter?

Stephen That damned interview.

Simon Interview?

Stephen For the assistant headmastership. You'd forgotten then!

Simon No, no of *course* I hadn't. When is it exactly?

Stephen (*looks at him*) Yesterday.

Simon Good God! Was it really? Well, what happened?

Stephen I didn't get it.

Simon Well, who did?

Stephen A chap called MacGregor. And quite right too, as he's already assistant headmaster of a small public school in Edinburgh, very capable, written a couple of textbooks – in other words he's simply the better man for the job.

Simon I don't see what that's got to do with it. I don't know how your headmaster had the face to tell you.

Stephen Oh, he didn't. Nobody's had the face or the grace. Yet.

Simon Then how do you know he's got it?

Stephen It was written all over MacGregor. I've never seen anyone so perky after an interview.

Simon Oh good God, is that all? Of course he was perky. He's a Scot, isn't he? They're always perky. Except when they're doleful. Usually they're both at once.

Stephen If you'd seen him come bouncing down the library steps.

Simon In my experience a bouncing candidate is a rejected candidate. No, no, Steve, my money's on your paddle feet. (*He sits.*)

Stephen Even though my interview lasted a mere half-hour although his lasted fifty-seven minutes? Even though I fluffed my mere half-hour, and before a hostile board? Do you know, one of the governors couldn't get over the fact that I'd taken my degree at Reading. He was unable to grasp that Reading was a university even, he referred to it as if it were some cut-price institution where I'd scraped up some – some diploma on the cheap. MacGregor went to Oxford, needless to say.

Simon Did he? Which college?

Stephen And then another governor harped on the number of our children – he kept saying *five* children, eh? Like that. Five children, eh? As if I'd had – I don't know – five – five –

Simon Cheques returned.

Stephen What?

Simon That's what you made it sound as if he sounded as if he were saying.

Stephen Anyway, there were the two governors manifestly hostile.

Simon Out of how many?

Stephen Two.

Simon Ah, but then your headmaster was on your side.

19

Stephen Perhaps. (*Pause.*) At least until I succeeded in putting him off.

Simon How?

Stephen By doing something I haven't done since I was twelve years old.

Simon (*after a pause*) Can you be more specific?

Stephen You will of course laugh, for which I shan't of course blame you, but I'm not sure that I can stand it if you do laugh at the moment. It was something very trivial, but also very embarrassing. (*Pause.*) You see, the governor who didn't feel Reading was up to snuff had a rather low, husky voice, and towards the end I bent forward rather sharply, to catch something he said, and this movement caused me to fart.

They stare levelly at each other. Simon's face is completely composed.

Simon You haven't farted since you were twelve?

Stephen In public, I meant.

Simon Oh. Loudly?

Stephen It sounded to me like a pistol shot.

Simon The question, of course, is what it sounded like to Headmaster.

Stephen Like a fart, I should think.

Simon Oh, he probably found it sympathetically human, you've no grounds for believing he'd hold anything so accidental against you, surely?

Stephen I don't know, I simply don't know. (*He gets up.*) But afterwards, when he had us around for some of his wife's herbal coffee –

Simon Herbal coffee?

Stephen They paid far more attention to MacGregor than they did to me. I had to struggle to keep my end up. Headmaster was distinctly aloof in his manner – and MacGregor, of course, was relaxed and I suppose a fair man would call it charming.

Simon What herbs does she use?

Stephen What? What's that got to do with it? How would I know?

Simon Sorry, I was just trying to imagine the – the setting, so to speak.

Stephen You know, what really hurts is that I can't complain that it's unfair. MacGregor really is better qualified, quite obviously an admirable bloke. But what I do resent, and can't help resenting, is the edge Oxford gives him – the simple fact that he went there improves his chances – but I suppose that's the way of the world, isn't it? Almost everybody goes along with it, don't they?

Simon Oh, I don't know –

Stephen Of course you know. You subscribe to it yourself, don't you?

Simon Certainly not. Why should I?

Stephen Because you went to Oxford yourself.

Simon Good God, so what?

Stephen Well, how many other members of your editorial board also went there?

Simon Only five.

Stephen Out of how many?

Simon Eight.

Stephen And where did the other three go, Cambridge?

Simon Only two of them.

Stephen And so only *one* of the nine went elsewhere?

Simon No, he didn't go anywhere. He's the Chairman's son.

Stephen I think that proves my point.

Simon It proves merely that our editorial board is composed of Oxford and Cambridge graduates, and a half-wit. It proves absolutely nothing about your chances of beating MacDonald to the assistant headmastership. And it's my view that poor old MacDonald, whether he be Oxford MacDonald or Cambridge MacDonald or Reading MacDonald or plain Edinburgh MacDonald –

Stephen MacGregor.

Simon What?

Stephen His name happens to be MacGregor.

Simon Absolutely. Has no chance at all. Even if they do believe you have too few qualifications and too many children, even if they suspect that your single fart heralds chronic incontinence, they'll still have to appoint you. And if they've been extra courteous to MacDonald it's only to compensate him for coming all the way from Edinburgh for a London rebuff. (*Stands up.*)

Stephen Actually it would be better, if you don't mind, not to try and jolly me along with reasons and reassurances. I shall have to face the disappointment sooner or later, and I'd rather do it sooner – wouldn't you?

Simon No, I have a distinct preference for later, myself. I really do think you'll get it, you know.

Stephen Yes, well thanks anyway. I'd better get back. What time's your friend coming?

Simon What friend?

Stephen When I phoned and asked whether I could come round, you said it mightn't be worth my while as you were expecting a friend.

Simon Good God! Yes. Still, he's one of those people who never turns up when expected. So if I remember to expect him I should be all right.

Stephen You mean you don't want him to turn up? Who is he anyway?

Simon Jeff Golding.

Stephen Oh *him*! Yes, well, I must say that piece he wrote in one of last week's Sundays, on censorship and children – I've never read anything so posturingly half-baked.

Simon Oh, I doubt if he was posturing, he really is half-baked.

Stephen I shall never forget – never – how he ruined the dinner party – the one time I met him – his drunkenness and his appalling behaviour. And I shall particularly never forget his announcing that people – he meant me, of course – only went into public school teaching because they were latent pederasts.

Simon Good God, what did you say?

Stephen I told him to take it back.

Simon And did he?

Stephen He offered to take back the latent, and congratulated me on my luck. That was his idea of badinage. By God, I don't often lose control but I made a point of cornering him in the hall when he was leaving. I got him by the lapels and warned him that I'd a good mind to beat some manners into him. If Teresa hadn't happened to come out of the lavatory just then – she'd rushed in there in tears – I might have done him some damage. I've never told you that bit before, have I?

Simon You haven't told me any of it before, it's very amusing. Tell me, who gave this memorable dinner party?

Stephen You did.

Simon Did I really? I don't remember it. It must have been a long time ago.

Stephen Yes, but I have a feeling your friend Jeff Golding will remember it all right.

The front door slams and Jeff Golding enters left.

Jeff Simon – ah, there you are. (*There is a pause.*) Weren't you expecting me?

Simon I most certainly was. Oh, my brother Stephen – Jeff Golding. I believe you know each other.

Stephen We do indeed.

Jeff Really? Sorry, 'fraid I don't remember.

Stephen A dinner party Simon gave – some years ago.

Jeff (*clearly not remembering at all*) Nice to see you again. (*To Simon.*) Could I have a Scotch, please?

Simon Of course. (*Goes to the drinks table.*) Steve?

Stephen No thank you.

Jeff (*collapses into a chair*) Christ! Christ! I've just had a session at the Beeb, taping a piece with Bugger Lampwith. I've got the goods on him at last.

Stephen Lampwith. Isn't he a poet?

Jeff Not even. He's an Australian. A closet Australian. Went to Oxford instead of Earls Court. Thinks it makes him one of us. Still, I got him out of his closet with his vowels around his tonsils, once or twice. Thrice, actually. (*Laughs at the recollection.*)

Stephen What exactly have you got against him?

Jeff Isn't that enough?

Stephen Simply that he's an Australian?

Jeff They're all right as dentists.

Stephen But could you please explain to me why you have it in for Australians?

Jeff Once you let them into literature they lower the property values.

Stephen Really? How?

Jeff They're too fertile, scribble, scribble, scribble like little Gibbons. They breed whole articles out of small reviews, don't mind what work they do, go from sports journalists to movie critics to novelists to poets to television pundits, and furthermore they don't mind how little they get paid as long as they fill our space. So you see, if there weren't any Australians around, sods like me wouldn't end up having to flog our crap to the *Radio Times* and even the *Shiterary Supplement*, let alone spend Saturday morning interviewing buggers like Bugger Lampwith.

Stephen We've got half-a-dozen Australian boys in our school at the moment. They're not only friendly, frank and outgoing, they're also intelligent and very hard-working.

Jeff Exactly, the little buggers. Hey! (*To Simon.*) Roger's been going around telling people I can't face him since my review of his turgid little turd of a novel. Have you read it?

Simon Which?

Jeff My review – first things first.

Simon Yes, I did.

Jeff Well?

Simon Some good jokes, I thought.

Jeff Weren't there? And what did you honestly, frankly and actually think of his turd?

Simon I haven't read it.

Jeff Didn't you publish it?

Simon Yes.

Jeff Well, if you ask me, the bloke you got to write the blurb hadn't read it either, bloody sloppy piece of crap, who did it anyway?

Simon Actually I did.

Jeff D'you know what it bloody is – I'll tell you what it bloody is – I wish I'd come out with it straight when I wrote about it – it's a piece of – *literature*, that's what it bloody is!

Stephen You don't like literature?

Jeff (*pause*) I don't like literature, no.

Stephen Why not?

Jeff Because it's a bloody boring racket.

Stephen You think literature is a *racket*?

26

Jeff Are you in it too?

Stephen I happen to teach it, it so happens.

Jeff Does it, Christ! To whom?

Stephen Sixth-formers. At Amplesides.

Jeff What's Amplesides?

Stephen It happens to be a public school.

Jeff Does it? Major or minor?

Stephen Let's just say that it's a good one, if you don't mind.

Jeff I don't mind saying it even if it's not. It's a good one. Christ, I can't remember when I last met a public school teacher.

Stephen Probably when you last met me.

Jeff But I don't remember that, don't forget.

Stephen Would you like me to remind you? I'm the latent pederast.

Jeff (*after a pause*) Then you're in the right job.

Stephen (*to Simon*) I think I'd better go. Before I do something I regret. (*Turns and goes out through kitchen.*)

Simon Oh, right. (*Making an attempt to follow Stephen.*) Love to Teresa and the kids. (*Calling it out.*)

Sound of door slamming. Jeff helps himself to another Scotch.

Jeff Seems a real sweetie, what's he like in real life?

Simon Not as stupid as he seems.

Jeff That still leaves him a lot of room to be stupid in.

Simon He *is* my brother.

Jeff I'm very sorry.

Simon Actually, the last time he met you, he offered to fight you.

Jeff Then he's matured since then. Where's Beth?

Simon Gone to Canterbury.

Jeff With her woggies?

Simon Yes.

Jeff Never seem to see her these days. You two still all right, I take it?

Simon Yes, thanks.

Jeff Christ, you're lucky, don't know how you do it. She's so bloody attractive, of course, as well as nice and intelligent. I suppose that helps.

Simon Yes, it does really.

Jeff And she's got that funny little moral streak in her – she doesn't altogether approve of me, I get the feeling. Even after all these years. Christ, women! Listen, there's something I want to talk to you about, and I'll just lay down the guidelines of your response. What I want from you is an attentive face and a cocked ear, the good old-fashioned friendly sympathy and concern for which you're celebrated, O-bloody-K?

Simon Well, I'll do my best.

Jeff Remember Gwendoline?

Simon Gwendoline, no. Have I met her?

Jeff Hundreds of times.

Simon Really, where?

Jeff With me.

Simon Oh. Which one was she? – To tell you the truth, Jeff, there've been so many that the only one I still have the slightest recollection of is your ex-wife.

Jeff Are you sure?

Simon Absolutely.

Jeff Well, that was Gwendoline.

Simon Oh, I thought her name was Gwynyth.

Jeff Why?

Simon What?

Jeff Why should you think her name was Gwynyth?

Simon Wasn't she Welsh?

Jeff No, she bloody was not Welsh.

Simon Well, I haven't seen her for years, don't forget, not since the afternoon you threw your drink in her face and walked out on her.

Jeff And that's all you remember?

Simon Well, it *did* happen in my flat, a lunch party you asked me to give so that you could meet the then Arts Editor of the *Sunday Times*, and you did leave her sobbing on my bed, into my pillow, with the stink of Scotch everywhere –

Jeff Don't you remember anything else about my Gwendoline days, for Christ's sake? What I used to tell you about her?

Simon (*thinks*) Yes. You used to tell me that she was the stupidest woman I'd ever met.

Jeff *You'd* ever met.

Simon Yes.

Jeff And was she?

Simon Yes.

Jeff Well, you've met some stupider since, haven't you?

Simon Probably, but fortunately I can't remember them either.

Jeff So you rather despised my poor old Gwendoline, did you?

Simon Absolutely. So did you.

Jeff Then why do you think I married her?

Simon Because of the sex.

Jeff Did I tell you that too?

Simon No, you told her that, once or twice, in front of me.

Jeff Christ, what a bloody swine of a fool I was. (*Pours himself another drink.*) Well, now I'm suffering for it, aren't I? Listen, a few months ago I bumped into her in Oxford Street. I hadn't given her a thought in all that time, and suddenly there we were, face to face, looking at each other. For a full minute, just looking. And do you know something, she cried. And I felt as if we were – Christ, you know – still married. But in the very first days of it, when we couldn't keep our hands off each other. In a matter of minutes.

Simon Minutes?

Jeff Minutes. Bloody minutes. All over each other.

Simon In *Oxford* Street?

Jeff I'll tell you – I put my hand out, very slowly, and stroked her cheek. The tears were running down, her mouth was trembling – and she took my hand and pressed it against her cheek. Then I took her to Nick's flat – he's still in hospital by the way.

Simon Really? I didn't know he'd gone in.

Jeff They're trying aversion therapy this time, but it won't do any good. He's so bloody addictive that he'll come out hooked on the cure and still stay hooked on the gin, poor sod. Saline chasers. Anyway, I took her to Nick's, and had her, and had her, and had her. Christ! And when she left, what do you think I did?

Simon Slept, I should think.

Jeff I cried, that's what I did. Didn't want her to leave me, you see. I'm in love with her. I think I love her. And since then there have been times when I've thought I even liked her. Well?

Simon Well, Jeff, that's marvellous. Really marvellous.

Jeff Oh yes, bloody marvellous to discover that you want to marry your ex-wife.

Simon But why ever not? It just confirms that you were right the first time. Why not marry her?

Jeff (*taking another drink*) Because she's got a new bloody husband, that's why. In fact not so new, five years old. A bloody don in Cambridge called Manfred. Christ knows why he had to go and *marry* her!

Simon Perhaps he likes sex too.

Jeff According to Gwen he likes TV situation comedies, football matches, wrestling, comic books, horror films and sadistic thrillers, but not sex.

Simon What does he teach?

Jeff Moral sciences.

31

Simon Then there's your answer. Philosophers have a long tradition of marrying stupid women, from Socrates on. They think it clever. Does she love him?

Jeff Of course she does, she loves everyone. But she loves me most. Except for their bloody child. She bloody dotes on the bloody child.

Simon Oh. How old is it?

Jeff Two – three – four – that sort of age.

Simon Boy or girl?

Jeff Can't really tell. The one time I saw it, through my car window, it was trotting into its nursery school with its arm over its face, like a mobster going to the grand jury.

Simon Haven't you asked Gwen which it is?

Jeff Yes, but only to show interest. Anyway, what does it matter? What matters is she won't leave Manfred because of it. She's *my* wife, not his, I had her first, and she admits as much, she'll always be mine, but all I get of her is two goes a week when I drive up to Cambridge – Tuesdays and Thursdays in the afternoon, when Manfred's conducting seminars. In the rooms of some smartie-boots theologian.

Simon (*pacing up and down*) Do you mean Manfred conducts his seminars in the rooms of some smartie-boots theologian or you have Gwen in the rooms of some smartie-boots theologian?

Jeff I have Gwen there. He's a friend of Manfred's, you see.

Simon So Manfred's asked him to let you use his rooms?

Jeff Oh no, Manfred doesn't know anything about it. Or about me. No, smartie-boots seems to have some idea

that it's part of his job to encourage what he calls sin.
Oh Christ, you know the type, a squalid little Anglican
queen of a pimp, the little sod. Turns my stomach. (*Adds
more Scotch.*) Christ, you know, Simon, you want to
know something about me?

Simon What? (*Sinks into an armchair.*)

Jeff I'm English, yes, English to my marrow's marrow.
After years of buggering about as a cosmopolitan
littérateur, going to PEN conferences in Warsaw, hob-
nobbing with Frog poets and Eyetie essayists, German
novelists and Greek composers, I suddenly realise I hate
the lot of them. Furthermore I detest women, love men,
loathe queers. D'you know when I'm really at bloody
peace with myself? When I'm caught in a traffic jam on
an English road, under an English heaven – somewhere
between London and Cambridge, on my way to Gwen,
on my way back from her, rain sliding down the window,
engine humming, dreaming – dreaming of what's past or
is to come. Wrapped in the anticipation or the memory,
no, the anticipation *of* the memory.

Pause.

Oh Christ – it's my actual bloody opinion that this sad
little, bloody little country of ours is finished at last.
Bloody finished at last. Yes, it truly is bloody well
actually finished at last. I mean that. Had the VAT man
around the other day. That's what we get now instead
of the muffin man. I remember the muffin men, I'm old
enough to remember the muffin men. Their bells and
smells and lighting of the lamps – do you remember?
Sometimes I even remember hansom cabs and crinolines,
the music halls and Hobbes and Sutcliffe . . . (*Smiles.*)
Or the memory of the anticipation, I suppose. Stu
Lampwith. Christ, the bugger!

Pause.

Well, Christ – I suppose I'd better go and write my piece. (*He gets to his feet.*) Did I tell you what that cold-hearted bitch said last night, in bed? Christ!

Simon Who?

Jeff What?

Simon What cold-hearted bitch?

Jeff Davina. (*Takes another Scotch.*)

Simon Davina?

Jeff You don't know about Davina?

Simon (*wearily*) No.

Jeff You haven't met her?

Simon No, no – I don't think –

Jeff But Christ, I've got to tell you about bitch Davina. (*Sits down.*)

Simon Why?

Jeff Because she is actually and completely the most utterly and totally – (*Lifts his hand.*)

There is a ring at the doorbell.

What?

Simon Just a minute, Jeff. (*Goes to the door, opens it.*)

Davina Hello, is Jeff here, by any chance?

Jeff groans in recognition and sits down on the sofa.

Simon Yes, yes, he is. Come in.

Davina enters. Jeff ignores her.

Davina (*to Simon*) I'm Davina Saunders.

Simon I'm Simon Hench.

Davina I know.

There is a pause.

Simon Would you like a drink?

Davina Small gin and bitters, please.

Simon goes across to the drinks table.

Jeff How did you know I was here?

Davina You said you would be.

Jeff Why did I tell you?

Davina Because I asked you.

Jeff But why did I tell you? Because, you see, I wanted a quiet conversation with my friend, Simon, you see.

Davina You're all right then, are you?

Jeff What?

A pause. Simon brings Davina her drink.

Davina How did the interview go?

Jeff All right.

Davina What's he like?

Jeff Who?

Davina Bugger Lampwith.

Jeff OK.

Davina What's OK about him?

Jeff He's all right.

Davina Good.

Jeff What do you mean, good?

Davina That he's all right. (*Sits down.*)

Jeff Well, what d'you want me to say? You follow me across bloody London, you turn up when I'm having a private bloody conversation with my old friend Simon, you're scarcely in the room before you ask me whether I'm drunk –

Davina As a matter of sober precision, I did not ask you whether you were drunk. I asked you whether you were all right.

Jeff Then as a matter of drunken precision, no, I'm not all right, I'm drunk.

Davina That's surprising, as with you being all right and being drunk are usually precisely synonymous.

Jeff But now you're here, aren't you, and that alters everything, doesn't it?

Davina Does it?

Jeff I thought you were going to spend the morning at the British bloody Museum. I thought we'd agreed not to see each other for a day or two, or even a year or two –

　There is a pause.

Simon What are you doing at the BM, some research?

Jeff That's what she's doing. On Major bloody Barttelot. Got the idea from *my* review of that *Life* of Stanley – naturally.

Simon Really, and who is Major bloody Barttelot?

Davina Major Barttelot went with Stanley to the Congo, was left in a camp to guard the rear column, and ended up flogging, shooting, and even, so the story goes, eating the natives.

Jeff Pleasant work for a woman, eh?

Simon Major Barttelot was a *woman*?

Davina He was an English gentleman. Although he did find it pleasant work from what I've discovered, yes.

Simon Really? And are you planning a book?

Jeff Of course she is – cannibalism, sadism, doing down England all at the same time, how can it miss? Why do you think she's on to it?

Simon I must say it sounds quite fascinating. Who's your publisher?

Davina I haven't got one yet.

Jeff Is that what summoned you away from the BM, the chance of drawing up a contract with my old friend, the publisher Simon? (*Refills his glass.*)

Davina Actually, I haven't been to the BM this morning. I've been on the telephone. And what summoned me here was first that I wanted to give you your key back. (*Throws it over to him.*)

Jeff (*makes no attempt to catch it*) Thank you.

Davina And secondly to tell you about the telephone call.

Jeff What? Who was it?

Davina Your ex-wife's husband. Manfred.

Jeff What did he want?

Davina You.

Jeff Why?

37

Davina He wanted you to know the contents of Gwendoline's suicide letter.

Jeff (*after a pause*) What? Gwendoline – what – Gwen's dead!

Simon Good God!

Davina No.

Jeff But she tried – tried to commit suicide?

Davina Apparently.

Jeff What do you mean apparently, you mean she failed?

Davina Oh, I'd say she succeeded. At least to the extent that Manfred was hysterical, I had a wastefully boring morning on the telephone, and you look almost sober. What more could she expect from a mere bid, after all?

Jeff For Christ's sake, what happened, what actually happened?

Davina Well, Manfred's narrative was a trifle rhapsodic.

Jeff But you said there was a letter.

Davina He only read out the opening sentences – he was too embarrassed by them to go on.

Jeff Embarrassed by what?

Davina Oh, Gwendoline's epistolary style, I should think. It was rather shaming.

Jeff Look, where is she?

Davina In that hospital in Cambridge probably. And if you're thinking of going up there, you should reflect that Manfred is looking forward to beating you to a pulp. A *bloody* pulp was his phrase, and unlike yourself he seems to use the word literally, rather than for rhetorical effect or as drunken punctuation. I like people who express themselves limpidly – (*to Simon*) – under stress, don't you?

Jeff (*throws his drink at her, splashing her blouse, etc.*) Is that limpid enough for you?

Davina No, tritely theatrical, as usual. But if you're absolutely determined to go – and you might as well because what else have you to do? I advise you not to drive. Otherwise you may have to make do with one of the hospitals en route.

Simon Yes, you really shouldn't drive, Jeff . . .

Jeff turns, goes out, left, slamming the door. There is a pause.

I'll get you something to wipe your shirt –

Davina Don't bother, it's far too wet. But another drink please. (*Hands him her glass.*)

Simon Of course.

Takes it, goes to the drinks table. Davina takes off her shirt and throws it over a chair. She is bra-less. She goes to the large wall mirror, and dries herself with a handkerchief from her bag. Simon turns with the drink, looks at Davina, falters slightly, then brings her her drink.

Davina God, what a stupid man, don't you think?

Simon Well, a bit excitable at times, perhaps.

Davina No, stupid really, and in an all-round way. You know, when I was at Oxford one used to take his articles quite seriously – not very seriously but quite. But now of course one sees that his facility, though it may pass in the Arts pages as intelligence and originality, was something merely cultivated in late adolescence for the examination halls. He hasn't developed, in fact his Gwendoline syndrome makes it evident that he's regressed. Furthermore his drunken bravado quickly ceases to be amusing, on top of which he's a fourth-rate fuck.

Simon Oh well, perhaps he's kind to animals.

Davina (*sitting on the sofa*) To think I thought he might be of some use to me. But of course he's out of the habit, if he was ever in it, of talking to women who like to think and therefore talk concisely, for whom intelligence does actually involve judgement, and for whom judgement concludes in discrimination. Hence the appeal, I suppose, of a pair of tits from which he can dangle, with closed eyes and infantile gurglings. Especially if he has to get to them furtively, with a sense of not being allowed. Yes, stupid, don't you agree?

Simon Did you really go to Oxford?

Davina Came down two years ago, why?

Simon From your style you sound more as if you went to Cambridge.

Davina Anyway, he's nicely gone, you will admit, and four bad weeks have been satisfactorily concluded.

Simon Aren't you a little worried about him, though?

Davina Why should I be?

Simon Well, Manfred did threaten to beat him to a bloody pulp, after all. And it may not be an idle boast. Men whose wives attempt suicide because of other men sometimes become quite animated, even if they are moral scientists.

Davina Oh, I think the wretched Manfred will be more bewildered than belligerent. I composed that fiction between Great Russell Street and here. Of course I didn't know until I met his glassy gaze and received his boorish welcome whether I was actually going to work it through. It was quite thrilling, don't you think?

Simon You mean, Gwendoline didn't try to commit suicide?

Davina Surely you don't imagine that *that* complacent old cow would attempt even an attempted suicide?

Simon Why did you do it?

Davina Spite, of course. Well, he told me he wanted to bring it all to a climax, although he wanted no such thing of course, prolonged and squalid messes that lead least of all to climaxes being his method, so my revenge has been to provide him with one that should be exactly in character – prolonged, squalid and utterly messy even by Cambridge standards, don't you think? *You're* married, aren't you? To Beth, isn't it?

Simon That's right.

Davina I've only just realised she isn't here, is she?

Simon Well, I suppose that's better than just realising she was, isn't it?

Davina I'd like to have met her. I've heard a great deal about you both, you mainly, of course. Are you two as imperturbably, not to say implacably, *married* as he and everyone else says?

Simon I hope so.

Davina And that you've never been unfaithful to Beth, at least as far as Jeff knows.

Simon Certainly never that far.

Davina Don't you even fancy other women?

Simon (*sits in the armchair*) My not sleeping with other women has absolutely nothing to do with not fancying them. Although I do make a particular point of not sleeping with women I don't fancy.

Davina That's meant for me, is it?

Simon Good God, not at all.

Davina You mean you do fancy me?

Simon I didn't mean that either.

Davina But do you fancy me?

Simon Yes.

Davina But you don't like me?

Simon No.

Davina Ah, then do you fancy me *because* you don't like me? Some complicated set of manly mechanisms of that sort, is it?

Simon No, very simple ones that Jeff, for instance, would fully appreciate. I fancy you because of your breasts, you see. I'm revolted by your conversation and appalled by your behaviour. I think you're possibly the most ego-centrically unpleasant woman I've ever met, but I have a yearning for your breasts. I'd like to dangle from them too, with my eyes closed and doubtless emitting infantile gurglings. Furthermore they look deceptively hospitable.

Davina If they look deceptively hospitable, they're deceiving you. (*Comes over and sits on the arm of his chair.*) You're very welcome to a nuzzle.

Pause.

Go on then. And then we'll see what *you* can do.

Simon sits, hesitating for a moment, then gets up, gets Davina's shirt, hands it to her.

Because of Beth?

Simon This is her house, as much as mine. It's *our* house, don't you see?

Davina Fidelity means so much to you?

Simon Let's say rather more to me than a suck and a fuck with the likes of you. So, come to that, does Jeff.

Davina Yes, well, I suppose that's to be expected in a friend of his. He doesn't begin to exist and nor do you.

Simon That's excellent. Because I haven't the slightest intention of letting you invent me.

Davina And what about my Barttelot book?

Simon There I'm sure we shall understand each other. If it's any good, I shall be delighted to publish it. And if you've any sense, and you've got a hideous sight too much, you'll be delighted to let me. I shall give you the best advance available in London, arrange an excellent deal with an American publisher, and I shall see that it's edited to your advantage as well as ours. If it's any good.

Davina That means more to me than being sucked at and fucked by the likes of you.

> *They smile. Davina turns and goes out. Simon, with the air of a man celebrating, picks up the keys and glasses, puts them away. Makes to go to the gramophone, stops, goes to the telephone answering machine.*

Simon (*records*) 348 0720, Simon Hench on an answering machine. I shall be otherwise engaged for the rest of the day. If you have a message for either myself or for Beth, could you please wait until after the high-pitched tone, and if that hasn't put you off, speak. Thank you.

Puts the button down, then goes over to the gramo-
phone, bends over to put a record on. Dave enters.
Simon freezes, turns.

Dave She didn't show.

Simon What?

Dave Suzy. My girl. She didn't show. You know what I'd
like to do now? I'd like to get really pissed, that's what
I'd like to do.

Simon I don't blame you, and furthermore, why don't
you? You'll still catch the pubs if you hurry –

Dave Well, I'm a bit short, you see.

Simon But didn't you have a few pounds –?

Dave Yeah, well I spent those.

Simon Oh, what on?

Dave Usual sort of stuff.

Simon Well then, let me.

Pause.

I've got just the thing. (*Goes to the drinks table, fishes
behind, takes out a bottle of Cyprus sherry.*) Here. Go
on, one of Beth's students gave it to her – it's yours.
(*Hands it to Dave.*) A Cyprus sherry. Nice and sweet.
Now you settle down in some dark corner, with a
receptacle by your side, and forget yourself completely.
That's what I'd want to do if I were you. (*Points him
towards the door.*)

*Dave goes out. Simon turns back to the hi-fi. Voices
in the hall.*

Dave (*opens the door*) Bloke here for you. (*Withdraws.*)

Simon What? (*Turns.*)

44

Wood (*enters*) Mr Hench?

Simon Yes.

Wood Can you spare me a few minutes? My name is Wood. Bernard Wood.

Simon (*as if recognising the name, then checks it*) Oh?

Wood It means something to you, then?

Simon No, just an echo. Of Birnam Wood, it must be, coming to Dunsinane. No, I'm very sorry, it doesn't. Should it?

Wood You don't recognise me either, I take it?

Simon No, I'm afraid not. Should I?

Wood We went to school together.

Simon Did we really – Wundale?

Wood Yes. Wundale. I was all of three years ahead of you, but I recall you. It should be the other way around, shouldn't it? But then you were very distinctive.

Simon Was I really, in what way?

Wood (*after a little pause*) Oh, as the sexy little boy that all the glamorous boys of my year slept with.

Simon (*after a pause*) But you didn't?

Wood No.

Simon Well, I do hope you haven't come to make good, because it's too late, I'm afraid. The phase is over, by some decades. (*Little pause, then with an effort at courtesy.*) I'm sure I would have remembered you, though, if we had slept together.

Wood Well, perhaps your brother – Stephen, isn't it? – would remember me as we were in the same year. How is he?

Simon Oh, very well.

Wood Married, with children?

Simon Yes.

Wood And you're married?

Simon Yes.

Wood Good. Children?

Simon No.

Wood Why not?

Simon There isn't enough room. What about you?

Wood Oh, as you might expect of someone like me. Married with children.

There is a pause.

Simon Well . . . um – you said there was something –

Wood Yes, there is. It's of a rather personal – embarrassing nature.

Pause.

Simon (*unenthusiastically*) Would a drink help?

Wood Oh, that's very kind. Some sherry would be nice, if you have it.

Simon Yes, I have it.

Wood Then some sherry, if I may.

Simon Yes, you may. (*Pours Wood a sherry.*)

Wood My many thanks. Your very good health. I thought you might have heard my name the day before yesterday.

Simon Oh, in what context?

Wood From my girl, Joanna. In your office, at about six in the evening.

Simon Joanna?

Wood She came to see you about getting work in publishing. She's only just left art school, but you were kind enough to give her an appointment.

Simon Oh yes, yes. I do remember a girl – I'm terrible about names – a nice girl, I thought.

Wood Thank you. How did your meeting go? Just between us?

Simon Well, I thought she was really quite promising.

Wood But you didn't make her any promises.

Simon Well, no, I'm afraid I couldn't. What work of hers she showed me struck me as a – a trifle over-expressive for our needs. (*Pause.*) Why, is her version of our, um, talk different, in any way?

Wood She hasn't said anything about it at all.

Simon I see. And you've come to me to find out about her potential?

Wood Not really, no. I've come to ask you if you know where she is.

Simon Have you lost her, then?

Wood She hasn't been home since I dropped her off at your office.

Simon Well, I'm very sorry, but I haven't seen her since she left my office.

Wood I only have one rule with her, that she come home at night. Failing that, that at least she let me know where or with whom she is spending the night. Failing that,

that at least she telephone me first thing in the morning. Could I be more unreasonably reasonable? So before doing the rounds among her pals, from Ladbroke Grove to Earls Court, I thought it might be worth finding out from you if she let anything slip about her plans.

Simon Nothing that I can remember.

Wood She didn't mention any particular friend or boyfriend?

Simon Just the usual references to this drip and that drip in the modern manner. Look, from what one makes out of today's youth, isn't it likely that she'll come home when she feels in the mood or wants a good meal, eh?

Wood I suppose so.

Simon I can quite understand your worry –

Wood Can you? No, I don't think you can.

Simon No, perhaps not. But I really don't see how I can help you any further.

Wood Did you have it off with her?

Simon What? *What?*

Wood Did you have it off with her?

Simon Look, Wood, whatever your anxiety about your daughter, I really don't think, old chap, that you should insinuate yourself into people's homes and put a question like that to them. I mean, good God, you can't possibly expect me to dignify it with an answer, can you?

Wood In other words, you did.

Simon (*after a long pause*) In other words, I'm afraid I did. Yes. Sorry, old chap.

Curtain.

Act Two

Curtain up on exactly the same scene, Wood and Simon in exactly the same postures. There is a pause.

Wood Tell me, does your wife know you do this sort of thing?

Simon Why, are you going to tell her?

Wood Oh, I'm not a sneak. Besides, Joanna would never forgive me. She'd have told me herself, you know. She always does. She thinks it's good for me to know what she and her pals get up to. Do you do it often? (*Smiling.*)

Simon Reasonably often. Or unreasonably, depending on one's point of view.

Wood And always with girls of my Joanna's age?

Simon There or thereabouts, yes.

Wood Because you don't love your wife?

Simon No, because I do. I make a point, you see, of not sleeping with friends, or the wives of friends, or acquaintances even. No one in our circle. Relationships there can be awkward enough –

Wood It's a sort of code, is it?

Simon No doubt it seems a rather squalid one, to you.

Wood So that's why you chose my Joanna, is it?

Simon I didn't really choose her, you know. She came into my office, and we looked at her work, and talked –

49

Wood Until everybody else had gone. You decided, in other words, that she was an easy lay. And wouldn't make any fuss, afterwards.

Simon I also realised that I couldn't possibly do her any harm.

Wood What about the clap? (*Pause.*) I think I have a right to know.

Simon I keep some pills at my office.

Wood So your post-coital period together was passed gobbling down anti-VD pills.

Simon One doesn't exactly gobble them – one swallows them, as one might digestive tablets.

Wood What about going back to your wife, reeking of sex?

Simon What?

Wood What do you do about the stench of your adulteries?

Simon I confess I find this enquiry into method rather depressing. I'd willingly settle for a burst of parental outrage –

Wood And I'd far rather satisfy my curiosity. Won't you please tell me?

Simon Very well. I stop off at my squash club, play a few points with the professional, then have a shower.

Wood But you don't suffer from any guilt afterwards? No post-coital distress, no angst or even embarrassment?

Simon Not unless this counts as afterwards.

Wood So really, only your sexual tastes have changed, your moral organism has survived intact since the days when you were that lucky sod, the Wundale Tart?

Simon Look, are you here because I slept around at thirteen, with the attractive boys of your year, or because I sleep around with attractive girls of your daughter's generation, at thirty-nine? Good God, Wood, I'm beginning to find something frankly Mediterranean in this obsession with your child's sex-life – and mine – after all, let's face it, in the grand scheme of things, nothing much has happened, and in the Anglo-Saxon scheme of things, your daughter's well over the age of consent. That may sound brutal, but it's also true.

Wood Except in one important point. She's not my daughter.

Simon What? What is she then?

Wood My – (*hesitates*) – fiancée.

Simon Is it worth my saying sorry over again, or will my earlier apologies serve? (*Pause.*) But I thought you said her name was Wood –

Wood Yes.

Simon And your name is Wood.

Wood Yes. I changed my name as she refuses to change hers, and won't marry me.

Simon In that case you're not Wood of Wundale.

Wood No, I'm Strapley – Strapley of Wundale. Known as Wanker Strapley. Now do you remember me?

Simon Strapley – Strapley, Wanker Strapley. No.

Wood Well, your brother certainly would. He was known as Armpits Hench. We were two of a kind, in that we were both considered drips – what was the Wundale word for drip?

Simon I really can't remember.

Wood It was 'plop'.

Simon Plop.

Wood Those of us who were called it are more likely to remember it than those of you who called us it. Plop. Yes, I'm a plop, Hench. Whom one can now define, after so many years ploppily lived, as a chap who goes straight from masturbation to matrimony to monogamy.

Simon Oh, now there I think you're underestimating yourself. After all you have a wife, didn't you say, and now Joanna –

Wood I haven't got my wife any more. I doubt if I've got Joanna any more. But it's only appropriate that *you* should be the last common factor in our relationship. The first time I set eyes on her she reminded me of you.

Simon Where was that?

Wood At our local amateur theatricals. Joanna was playing in *The Winslow Boy*. She came on the stage in grey flannel bags, a white shirt and starched collar. She walked with a modest boy's gait, her eyes were wide with innocent knowledge. So did you walk down the Wundale Cloisters, that first year of yours. So I watched you then as I watched her. And there, on my one side, were my two poor old sons, who've never reminded me of anyone but myself. And on the other, my poor old wife, the female plop, who from that second on ceased even to remind me that we shared a ploppy past. The years we'd spent together brooding over her mastoids, my haemorrhoids and the mortgage on our maisonette, watching over our boys' sad little defeats, their failure to get into Wundale, their scrabbling for four O-Levels and then two A-Levels, their respective roles as twelfth man and scorer – they haven't even the competitiveness for sibling rivalry, poor old boys – all seemed, it all seemed such a waste, such a waste.

Simon But still you did succeed, to some extent at least, in breaking free. And you did succeed, to some extent I take it, with Joanna – so not altogether a case for predestination, when you think of it.

Wood Free meals, lots of gifts, little loans by the usual ploppy techniques of obligation and dependence – not that she felt dependent or obliged. She took what I offered and then asked for more. A generous nature. Did she get anything from you?

Simon She didn't ask for anything.

Wood Just as you never asked for anything from those boys – Higgens, Hornby, Darcy.

Simon It's true that Darcy was very kind with his tuck, but I hope I never took it as payment, nor did he offer it as such.

Wood (*pause*) What was it like with Joanna?

Simon Well, it was, um, I'm sure you know – she's a very uninhibited, um –

Wood It was, then, satisfactory?

Simon Well, as these things go.

Wood They don't for me. I'm incapacitated by devotion.

Simon But you live together?

Wood She allows me to share the flat I've leased for her. We have different rooms – I sometimes sit on the side of her bed when she's in it. More often when she's not.

Simon You're obviously in the grip of a passion almost Dante-esque in the purity of its hopelessness. You know,

I really feel quite envious – for you every moment has its significance, however tortured, I just have to get by on my small pleasures and easy accommodations, my daily contentments –

Wood So she actually talks of me as a drip, does she?

Simon The ignorance of youth. Drips have neither your capacity for ironic self-castigation, nor more importantly your gift for the futile grand gesture.

Wood If she comes back, do you know what she'll do? She'll tell me about the boys she's slept with, the adults she's conned, the pot she's smoked. She'll tell me what a good time she had with you on your office floor –

Simon Sofa, actually.

Wood If she comes back. And I'll sit listening and yearning and just occasionally I'll soothe myself with the thought that one day she'll be dead or, even better, old and unwanted and desperate – what I resent most about you, little Hench, is the way you seem to have gone on exactly as you promised you would at Wundale. If life catches up with everybody at the end, why hasn't it with you?

Simon But I haven't got to the end yet, thank God. I'm sure it will eventually.

Wood Sweet little Hench from Wundale, who picks off my Jo in an hour at his office, munches down a few pills, and then returns, without a worry in his head, the whole experience simply showered off, to his wife, who is doubtless quite attractive enough – is she?

Simon I find her quite attractive enough for me. Though taste in these matters –

Wood I'd like to kill you, Hench. Yes – kill you!

Stephen (*enters through the kitchen*) Si – (*Sees Wood.*) Oh sorry, I didn't realise . . . Good God, it is, isn't it? Old Strapley, from Wundale?

Wood The name's Wood.

Stephen Oh, sorry. You look rather like a chap who used to be at school with us, or rather me, in my year. Strapley.

Wood Really? What sort of chap was he?

Stephen Oh, actually, a bit of what we used to call a plop, wasn't he, Simon? So you're quite lucky not to be Strapley, who almost certainly had a pretty rotten future before him. (*Laughs.*)

Wood Thank you for the sherry. (*Turns quickly, goes out.*)

Simon Not at all.

Stephen I hope I haven't driven him off.

Simon Mmmm. Oh no, it's not you that's driven him off.

Stephen What did he want?

Simon He was looking for somebody I once resembled. A case of mistaken identity, that's all.

Stephen Well, if he had been Strapley, he'd hardly have changed at all, except that he's a quarter of a century older. Poor old Wanker Strapley.

Sits down. There is a pause.

Well, Si, you were quite right, of course.

Simon Mmmm?

Stephen I got it.

Simon Got what?

Stephen The assistant headmastership.

Simon Oh. Oh good! (*Pause.*) Goody.

Stephen You can imagine how stunned I was. I was so depressed when I got home, not only because I thought I'd lost the appointment, but because of that friend of yours –

Simon What friend?

Stephen Golding. Jeff Golding. That he didn't even remember me, let alone what I'd threatened to do to him – and I could hear the children quarrelling in the garden, the baby crying in her cot, and when I sat down in the sitting room there was a piece in *The Times* on the phasing out of public schools and private health, lumped together, and it all seemed – well! Then Teresa called out. I couldn't face her, you know how lowering her optimism can be – but I managed to drag myself into the kitchen – she had her back to me, at the oven, cooking up some nut cutlets for the children's lunch – and she said: 'Greetings, Assistant Headmaster of Amplesides.' Yes, Headmaster's wife had phoned while I was here, isn't that ironic? I could hardly believe it. So. I crammed down a nut cutlet –

Simon What was it like?

Stephen What?

Simon The nut cutlet.

Stephen Oh, it was from one of Headmaster's wife's recipes. They're semi-vegetarian, you know.

Simon What did it *taste* like?

Stephen Rather disgusting. But she's going to give us some more recipes if we like this one. Perhaps they'll be better.

Simon But you didn't like this one.

Stephen (*pause*) Aren't you pleased or even interested in my news?

Simon Of course I am.

Stephen In spite of thinking MacDonald the better man? Well, you needn't worry about him, he's been offered a job too. As head of sixth form English.

Simon But you're head of sixth form English.

Stephen Not any more. Headmaster reckons that with my new responsibilities I should step down from some of my teaching. I shall be head of fifth form English.

Simon Ah, fewer hours then.

Stephen Actually more hours, but at fifth-form level.

Simon Ah, less cerebration. That's even better. So . . . (*Loses thread, picks it up.*) So justice has been done to two excellent candidates.

Stephen I shall still be senior to MacDonald, you know.

Simon Isn't his name MacGregor?

Stephen Yes. (*Little pause.*) Thanks, Si. (*Ironically.*)

Simon What for?

Stephen Sharing my triumph with me.

Simon Why don't you – have a drink?

Stephen No, thank you. Headmaster's asked Teresa to ask me to look in after lunch for a celebration glass.

Simon Oh. Of what?

Stephen Pansy wine, I expect, as that's their favourite tipple.

Simon (*after a pause*) Do they make it themselves?

Stephen Headmaster's wife's aunt's husband does.

Simon Does he? (*Little pause.*) What's it like?

Stephen You know what it's like.

Simon No, I don't. What's it like?

Stephen Why do you want to know what it's like?

Simon Because I can't imagine what it's like, I suppose.

Stephen Oh yes you can. Oh yes you can.

Turns, goes out through the kitchen. Dave enters left. He's slightly drunk. There is a pause.

Dave (*swaying slightly*) She's come. She's upstairs. She came all by herself.

Simon Who?

Dave That girl. Suzy. She dropped in for a cup of Nescafé.

Simon That's very good news, Dave. But should you, now you've got her, leave her to have it all by herself. She sounds a highly strung creature –

Dave Yeah, well, the only thing is, I'm out of Nescafé.

Simon Oh.

Dave Well, have you got any, man?

Simon No, I'm sorry, we don't drink it.

Dave Anything else?

Simon Nothing at all like Nescafé, I'm afraid.

Dave What, no coffee at all?

Simon Oh yes, we've got coffee. But we use beans, a grinder, and a rather complicated filter process. Metal holders, paper cones –

Dave That'll do. Is it in the kitchen? (*He moves towards kitchen.*)

Simon Actually, it's rather a precious set.

Dave (*returning*) What?

Simon It's one of those few things I feel rather specially about.

Dave You mean you've got something against lending it to me?

Simon Not at all. The beans are in a sealed bag in an airtight tin –

Dave Oh yes you have. I can tell by your – your tone.

Simon My tone? Oh come now, Dave, that's only one possible gloss of my tone. No, you take the grinder, take the filters, the jug, the paper cones and the metal holders, and the coffee beans which come from a small shop in Holborn that keeps uncertain hours and can therefore be easily replaced with a great deal of difficulty, and don't addle your head with questions about my tone, good God! (*Pause.*) Go ahead. Please. (*Wearily.*)

Dave No thanks. No thank you! Because you do mind all right, you bloody mind all right.

Simon No, I don't.

Dave No, you don't, no, you don't bloody mind, do you? Why should you, you've got it all already, haven't you? Machines for making coffee, a table covered with booze, crates of wine in your cellar, all the nosh you want, all the books you want, all the discs, the best hi-fi on the bloody market, taxis to work every morning, taxis home in the evening, a whole bloody house just for you and your sexy little wife – oh, you don't bloody mind anything, you don't, what's there for you to mind, you shit you!

Simon Now that's not quite fair, Dave. It's not really a whole house, you know, since we converted the top floor at considerable expense and turned it over to you at an inconsiderable rent which you don't pay anyway. But then I don't mind that either.

Dave Course you bloody don't, why should you? You bloody like to run a pet, don't you, your very own special deserving case.

Simon I swear to you, Dave, I've never once thought of you as my pet or as a deserving case. If we'd wanted the former to occupy our upstairs flat we'd have got a monkey, and if we'd wanted the latter we'd have selected from among the unmarried mothers or the dispossessed old-age pensioners. We thought quite hard about doing that, in fact.

Dave Then why didn't you?

Simon Because unmarried mothers mean babies, and babies mean nappies, and crying. While old-age pensioners mean senility and eventual death.

Dave So I salve your bloody conscience without being a nuisance, eh? Right?

Simon Wrong. You salve my conscience by being a bloody nuisance. Your manners irritate me, your smell is unusually offensive, you're extremely boring, your sex-life is both depressing and disgusting, and you're a uniquely ungrateful cadger. But you really mustn't mind, because the point is that I don't, either. You have your one great value, that you run a poor third to recent births and imminent deaths.

Dave I'm not staying – I'm not staying – I'm not staying in the fucking top of your fucking house another fucking minute. You – you –

> *Makes as if to hit Simon. Simon remains impassive. Dave turns, goes out left. Noise of door slamming. Simon closes door left. As he does so, Stephen enters right.*

Stephen It's sugary and tastes of onions. And it's quite revolting, just as you imagine.

Simon Well, I did imagine it would be revolting and probably sugary, but it never occurred to me it would taste of onions. But you can't have come back to report on its flavour already, you've only just left.

Stephen I've been sitting in the car, thinking.

Simon What about?

Stephen You, and your sneers. Oh, I don't altogether blame you, but I wish – (*Sits down, looks at Simon.*) – you'd had the guts to say it outright.

Simon Say what?

Stephen That it's taken me twenty-four years to advance from Second Prefect of Wundale to Assistant Headmaster of Amplesides.

Simon (*sitting down*) But that seems very respectable progress to me. At that rate you should make it to Eton, if it still exists, by your mid-fifties. And as that's what you want, why should I have a word to say against it?

Stephen Nor against the way I'm doing it? My stuffing down nut cutlets, and herbal coffee and pansy wine. And then coming back for seconds.

Simon But you do rather more than eat the inedible and drink the undrinkable. You're among the best Junior Colts football managers in the country.

Stephen You despise my job.

Simon You've a family to support.

Stephen So you do despise my job, and despise me for doing it. Why don't you say it? That's all I'm asking you to do.

Simon But I don't want to say it! I can't remember when you were last as you've been today, or what I said then to make you feel any better. I wish I could, because that's what I'd like to say now.

Stephen The last time I felt like this was eleven years ago, after Teresa had broken off our engagement, and you didn't say anything to make me feel any better. What you did say was that I was well out of it.

Simon Well, as you've been back in it for eleven years, you'll agree that it has little relevance now.

Stephen It had little relevance then, either. As I was desperately in love with her.

Simon Good God, all I probably meant, and I don't even remember saying it, was that if she didn't want to marry you then it was better to be out of it before the wedding.

Stephen Oh no, oh no, all you meant was that *you* were relieved to be out of it.

Simon Out of what?

Stephen Out of having for your sister-in-law a girl you thought tedious and unattractive. And still do. And still do.

Simon Look, Stephen, this is really rather eccentric, even in the English fratricidal tradition. First you hold it against me that I won't join you in abusing yourself, and then you hold it against me that not only did I fail to abuse your intended wife eleven years ago, but won't join you in abusing her now that she is your wife and has borne you seven children –

Stephen Six children.

Simon Nearly seven.

Stephen Nearly six.

Simon Well, straight after the sixth, it'll be nearly seven. (*He gets up.*)

Stephen Teresa's absolutely right about you. She always has been. You're just indifferent. Absolutely indifferent!

Simon In what sense? As a wine is indifferent, or prepositionally, as in, say, indifferent to –

Stephen Imbeciles like Teresa. Go on, say it!

Simon But I don't want to say it.

Stephen Not to me, no. But that's what you tell your clever-clever metropolitan Jeff Goldings, isn't it? That Teresa and I are imbeciles.

Simon I swear to you, Stephen, I've never told a soul.

Stephen Answer me one question, Simon. One question! What have you got against having children?

Simon Well, Steve, in the first place there isn't enough room. In the second place they seem to start by mucking up their parents' lives, and then go on in the third place to muck up their own. In the fourth place it doesn't seem right to bring them into a world like this in the fifth place, and in the sixth place I don't like them very much in the first place. OK?

Stephen And Beth? What about her?

Simon (*after a little pause*) Beth and I have always known what we're doing, thank you, Stephen.

Stephen You think she's happy, do you?

Simon Yes, I do. And let's not let you say another word about her, because I don't want to hear it. Have you got that, Steve? (*With low emphasis.*) *I don't want to hear it.*

Stephen No, I'm sure you don't. I'm sure you don't. The last thing you want to hear is how unhappy she is.

Simon Steve!

Stephen Well, she is! So unhappy that last week she came around to Teresa and sobbed her heart out!

Simon Steve!

Stephen She's having an affair, Simon. An affair with that Ned whom you so much despise. *That's* how unhappy your happy Beth is.

There is a long pause.

Simon With Ned. (*Pause.*) Beth's having an affair with Ned? (*Pause.*) Really? With Ned? Good God! (*Sits down.*)

Stephen It's time you knew.

Simon No it isn't.

There is a pause.

Stephen I had to tell you.

Simon Now that's a different matter.

There is the sound of a door opening left. Beth enters.

Beth Hello. Hello, Stephen.

Stephen Hello, Beth.

Simon (*goes over, gives Beth a kiss*) You're back nice and early, aren't you?

Beth Yes, I got an earlier train.

Simon Ah, that explains it. How was it, then, old Salisbury?

Beth Old *Canterbury*, actually. Much as it ever was, except for the parts they've turned into new Canterbury.

Simon But the Cathedral's still there?

Beth Although the French students were more interested in the new Marks and Spencer's.

Simon And Ned?

Beth Oh, he preferred the Cathedral.

Stephen I really must be getting along. Headmaster will be wondering what's happening to me.

Simon Oh, but first you must tell Beth your news. (*There is a slight pause.*) The assistant headmastership, Steve.

Stephen Oh. Oh yes. I got it.

Beth Steve – how marvellous! (*Comes over, gives him a kiss.*) Congratulations – Teresa must be thrilled!

Stephen Yes, she is. I've had some black moments since the interview, but she was absolutely sure – and old Si jollied me along a bit this morning. It's all a great relief, more than anything. Well, I really must dash – see you both very soon – (*Goes towards the kitchen door.*) Oh, by the way, Si – I was a bit carried away just now, spoke a lot of nonsense, don't know why I said it.

Simon Don't you?

Stephen Yes, well I suppose I meant to hurt, but I didn't mean harm, if you see.

Simon Well then, that's fine, because no harm's been done. I didn't take it seriously.

Stephen Good. (*Hesitates, turns, goes out.*)

Beth What did he say? (*Sits and lights a cigarette.*)

Simon Actually I could hardly make out – he was in a post-success depression, I think, suddenly realising that what he's got can therefore no longer be striven for. He'll be all right the moment he sets his sights on a full headmastership. Or Amplesides is abolished. Triumph or disaster – you know, like a drug. What about tea or coffee?

Beth No, I've had some, thanks.

Simon Where?

Beth On the train.

Simon Oh, then you're probably still trying to work out which it was.

Beth Did you enjoy your Wagner?

Simon I enjoyed some things about it, very much. The picture on its cover for example, its glossy and circular blackness when unsheathed, its light balance – and if the sound is any good it'll be quite perfect.

Beth You haven't managed to play it, then?

Simon Very nearly, very nearly. But what with Dave and Stephen, Jeff and Davina, the odd bod and sod, you know –

Beth Oh, you poor thing, and you'd been looking forward to it all week.

Simon Still, one mustn't snatch at one's pleasures, nor over-plan them, it seems. (*He puts the record away in its box.*)

Beth (*pause*) How was Jeff?

Simon Oh, in excellent form, really. He got drunk, threw his Scotch in his girl's face, dashed off to Cambridge where he's been having it off with his ex-wife, Gwynyth. Did you know Gwynyth, or was she a little before your time?

Beth Isn't it Gwendoline?

Simon Yes, yes, Gwendoline. Anyway, usual sort of Jeff saga, quite droll in its way.

Beth And what's his girl like?

Simon She's got good tits and a nasty sense of humour.

Beth And did she try to get you to bed?

Simon She did.

Beth And how did you get out of it?

Simon Rudely, I'm afraid, as she's on to rather a good book, from the sound of it. Ah well –

Beth Ah well, you can play your records now, can't you?

Simon Oh no. Wouldn't dream of it.

Beth Why not?

Simon Well, for one thing, you hate Wagner.

Beth Well, I'm going to have a bath.

Simon A four-hour bath?

Beth Afterwards I've got to go along to the school – sort out the fares and docket them, that sort of thing.

Simon Ah! Well, in that case –

Simon moves to hi-fi and takes out record. Beth rises, hesitates, and moves towards him.

Beth (*stops, looks at Simon*) Stephen told you, didn't he? About me. At least I hope he has.

Simon Why?

Beth So I shan't have to tell you myself.

Simon You don't have to.

Beth What?

Simon Tell me.

Beth What?

Simon Tell me anything you don't want to tell me. Stephen said nothing of significance about anything.

Beth But you see, I may not want to tell you, but I do want you to know.

Simon Why?

Beth Because there's an important problem we shall have to discuss. And I want you to understand. (*Sits on sofa.*)

Simon In my experience, the worst thing you can do to an important problem is discuss it. You know – (*sitting down*) – I really do think this whole business of non-communication is one of the more poignant fallacies of our zestfully over-explanatory age. Most of us understand as much as we need to without having to be told – except old Dave, of course – now I thought he had quite an effective system, a tribute really to the way in which even the lowest amongst us can put our education (or lack of it, in Dave's case) and intelligence (or lack of it, in Dave's case) to serving our needs. He's done really remarkably well out of taking the metaphors of courtesy literally, as for example when he asks for a loan that is in fact a gift, and one replies, 'Of course, Dave, no trouble, pay it back when you can.' *But* this system completely collapses when he's faced with a plainly literal reply, as for example when he asks to borrow our coffee set, and he's told that it'll be lent with reluctance and one would like him to be careful with it. Weird, isn't it, he can take one's courteous metaphors literally, but he can't take one's literals literally, he translates them into metaphors for insults, and plans, I'm reasonably happy to inform you, to move out at once. So I've managed one useful thing today, after all. When we come to think of his replacement, let's narrow our moral vision slightly, and settle for a pair of respectably married and out of date homosexuals who still think they've something to hide. They'll leave us entirely alone, and we can congratulate ourselves on doing them a good turn. We'll have to raise the rent to just this side of exorbitant, of course, or they'll smell something fishy, but we'll pass the money straight on to charities for the aged, unmarried mothers, that sort of thing, and no one need be the wiser, what do you think?

Beth In other words, you do know.

Simon In other words, can't we confine ourselves to the other words?

Beth What did Stephen tell you, please, Simon?

Simon Nothing. Nothing, except for the odd detail, that I haven't known for a long time. So you see it's all right. Nothing's changed for the worse, though it might if we assume we have to talk about it.

Beth (*long pause*) How long have you known for?

Simon Oh – (*Sighs.*) – about ten months it would be, roughly. (*Pause.*) How long has it been going on for?

Beth For about ten months, it would be. (*Pause.*) How did you know?

Simon There's no point, Beth –

Beth Yes, there is. Yes, there is. How did you know?

Simon Well, frankly, your sudden habit, after years of admirable conversational economy on such day-to-day matters as what you'd done today, of becoming a trifle prolix.

Beth You mean you knew I was having an affair because I became boring?

Simon No, no, over-detailed, that's all, darling. And quite naturally, as you were anxious to account for stretches of time in which you assumed I *would* be interested if I knew how you'd *actually* filled them, if you see, so you sweetly devoted considerable effort and paradoxically imaginative skill to rendering them – for my sake, I know – totally uninteresting. My eyes may have been glazed but my heart was touched.

Beth Thank you. And is that all you had to go on?

Simon Well, you have doubled your bath routine. Time was, you took one immediately before going out for the day. These ten months you've taken one immediately on return, too. (*Pause.*) And once or twice you've addressed me, when in the twilight zone, with an unfamiliar endearment.

Beth What was it?

Simon Foxy. (*Little pause.*) At least, I took it to be an endearment. Is it?

Beth Yes. I'm sorry.

Simon No, no, it's quite all right.

Beth You haven't felt it's interfered with your sex-life then?

Simon On the contrary. *Quite* the contrary. In fact there seems to have been an increased intensity in your –

(*Gestures.*) Which I suppose in itself was something of a sign.

Beth In what way?

Simon Well, guilt, would it be? A desire to make up –

Beth (*after a pause*) And did you know it was Ned, too?

Simon Ned *too*? Oh, did I also know it was Ned? No, that was the little detail I mentioned Stephen did provide. Ned. There I *was* surprised.

Beth Why?

Simon Oh, I don't know. Perhaps because – well, no offence to Ned, whom I've *always* as you know thought of as a very engaging chap, in his way, no offence to *you* either, come to think of it, I'd just imagined when you did have an affair it would be with someone of more – more –

Beth What?

Simon Consequence. *Overt* consequence.

Beth He's of consequence to me.

Simon And *that's* what matters, quite.

Beth What did you mean, when?

Simon Mmmm?

Beth *When* I had an affair, you said.

Simon A grammatical slip, that's all. And since the hypothesis is now a fact –

Beth But you used the emphatic form – when I *did* have an affair – which implies that you positively assumed I'd have an affair. Didn't you?

Simon Well, given your nature, darling, and the fact that so many people do have them these days, I can't see any reason for being *bouleversé* now that you're having one, even with Ned, can I put it that way?

Beth Given what about my nature?

Simon It's marvellously responsive – warm, a warm, responsive nature. And then I realised once we'd taken the decision not to have children – and the fact that you work every day and therefore meet chaps – and pretty exotic ones too, from lithe young Spanish counts to experienced Japanese businessmen – not forgetting old Ned himself – it was only realistic –

Beth From boredom, you mean? You know I'm having an affair because I'm boring, and you assumed I'd have one from boredom. That's why I'm in love with Ned, is it?

Simon I'm absolutely prepared to think of Ned as a very, very lovable fellow. I'm sure *his* wife loves him, why shouldn't mine?

Beth You are being astonishingly hurtful.

Simon I don't want to be, I don't want to be! That's why I tried to avoid this conversation, darling.

Beth You'd like to go back, would you, to where I came in, and pretend that I'd simply caught the early train from Salisbury, and here I was, old unfaithful Beth, back home and about to take her bath, as usual?

Simon Yes, I'd love to. (*Little pause.*) I thought it was Canterbury.

Beth It was neither. We spent the night in a hotel in Euston, and the morning in Ned's poky little office at the school, agonising.

Simon Agonising? Good God, did you really?

Beth About whether we should give up everything to live together properly.

Simon Properly?

Beth We want, you see, to be husband and wife to each other.

Simon Husband *and* wife to each other? Is Ned up to such double duty? And what did you decide?

Beth Do you care?

Simon Yes.

Beth His wife isn't well. She's been under psychiatric treatment for years. And his daughter is autistic.

Simon Oh. I'm sorry. I can quite see why he wants to leave them.

Beth But I could still leave you.

Simon Yes.

Beth But you don't think I will. Do you?

Simon No.

Beth And why not?

Simon Because I hope you'd rather live with me than anybody else, except Ned, of course. And I know you'd rather live with almost anyone than live alone.

Beth You think I am that pathetic?

Simon I don't think it's pathetic. I'd rather live with you than anyone else, including Ned. And I don't want to live alone either.

Beth But do you want to live at all?

Simon What?

Beth As you hold such a deeply contemptuous view of human life. That's Ned's diagnosis of you.

Simon But the description of my symptoms came from you, did it?

Beth He says you're one of those men who only give permission to little bits of life to get through to you. He says that while we may envy you your serenity, we should be revolted by the rot from which it stems. Your sanity is of the kind that causes people to go quietly mad around you.

Simon What an elegant paraphrase. Tell me, did you take notes?

Beth I didn't have to. Every word rang true.

Simon But if it's all true, why do you need to keep referring it back to Ned?

Beth It's a way of keeping in touch with him. If I forgot in the middle of a sentence that he's there and mine, I might begin to scream at you and claw at you and punch at you.

Simon But why should you want to do that?

Beth Because I hate you.

The telephone rings. Simon makes a move towards it. After the fourth ring, it stops.

Simon Oh, of course. I've put on the machine.

Pause.

Beth (*quietly*) You know the most insulting thing, that you let me go on and on being unfaithful without altering your manner or your behaviour one – one – you don't care about me, or my being in love with somebody else, or my betraying you, good God! Least of all that! But

74

you do wish I hadn't actually *mentioned* it, because then
we could have gone on, at least *you* could, pretending
that everything was all right, no, not even pretending, as
far as *you* were concerned, everything was all right, you
probably still think it is all right – and – and – you've –
you've – all those times we've made love, sometimes the
very same evening as Ned and I – and yet you took me –
in your usual considerate fashion, just as you take your
third of a bottle of wine with dinner or your carefully
measured brandy and your cigar after it, *and* enjoyed it
all the more because I felt guilty, God help me, *guilty*,
and so tried harder for your sake – and you *admit* that,
no, not admit it, simply state it as if on the difference
made by an extra voice or something in your bloody
Wagner – don't you see, don't you see that that makes
you a freak! You're – you're – oh, damn! Damn. Damn
you. (*Pause.*) Oh, damn. (*There is a silence.*) So you
might as well listen to your Wagner.

Simon I must say you've quite warmed me up for it.
And what are *you* going to do, have your cleansing
bath?

Beth No, go to Ned for a couple of hours.

Simon Oh dear, more agonising in his poky little office.
Or is that a euphemism for Ned's brand of love-play?
Excuse me, but what precisely has all this been about?
You complain of my reticence over the last ten months,
but what good has all this exposition served, what's it
been for, Beth? Ned's not going to leave his wife, I don't
want you to leave me, you don't even think you're going
to leave me – we have a perfectly sensible arrangement,
we are happy enough together, you and I, insultingly so,
if you like, but still happy. We could go on and on, with
Ned, until you've gone off him. Why, why did you have
to muck it up between you with your infantile agonisings?

Beth Because there's a problem.

Simon What problem?

Beth I'm going to have a baby.

Simon (*stares at her for a long moment*) What? (*Another moment.*) Whose?

Beth *That* is the problem.

> *She goes out. Simon sits in a state of shock. Dave enters left.*

Dave (*stands grinning at Simon*) Well, I worked it out, you'll be unhappy to hear. Suzy put me on to you. She just laughed when I told her the stuff you'd said, she and her bloke had dealings with your type in their last place. You were trying to get me out, that's all. Well, it hasn't worked, see. I'm staying. See. And another thing, Suzy and her bloke are looking for a new place. I said they could move in upstairs with me. Got that? Got that? You won't like tangling with them either. (*Stares at Simon.*) Having a bit of trouble sinking in, is it?

> *Turns, goes out, leaving the door open. Simon remains sitting, dazed. Then he goes to the drinks table, pours himself a small Scotch. Looks at it. Frowns. Adds some more. Stands uncertainly, looks at the telephone, goes over to it. Remembers something vaguely, presses the play-back machine.*

Wood (*his voice*) Hello, Hench, Bernard Wood, *né* Strapley here. I expect by now my little visit has passed entirely out of your consciousness, it was all of an hour ago that I left, and you've no doubt had any number of amusing little things to engage your attention. Your life goes on its self-appointed way, as I sit in my empty flat, my home. I've taken off my jacket, and I've lowered my braces so that they dangle around me – a picture, you might say, of old Wood, *né* Strapley, quite abandoned at the last. Imagine it, the jacket off, the braces down, thinking of you as I speak into the telephone, clasped tightly in my left hand as my right brings up, not trembling too much – Hench – sweet little Hench – and point the gun at my forehead – no, through the – no, I can't do the mouth, the metal tastes too intimate – it'll have to be – picture it – picture it – and as I – as I – Hench, as I squeeze – squee—

Simon switches off the machine, interrupting the message. He sits motionless. Jeff appears in the doorway, left.

Simon (*sees him, gets up slowly*) Ah yes. Jeff. All right, are we then? Get back to – (*Thinks.*) – Oxford, did you?

Jeff I didn't get to the bloody corner.

Simon Oh really. Why not?

Jeff There was a police car, Simon, right behind me, then right beside me, then right on bloody top of me with the cops all bloody over me, breathalysing me, shaking me about, and then down at the station for the rest of it. That's why bloody not. And you tipped the buggers off, friend, Christ!

Simon (*vaguely*) What? What?

Jeff No, don't deny it, don't deny it, please Christ don't deny it. Davina told me when I phoned her. She told me – you tipped them off. Christ!

Simon Oh. (*Thinks.*) That's what you believe, is it?

Jeff That's what I bloody know, Simon.

Simon (*calmly*) What sort of man do you think I am? (*He throws his Scotch in Jeff's face.*) What sort of man do you think I am?

Jeff (*sputtering, gasping*) Christ, Christ! My eyes! My eyes!

Simon watches him a moment, then takes out his handkerchief, gives it to Jeff.

Christ – (*Takes the handkerchief.*) Thanks. (*Little pause.*) Thanks. (*Little pause.*) Sorry. Sorry, Simon. (*Pause, goes and sits down.*) Can I have a drink? (*Pause.*) The bitch.

Simon hesitates, then goes and gets him a Scotch, brings it to him.

Thanks.

There is a pause.

Don't throw me out, eh? I've got nowhere to bloody go, and I don't want to go there yet.

Simon I'm going to play *Parsifal*. Do you mind?

Jeff No, lovely. Lovely.

Simon You sure?

Jeff Christ, yes. You know I adore Wagner.

Simon No, I didn't know that.

Jeff Christ, I introduced you. At Oxford. I bloody introduced you.

Simon Did you really? (*Looks at him.*) Such a long time ago. Then I owe you more than I can say. Thank you, Jeff.

Goes over to the hi-fi, puts on the record. The opening bars of Parsifal *fill the theatre. They sit listening as the music swells.*

The light fades. Curtain.

DOG DAYS

To Ian Hamilton,
in whose *New Review* the play was first published,
my thanks for many other things

Introduction

Dog Days was begun before the final draft of another play –
Butley – was in production, was continued at odd moments
during rehearsals and completed – frequently and variously
– during the next two years or so. It was just one of a number of plays I was working on in an increasing state of
muddle that was eventually like a madness. There were
moments when, nauseated into lucidity by the piles of typescript that filled my drawers, my cupboard, an antique
chest and two pinewood coffins, I swore I'd never write
again; which I would have to amend, as I crouched a few
minutes later at my typewriter, into the more calming proposition that I would merely never finish anything again.

So I went on and on, covering page after page. Charac-
ters from one play would slip into another, change name,
age, occupation and even sex, before either slipping into
yet another play or back into the first. The same passages
of dialogue cropped up in different scenes, in different
plays, sometimes in different scenes in the same play or
plays. At the end of each session I squirrelled the newly
written pages away for tomorrow or next week; for whenever I might be short. I was the Casaubon of show business.

I doubt if I could ever have stopped, if I hadn't had to go
to New York. In the ten days before my departure I wrote
an entirely new and above all freshly conceived piece that
probably differed only in the odd passage here and there
from its first version, dropped it off at my agent's on the
way to the airport, and left him to decide whether to pass
it to a producer or return it to me. Both agent and producer
cabled me in New York, I remember settling into an armchair in the lobby of the Algonquin and toasting their

adjectives – routinely intoxicating – in champagne, before going on to glare, several stages later and through a brandy fog, at their noun; which was 'draft'. As its implications became increasingly distinct, so did my future as a writer. I would never finish anything again. I would never write anything again.

Back in London I was given lunch with my agent by the producer in an expensive Spanish restaurant (a good omen, but not conclusive: an invitation to the Café Royal would, in a sense, have made the lunch unnecessary). A copy of *Dog Days*, that the producer had had retyped and bound (also a good omen) lay between us as we pursued the preliminary courtesies that always run, in these situations, from the first handshake through to coffee. They had both read the play again ('several times', but that was a metaphor) and were prepared to add a few more adjectives to their cabled lists. It seemed to them, too, to be far less of a 'draft' than they had first thought it. 'It was all there.' So much so, in fact, that we must think about a director, and could certainly talk about casting, dates, venues, etc. But perhaps a director first, with whom I could collaborate – if I were 'too close to the script to face it alone' – on whatever needed doing.

What needed doing? Oh, a little work, no more – a revision in the second scene of the first act, did I think? The mildest of personality changes to the central character (a dash of motivation, perhaps) – and, well, a touch of economy and a modicum of expansion – in different places, of course. Certainly nothing more than most plays needed in rehearsal anyway, for, after all, it was from 75 to 95 per cent *all there*. Good.

I took the producer's copy with me when I left – that night I threw it, along with everything I'd written in the two years since *Butley*, out with the other rubbish. Some day I might begin again. But not in my lifetime, as I saw it. At least, I hoped not.

It was extraordinary to be free. In my study now only the usual bottles, books; empty drawers and chests; a clear desk; a typewriter which could at last be put to proper use (abusive letters to friends, relatives and other strangers, for instance). It was as if I had rid myself of an aged and incontinent alter ego. Halved hack to my only self, I could keep things clean.

My agent sent me his copy of *Dog Days*. I tossed it unopened into a chest. The director of the Palace Theatre, Watford, telephoned to arrange a lunch. Over it he reminded me that I owed him a play. It had been promised years before, but he'd tactfully held back until I had nothing left to give. We went to my house and into my study and opened the chest. We met shortly afterwards to arrange a production.

Within two or three months I'd finished two television plays – *Plaintiffs and Defendants* and *Two Sundays* – and a stage play, *Otherwise Engaged*. It is possible that these three pieces evolved out of the unrelated labour that preceded them, but it is far more likely that I embarrassed myself into them at the prospect of *Dog Days* being performed.

My agent sent the two television plays to the BBC, and I hurried *Otherwise Engaged* off to Watford. But the director of its Palace Theatre was by this time passionately committed to *Dog Days*, and would accept no substitute. So *Otherwise Engaged* went to the producer who had talked of doing *Dog Days*, and the Director of the Palace Theatre, Watford, generously agreed to postpone his production until the year after *Otherwise Engaged* had opened in London.

December 1975

Postscript. It was not, after all, to be so easy. I went on behaving badly towards the Watford Palace Theatre and its director during the year that followed the opening of *Otherwise Engaged*, pleading that I wasn't yet up to discussions about a production of another play, with all the concentration it demanded and all the prospects (of casting, rehearsals, etc) it opened out, until he became increasingly cynical about my intentions (while remaining admirably a friend) and went off to the States on a year's visiting scholarship. And that was that. Until some time later a sudden show of interest from the Oxford Playhouse revived my own interest. I agreed to do it there, and to direct it myself. The by-now-habitual reaction followed. Almost at once I dispatched a grovelling message through my agent withdrawing the piece. One of the Playhouse directors came down to London to see me, we talked over lunch, and at its conclusion I agreed to restore the play to him, with the understanding that I shouldn't direct it myself (after such a display of doubt how could I?) and that I shouldn't again change my mind. I shan't. *Dog Days* will open at the Oxford Playhouse in October 1976 – God and the other devils willing; and I shall find out for myself at last what it is precisely I've been dreading all this time.

August 1976

From the Eyre Methuen edition of 1976.

84

Dog Days was first performed on 26 October 1976 at the Oxford Playhouse. The cast was as follows:

Peter Charles Kay
Hilary Gayle Hunnicutt
Charles Richard Wilson
Joanna Emma Williams

Director Gordon McDougall
Designer Saul Radomsky
Lighting David Colmer

Characters

Peter

Hilary

Charles

Three girls called
Joanna

Act One

SCENE ONE

Joanna is standing holding her folio under her arm. She puts it down next to the sofa and tentatively begins to wander around the room. There are sounds of clattering from the kitchen. She wanders over to the desk and looks at the photos. She picks one up. Peter enters from the kitchen with two mugs of coffee.

Peter Only instant, I'm afraid. The trick is to pretend it's not coffee at all, but a quite other beverage. The next trick is to like the other beverage.

Joanna Sorry, I'm being nosy. I can never resist old snapshots – are these your parents, then?

Peter That's right. It was taken in the garden of our house in Bromley, Kent.

Joanna Your dad is a fine figure of a man, isn't he? And I love his woollen cap – is it from the war or something?

Peter Well, actually that's my mother, in her gardening gear. Though you're right, she was a fine figure of a man. That's my father there. On the edge of the picture, as usual. In the fine figure of the little drunk.

Joanna Do they still live there?

Peter No. They're both dead. Killed in a car crash a few years back. And that's me, sitting on his shoulders, to give us both a mite of extra stature. And there's my brother Charlie, lurking between my mother's legs. He's still something of a homebody, with lots of children of his own now. I'm never sure how many, but it works on the opposite system to one's bank account – more than one expected. So there we are – a pretty typical suburban English family, eh? With its normal whiffs of incest, alcoholism and despair. (*He laughs and puts photo on desk.*) I'm so glad we decided to come back here. So much nicer than that dreadful pub, isn't it?

Joanna So you have this place all to yourself then, right?

Peter Right. Oh, except for upstairs. That belongs to someone else.

Joanna Oh. Who?

Peter My – um – landlady.

Joanna What does she do?

Peter What – oh, she teaches English to foreigners. In one of those dingy academies off Oxford Street. And then she has to pick up her little boy from school, so she won't be back for ages, you see. So . . .

He gestures to Joanna to sit on the sofa. She sits on the arm.

Joanna She's married then?

Peter Mmm? Oh yes. Yes, she is. But somehow one never thinks of him as one's landlord.

Joanna Why, what's he like?

Peter Well, rather like most husbands in these parts. Not much on the surface, but probably simmering away, you know, beneath. But a decent enough chap . . . so why don't you tell me about yourself, it's your turn. (*He puts his hand on her knee.*)

Joanna (*getting up*) Oh, there's not much to tell, really. Anyway, I'd rather get straight in and show you my work – I mean, if you're really interested.

Peter Of course I am. Indeed I am.

Joanna Right. (*She opens folio.*) These are just drawings and designs, you know, from my school portfolio – before it struck me to try to get into publishing.

Peter (*getting up and taking folio from her*) I'm so glad it did. (*He turns over drawings.*) Now that is lovely. What a marvellous colour sense you've got. All those greys and reds. By God, you can draw too. That's super. Ah, nudes. I like nudes. The one on the left, though, the chap's a bit fat, isn't he – oh, they're both chaps. What's it for, a homosexual sex manual?

Joanna No, the idea is it's for one of those dieting books. Those blokes are before and after, you see.

Peter Oh, I see. Before looks altogether nicer. I like that. I like that very much indeed.

He puts folio down and grabs her and kisses her.

Joanna (*freeing herself*) Are you the slightest bit interested in my work?

Peter Yes, I am. Indeed I am. I've seen quite enough of it to know you're very talented – in fact I've already made up my mind. We've got a sociologist called Nuzek who delivered his latest book only this morning. On Protestantism and pornography. I'm going to see what I can do to get you the dust jacket. And the paperback cover. If it goes into paperback. Something on the lines of that dieting one might do perfectly. I mean the thin nude could be Protestantism and the fat one Pornography, or the other way around even. I'm pretty sure I can get you lots of commissions.

Joanna In exchange for going to bed with you.

Peter Well, it would have to be the sofa, actually. But we could plump up the cushions . . .

He kisses her again. She punches him. He doubles up in pain.

I gather the idea doesn't appeal to you.

Joanna No.

Peter I see. Anything personal?

Joanna You're married, aren't you? To that landlady of yours!

Peter Yes. So I'm very well trained.

Joanna And that little boy's your son?

Peter Yes but he's very little. If you look straight ahead you can't even see him. (*Little pause.*) You don't sleep with married men, is that it?

Joanna Of course I do. It's just that I like to be asked first. Politely. I don't put out every time somebody just clutches at me.

Peter Oh, I see. Well – in that case – would you do me the honour of accompanying me to the sofa? We've got a good hour.

Joanna No, thank you. Right now I'm interested in getting into publishing and I have to meet someone on the other side of London in an hour. But give me a ring when you have something for me.

Peter I'll do that.

Joanna Good. (*Nods, goes to door.*) You know you're a bit of a prick, aren't you?

Peter (*angrily*) What!

Joanna I said you're a bit of a prick.

Peter Oh. Thank God. I thought you said prig.

Joanna laughs, exits. Peter runs after her, exiting.

(*Off.*) Hey – what's your number?

Joanna, off, very faint, calls out number.
  Lights down.

Lights up. The room full of sunlight. Outside the sound of children's voices at play. Toys and Sunday bits and pieces scattered around the room.
  After a moment, Peter enters, left, in weekend wear and very sloppy. He is smoking. He looks towards the window, winces, goes to the drinks table, pours himself a Scotch, squirts in soda water, turns, goes to the sofa.

Charles (*off, outside the window, right*) Nindy, what a clever girlie, did you do this just for Daddy? Thank you, darling, thank you. Now you go and watch the big ones play football while Daddy takes this in and looks for Uncle Peter.

There is a crashing sound from the kitchen. Peter listens to this, then rolls off the sofa, cupping his cigarette and drink.
  Charles enters, carrying a plastic pot. He goes through and out, left. He is also in weekend wear, but neat, short-haired and springy of step.
  Peter adjusts himself more comfortably, sips from his drink, puffs on his cigarette.
  Sound of tap running, lavatory flushing, left.
  Charles re-enters, carrying the pot. He hesitates, goes to the drinks table, then puts the pot down on it as he squirts himself an enormous soda water. He drains it off and then squirts himself a second glass. Peter coughs and Charles walks over to the sofa, and sees Peter.

Charles What on earth are you doing?

Peter Practising.

Charles Practising what?

Peter Secret drinking.

Charles Oh, I see. Not feeling very sociable, are we?

Peter On the contrary, but it's such a rare feeling I like to savour it on my own. (*Gets up, goes to the window.*)

Charles (*watches him*) I must say, you've been acting very strangely today. We've scarcely seen you except at lunch. Is something the matter?

Peter No.

Charles Frankly, some of your remarks were a bit off.

Peter Really? Probably because I've kept them in too long. Did you know that Alison's joined the boys in football? Is that wise at seven months gone?

Charles Oh, she'll be all right, you know how active she is during her pregnancies. Peter . . .

Peter And between them too, to get to them so quickly. When do you intend to stop exactly? I realise Alison's a practising Catholic, but this'll make six in five years . . .

Charles Four, actually. In six years. As I'm sure you realise. And you also realise, because I've told you often enough, that we both happen to believe in letting them come as they please.

Peter Well, you certainly do please them, from the speed at which they keep coming.

Charles The important thing is that they please us. Anyway, now that you've chosen to raise the subject, Alison and I sometimes wonder what you two have got against having more.

Peter Contraceptives, and they work miracles.

Charles Oh, ha ha. But has it ever occurred to you that it might turn out a little hard on Jeremy himself? He'll be the one that'll have to cope with being an only child.

Peter If I can cope with being an only father, when we need two or three, he can cope with being an only child when we don't need any more. (*He coughs.*)

Charles Something's the matter, isn't it?

Peter With what?

Charles With you. For one thing you're smoking and drinking far more than usual.

Peter Oh, that's quite usual with smoking and drinking.

Charles But Pete, think of your health! I'm sure you would feel much better if you cut down.

Peter Ah, but then I wouldn't have the Scotch and fags I need to help me endure it.

Charles Endure what?

Peter My health. (*Toasts himself.*) And yours. I notice you've cut down again, though. The last time you were here you'd fought your way up to a five a day, wasn't it?

Charles Only because I was under some stress.

Peter What stress?

Charles I was still waiting to hear whether I'd got it.

Peter Got what?

Charles The assistant headmastership at Amplesides.

Peter And did you?

Charles Not only did Alison phone Hilary as soon as I'd phoned her, but before lunch today Alison actually described a sort of informal interview she'd had with Headmaster.

Peter Oh, that was with Headmaster!

Charles Who did you think it was with?

Peter Her gynaecologist.

Charles That was during lunch.

Peter She had an interview with her gynaecologist during lunch . . . ?

Charles Oh, ha ha. She described her interview with the gynaecologist during lunch – I mean during lunch she described her interview – (*Stops.*)

Peter Well anyway, Charlie, congratulations. I know how much you respect that Headmaster of yours. It'll be wonderful to work so closely with him, won't it?

Charles Yes, it will.

Peter He's a great influence over your life, isn't he?

Charles In some things, perhaps. I don't deny it.

Peter How can you, when there's scarcely a decision, large or small, on which you don't consult him – where he leads, you follow, eh?

Charles I wouldn't go that far.

Peter Really? How far has he gone?

Charles It's no good, you won't get at me through Headmaster, you know.

Peter Does he smoke?

Charles He's got far too much sense.

Peter Does he drink?

Charles Yes, he does.

Peter What does he drink?

Charles The odd wine.

Peter That wine you brought along for lunch was odd, was it one of his?

Charles That was a retsina.

Peter Home-made, though, wasn't it?

Charles How on earth would one home-make a retsina?

Peter Exactly as the Greeks do, I should think. By boiling up some tree bark. They're vegetarian, aren't they, Headmaster and wife?

Charles Yes, they are, so what?

Peter And that's why you and Alison have given up meat, is it?

Charles Given up meat?

Peter You've got that smirk on, Charlie.

Charles What smirk?

Peter Your lying smirk.

Charles Lying – what lie, for heaven's sake? Didn't you see me put Hilary's casserole away?

Peter Yes, first into your handkerchief, then into your pocket. You used to employ the same technique with Mummy's Friday-night fish stews – until she asked you to explain why your trousers smelt of haddock.

Charles (*long pause*) Yes, well I do apologise for that. The truth is, as we'd forgotten to warn Hilary that we'd turned vegetarian, and as we realised she'd gone to a lot of trouble to cook for us, we felt it a matter of common courtesy to go through with it. Frankly, we knew the children would more than make up for us. (*Little pause.*) I do hope she didn't notice, though.

Peter Oh, you were as skilful as ever. The funny smile, the elaborate chewing, the dabs at your lips. You may have made her casserole look inedible, but you did look as if you were managing to eat it. Is it still in your pocket?

Charles Yes.

Peter Well, you can chuck it into the garbage now, I won't sneak.

Charles Actually, I'd rather keep it.

Peter Keep it!

Charles Yes.

Peter In your pocket?

Charles For the time being.

Peter (*after a pause*) Oh I see, no cloistered and fugitive virtue for you, eh, Charlie? You like to carry your vice around with you, to fight every moment of the day. A handkerchief full of temptation! I just hope you don't spill it out in front of Headmaster when you have to blow your nose. He might not believe your story.

Charles (*slowly*) Ha. Ha. Ha. I happen to want it for a dog.

Peter You haven't got a dog.

Charles No, but the school has. Alfonso – at least that's what I call him. He's a sort of stray that's always in and out of Headmaster's garden. Somebody's got to feed him.

Peter And you've chosen my wife? Why can't Headmaster do the job? It's his garden. Or doesn't he like animals?

Charles I'm sure he loves them. And I know his wife does. So I expect they do feed him. But I also expect he'd be grateful for any little titbits. Does that clear that up? There can't be any further questions, Pete – now that you've managed to embarrass me, after all.

Peter Well, just one.

Charles I don't think I want to hear it.

Peter OK.

He goes and stands by the window. Charles stands uncertainly, then goes to the soda water, takes a swift draught from his glass, looks at Peter.

Charles All right, what is it?

Peter Mmmm?

Charles Your last question.

Peter Mmm. Oh yes. Did you give up meat before your appointment as Assistant, to ingratiate yourself with Headmaster? Or afterwards, on orders from Headmaster? Or did you do it during the interview with Headmaster, in a dramatic renunciation?

Charles I didn't give up, or have to give up, anything to get the assistantship. Alison and I merely observed how well Headmaster and his wife looked on their regimen and drew the same conclusion. Which would doubtless have escaped you. Furthermore, far from feeling ashamed of it, I don't mind telling you that I, personally, feel absolutely marvellous for it. As if I were fifteen again!

Peter I'm sorry to hear that. You were particularly ghastly at fifteen. Even Mummy thought so.

Charles At least I see the world properly, in its vivid details. And most of what I see, I like. What do you see at the moment, Pete?

Peter Nothing much to like, I admit, Charles. (*Little pause.*) Actually, from my recollection of Alison's gynaecological anecdotes, delivered during the lunch she was presumably pocketing in her pregnancy trousers, you don't have to give up anything to get the vivid details, Charles. As long, that is, as you don't give up your Alison.

Charles Right! That does it! I've spent the whole morning trying to overlook your bloody nasty remarks –

Peter Spoilsport.

Charles But don't worry, I'm not going to overlook that one. You jeer at my feeling fifteen, but you have gone right back to the nursery to insult my wife like that.

Peter You didn't have a wife like that in the nursery, Charlie. Or are you about to spring into the Freudian open by naming Mummy?

Charles You little – (*Pulls himself together, and with dignity.*) If it weren't for Hilary's feelings, and Jeremy's – I wouldn't set foot in this house again.

Turns, goes towards exit kitchen, right.

Peter Those are my own sentiments exactly.

As Charles, unhearing, exits, he collapses on sofa.

There is a lighting change, to suggest time passing. Peter turns on lights. Much activity from the kitchen, right. Hilary enters. Looks at Peter, and as she begins to clear up toys and bits and pieces:

Hilary Jeremy is in bed, I trust.

Peter (*not stirring*) Hours ago.

Hilary And did you bother to get him to read to you?

Peter Until we both realised he still couldn't.

Hilary Of course he can.

Peter Then we have a wunderkind who can read with his eyes shut. My own view is that he was reciting.

Hilary You probably made him nervous.

Peter Not as nervous as he made me. 'This is Janet. This is John. That is Janet. That is John.' (*In a sing-song.*) I thought he was trying to put me under a spell. I'd learnt to read by four. So had you. So had everybody in our day, except Charlie, and even he made it by five and a half.

Hilary *And* except those who never learnt to read. Because they were never taught.

Peter Oh, I recognise the modern system is more democratic. Now everybody gets taught but nobody reads.

Hilary What would you know about the modern system? You don't even go to the lectures the school lays on to explain it.

Peter I went to the first, if you remember, in which case you'll also remember that it was doubtful whether the lady who gave the lecture could read, she could scarcely speak. But don't worry, darling, it's all being attended to. We publishers are working hand in hand with the Department of Education. They're making it their job to ensure that our Jeremy won't read when he grows up, and we're making it ours to ensure that when he grows up there won't be any books around worth his reading. I promise you our son shall not feel deprived! The rest can be read by those foreigners you teach, most of whom seem to be writing them anyway, judging by the standard of the English I'm called on to edit.

Hilary has gone to the door, toys, etc., in her arms. Turns, glares at him.

By God, I believe that's what's known as a level look. Or would be if it weren't for your slight squint, now you're tired.

Hilary (*sees the pot, manages to pick it up*) Do you mean you've just lolled there, letting it stare you in the face?

Peter I did try staring back, but it remained unmoved.

Hilary Could you please open the door?

Peter gets up, saunters over, opens the door, swivelling at the same time to pick up the Scotch. As Hilary exits, pours himself a glass, lights a cigarette. Goes back to sofa. Hilary off, calls something.

Peter Wha –?

Hilary continues to call, and Peter answers without listening.

Right, fine, fine.

Goes back to the sofa, settles onto it. Hilary enters, stage left.

Hilary God, I wish you'd at least answer me.

Peter I did.

Hilary And what did you say?

Peter Wha –? Right, fine and fine.

Hilary And what sort of answer is that?

Peter What sort of question was it?

Hilary That typescript that's been lying in the lavatory since Thursday, how important is it?

Peter To Nuzek, the Polish socio-prophet, very. Because he wrote it. To me, not at all. I'm merely its editor.

Hilary So you won't have to read it then?

Peter Nobody who buys it will read it, why should I?

Hilary And those reviewers you used to worry about? Won't they notice if it's not edited?

Peter Oh, they can write their reviews from my blurb.

Hilary And what will you write your blurb from?

Peter Their last reviews. It's what's known in publishing as a benign circle. Nuzek's reputation depends on nobody reading him. His prose guarantees that nobody will. You're taking an unusual interest in the mysteries of my little trade, darling, how come?

Hilary Because I want to find out whether 'Wha –? Right, fine, fine' were reasonable answers to my question.

Goes over to the desk, picks up a briefcase beside it, takes out some papers.

Peter And how did I do?

Hilary All right, it appears. (*Beginning to sort through.*) As it clearly doesn't matter that either Jeremy or one of your nephews blocked the lavatory with it this afternoon.

Peter Christ, they didn't!

Hilary I thought you said it didn't matter.

Peter But he's coming to our six simultaneous publications party in a couple of weeks. It would ruin it if he finds out about this. He's very vain, you know, Nuzek. Ah well, I'll just have to explain that our son mistook it for a bottom copy. (*Gets up, goes to the drinks table.*) Drink?

Hilary No thanks.

Peter (*pouring himself a large one, adding soda water*) Ah, I've been looking forward to this all day.

Hilary Really? What's so special about the fifth or sixth?

Peter It's backed up by four or five others. By the way, how do you think your casserole went down with Charlie and Alison? (*Sitting down again.*)

Hilary You needn't bother.

Peter What?

Hilary Alison confessed in the garden.

Peter Oh. (*Little pause.*) In the garden she confessed, did she? She really does practise away at her Catholicism, in Church, in the open air, in bed – I must say, she's pretty swollen, even for seven months swollen older Alison. Do you think that gynaecologist of hers has taught her how to begin the next before delivering the last? She surely doesn't bother with such fripperies as labour any more – just a brief muscular spasm, something like a hiccup. Oh, I remember when she was a mere slip of a lump of a thing – studying Charlie and English at Reading University, who would have believed – why even prophetic Nuzek will be a mite perplexed to hear – that because my brother happened to marry a lump of a slip whose reproductive organs might have been plumbed by the Vatican itself, his masterwork on Protestantism and pornography is currently washing through the sewers of London.

Hilary has got together her papers, and is on her way out.

What about some supper, I'm peckish. (*Taking her by the wrist.*)

Hilary Are you? Then you'll have to get it yourself.

Peter Why?

Hilary Because I've got to finish these tonight.

Peter Why?

Hilary So that I can brush up on some phonetics tomorrow before taking Jeremy to school. Unless of course you take him for once. Can you?

Peter Darling, I don't drive, remember. You do.

Hilary It's within walking distance. He could easily manage it.

Peter But I couldn't. Besides, he'd use up my whole day's supply of artless prattle, which I'm going to need for the office. (*Little pause.*) Surely even in these glum days a wife can rustle up a sandwich and cocoa for hubby, before hurrying off to her diversions.

Hilary Diversions! My diversions! Do you mean these! (*Shakes essays at him.*)

Peter (*pretending to peer closely*) If those include the essay I glanced at last night, on *Lady Windermere's Fan*. By some Swiss or Swede or Frog. Or Hun or Finn or other wog. He concludes that Oscar Wilde was a bit of a humbugger. You know, darling, they really shouldn't have to pay you for reading, you really ought to pay them for writing, lines like that. (*Reaches behind, pours Scotch into his glass.*)

Hilary Is it any good telling you you'll be sorry in the morning, if you drink that?

Peter I'll be sorry now, if I don't.

Hilary Not too nice though, for Jeremy, at breakfast.

Peter Then I shan't let him have it for breakfast.

Hilary (*makes to go to door, stops, comes back*) Just because you've started being contemptuous of your work, don't you dare start showing me your contempt for mine. Because not only am I not contemptuous of it, no I'm not, but also –

Peter Perhaps you should practise a little contempt for it. Taking it seriously is beginning to affect your conversational style. That last sentence was like the other half of a simultaneous translation.

Hilary I started to tell you something and I'm going to finish.

Peter OK. But keep your head. Now – 'Not only do you have a job which not only are you not contemptuous of, no you're not, but also –' Can you pick it up from there? But also?

Hilary But also I have this home to run, and I'm sick to death of your contempt for that too. It's a difficult enough proposition at the best of times, but it's virtually impossible since you've taken to sneering at me for trying to do it while refusing to make even a gesture towards actually helping.

Peter Actually helping in what?

Hilary Everything. As for instance taking Jeremy to school and fetching him. Every day. With four hours hard teaching between. Then there's the ironing, some of which you actually used to do at one time, remember, the twice-a-week drag through Sainsbury's now that you refuse to accompany me for one big load on Saturdays, then the cooking for Jeremy at teatime, and preparing something for you later on, with tomorrow's teaching to get ready in the evening. On top of which I still do my best to look attractive –

Peter On top of which on top of what, out of that assortment of recriminations and accolades? I know what else you've been doing, you sly boots you, you've been mugging up on the rhetoric of the new woman. A tirade in the form of a curriculum vitae. Wherever have you found the time? (*Pause.*) Actually, now you mention them, some of those meals you've been preparing recently were first prepared by Indians or Chinese, in those take-away restaurants. All you've had to do was to bring them home and then take them away. Usually uneaten. Before throwing them out. Why, if Charlie's doggie knew about your catering arrangements, he'd give up Headmaster's garden and lope straight up Muswell Hill.

Hilary (*after a long pause*) Tell me – how long do you intend to keep this up?

Peter What up?

Hilary This – this pose of yours.

Peter What pose of mine?

Hilary I don't know what you're aiming at, but the result is somewhere between Falstaff and a spiteful woman columnist.

Peter Falstaff. But I was only aiming for the spiteful woman columnist. (*Shakes his head effeminately.*)

Hilary God, I wish you knew how you looked.

Peter A wish you're about to make come true, from the look of you. (*Settles back as if comfortably.*) Well?

Hilary You've got a – what? – two-day stubble over your face, your eyes are bloodshot, you've got dandruff and a smoker's cough, which I've been hearing develop almost by the week. (*Pause.*) Like your paunch.

Peter You've been hearing my paunch develop? So that's why you've been sleeping so far down the bed, eavesdropping?

Hilary No, keeping away from your breath. Which reeks of nicotine and booze.

Peter Now that's dandruff, bad breath, smoker's cough, stubble and paunch. (*Ticking them off on his fingers.*) But those details apart, do you find me as winsome as ever?

Hilary I find you quite disgusting.

Peter Careful, sweetling, or in a second you'll say something you'll regret.

Hilary I regret not having said it to you weeks ago. I don't know what's the matter with you, but I can't stand it any more. Not the sight of you, nor the nagging it provoked from me at first, nor the contempt I've felt for you recently. Because that's what *my* contempt has been for, you. We haven't been to a dinner party recently at which you haven't ended up drunker than anyone else, or any social occasion at which you haven't contributed to insult half the people in the room. I've been ashamed.

Peter Well, some of those rooms were pretty large. Look at it this way, if they'd been half the size I'd have managed to insult the lot.

Hilary But you haven't done it with style, Peter, don't delude yourself.

Peter Quantity these days, darling, a lot of those people I scarcely knew.

Hilary But why? Why? Today, with your brother and his family around – I don't know what you said to him when he came in here, but he was in a dreadful state when he came out – and before that at lunch, the way you sat lolling forward, your eyes glassy with too much drink and too much food.

Peter And too much boredom! Don't forget the too much boredom!

Hilary The real bore was you! Stirring yourself only to bait Charlie, completely ignoring Alison –

Peter Not fair! I tried to bait Alison too. She chose to ignore it.

Hilary I can't go on like this!

Peter Really? I thought you were just warming up.

Hilary You're poisoning my life. And Jeremy's. He doesn't even want you to read to him in the evenings any more. He actually cried when I said tonight you might be doing it. Or does that make you pleased with yourself too? (*Pause.*) Neither of us can bear you as you are.

Peter Well, neither of you will get me as I might have been, because that's over. And as for how I was –

Hilary (*after a pause*) Well?

Peter That's over too. So far over, I've forgotten how I did it.

Hilary Very well. (*Turns, goes towards the door.*)

Peter Oh, just a minute, darling!

Gets up, goes towards her, stands staring at her, then begins to unbutton her blouse.

Hilary What are you doing?

Peter Stripping you down.

He stops, then puts his arms around Hilary, pulls her to him, kisses her.

Before having you off.

Hilary beats him off savagely.

Hey – hey – (*Defending himself.*) This is fun! (*Advances on her again.*)

Hilary (*strikes out at him again*) Stop it, stop it, stop it!

Peter backs away. They stand, breathing heavily, staring at each other.

How dare you!

Peter How dare I what?

Hilary Grab at me as if I were – were – (*Slight pause, then witheringly.*) Like some dirty old man.

Peter But you're not at all like some dirty old man. If you were I'd grab him instead. (*Little pause.*) Well, it is Sunday, isn't it? And therefore about the hour for our Sunday-evening sex. Distinguishable from our Wednesday-evening sex by its venue. Wednesday evening we have workday sex, upstairs in bed after a dinner out. If we can arrange a babysitter and you have no marking to do. Sunday evening we have sabbatical sex down here on the sofa in a spontaneous tussle after you've shyly removed the sofa cushion. (*Little pause.*) At least so we used to not too long ago.

Hilary Well, not any more.

Peter Now let's see – that's no cooking any more and no love-making any more –

Hilary Love-making? You haven't made love to me for months. You just use me as a stage towards one of your post-coital cigarettes. That is, when you've been conscious. Otherwise you merely roll on top of me yawning and away from me snoring.

Peter What do you do between my yawn and my snore, I wonder, in the short period when I tend to be quite active? Draw up your Sainsbury's shopping list. I recall catching the odd murmur, though your limbs remain supine.

Hilary It isn't a murmur. It's a mutter.

Peter But what? Directions? Encouragement?

Hilary 'Hurry up, pig, or get it over with.' That sort of encouragement.

Peter I see. Less of an effort then than actually resisting.

Hilary At least quicker than all the rows and explanations that dragged on until dawn.

Peter Which you now, you ageing paradox you, seem bent on having. Well then, let's discuss your past bedtime froideurs – the ones that led to the rows, and for which everything from Victorian headaches to brutally contemporary ailments were offered in explanation.

Hilary The most usual explanation was that I was tired after a day out at work and a day of domestic duties. A simple matter which you were incapable of understanding.

Peter Which I suppose is why you had to put more effort into a normal marital fuck.

Hilary Do you honestly mean that you're going in for all this – smoking and drinking and spite – to make up for your sex-life?

Peter My lack of it, perhaps.

Hilary How childish you really are.

Peter Do you think it's been fun sharing a bed with you?

Hilary Then don't. You can sleep down here.

Peter Down here!

Looks around him, laughs incredulously.

Hilary I'll make up the sofa.

Peter The sofa!

Hilary Or on the floor, if you prefer.

Peter If I don't sleep in our bed, I don't stay in this house.

Hilary Very well.

She exits, returns with blankets and pillow.

Jeremy and I will go to my mother's tomorrow. I'll give you a week to find somewhere else.

Jeremy's Voice Mummy, Mummy . . .

Hilary It's all right, darling, nothing to be frightened of, Mummy's coming. (*Exits.*)

Peter Sounds bloody frightening to me.

Lights.

SCENE TWO

Lights up. Sofa covered in blankets and sheets. There is a suitcase packed but open on the floor by the sofa.

Peter enters in socks, trousers and vest, wiping shaving soap off his face. Throws towel onto bed. Picks up shirt. There is a ring on the doorbell. He looks at his watch. Hurriedly buttons up shirt. Goes to front door, singing cheerfully. Sound of door opening.

Peter *(off)* Oh.

Charles *(off)* May I come in?

Peter enters, continuing to dress, followed by Charles.

I didn't really expect to catch you in. I thought you'd be at work.

Peter I didn't really expect you to catch me in. I thought you'd be at work.

Charles Actually, I've got a free morning. At least until lunch, when I have to see Headmaster.

Peter Have to, do you, Charlie?

Charles That's right, Peter. It's a personal matter. What are you doing at home?

Peter Dressing. To go to a party.

Charles *(shocked)* Party?

Peter With a young lady friend.

Charles Where's Hilary?

Peter But Charlie, I told you when you phoned the other night. She's gone to stay with her mother while I look for a flat. Didn't you believe me?

Charles You were drunk. I hoped it was one of your jokes.

Peter Well, it may be a joke, Charlie, but it also happens to be true. I'm moving into a flat in Notting Hill Gate, as soon as it becomes free. Which it will be this evening at six p.m.

Charles Is it any use asking you to explain?

Peter Explain what?

Charles Why you've left Hilary.

Peter Certainly, as it's easily explained. She asked me to leave her bed and sleep down here but I've decided to keep on going right out of the house. All right?

Charles No, it's damned well not all right. For one thing, what about Jeremy?

Peter Oh, she won't be turning *him* out of her bed for some years yet, if then.

Charles Look, Pete – is it because of her job? You don't resent that, do you? Because you feel less important now that she's meeting new people – her colleagues –?

Peter Oh, they don't sound particularly new. In fact, most of them sound old and weary, except for the students, who just sound foreign.

Charles Oh come on, Pete, come on, I don't believe it's as simple as you make it seem. You can't tell me you're just going to walk out. Not just like that. There must be something really terrible between you suddenly, after so many years of happy marriage. What is it?

Peter Oh, perhaps just so many years of happy marriage between us, eh, Charlie? And perhaps so many turned out to be more than our fair share.

Charles So what now? A return to a bachelor pad and your old ways?

Peter What old ways?

Charles Your promiscuous old ways. Do you really think at your age you can just go back to a life of short affairs and – what was that hideous phrase you used to use? – easy lays. Well, you're not an Oxford undergraduate any longer, Peter, you won't find it easy with the Friedas.

Peter Frieda? Who's Frieda?

Charles Gerta, whoever she was, the German ballerina.

Peter Oh, Gretel it was. Wasn't it?

Charles (*contemptuously*) And that Italian painter who was old enough to be your mother. Do you think it's going to be like that all over again? And that wretched business with André Gide's daughter.

Peter André Gide's daughter! (*Laughs.*) Charlie, I assure you, André Gide never had a daughter.

Charles Well, some French writer who was in vogue a dozen years ago. Well, you're a married man now, that's what you are.

Peter Am I? Charlie, you know nothing about any of it.

Charles Don't I? I remember the states you used to get into. It's a lucky thing for you you married Hilary when you did – your bachelor days nearly killed you.

Peter Now I've got them back, perhaps they'll finish the job. You're not still jealous, are you, Charlie, of those old passions of mine?

Charles Jealous? What should I be jealous of?

Peter Well, you never slept with a woman before you married Alison, did you? You had no premarital sex at all, did you? Well, did you?

Charles As a matter of fact I did, yes.

Peter You didn't! Christ, who with?

Charles Alison.

Peter Why, you rascal! You used to boast that yours was a real wedding night, in the old-fashioned sense of the term. Which I always took to mean a disaster, by the way.

Charles It only happened the once. One Sunday in my room in Reading we went – without meaning to – we went all the way. Afterwards we talked the whole thing through and decided that what with Alison's Catholicism and Mummy's desperation about your behaviour and my own – no doubt from your point of view – simple-minded principles, I'd have to control myself a little.

Peter A little? That's not very flattering to either of you. Anyway, Charlie, you see how unqualified you are to judge other people's sexual lives. Your own having consisted of ten years of marriage to Alison, preceded by two or three years of light to heavy necking with Alison preceded by – (*little pause*) Jane Russell, wasn't it? Into a jam jar.

There is a pause.

Charles How did you know that?

Peter What?

Charles About the – the –

Peter Jane Russell jam jar? Mummy told me you'd confessed.

Charles When?

Peter After she'd interrogated you about the jam jar and the Jane Russells she found under your floorboards.

Charles No, no. I mean when did she tell you?

Peter Oh, immediately after *I'd* confessed. Which was after she'd interrogated me about the old sock and the Betty Grables she found on top of my cupboard. But why look so troubled, Charlie? Everybody wanked at Wellington, including most of the staff, from a memory of their complexions. Do you remember that scandal when it was discovered that some of the older boarders had established it as a competitive sport and were awarding House Colours?

Charles But she promised me she'd never say a word about it to anyone, especially you.

Peter And I promised her I'd never tell you she told me. So now we're all square, two decades on. What exactly did she say to you?

Charles That if I went on doing it, I'd never get into the Wellington First for football.

Peter And she was quite right, you didn't. Although I suppose you didn't go on masturbating either?

Charles What did she say to you?

Peter That I'd ruin my eyes, lose my concentration, and wouldn't get a scholarship to Oxford. Of course I didn't know then what Oxford was like, or I'd have settled for spectacles and a job in a shoe shop.

Charles You were bloody lucky to get into Oxford.

Peter Really? Your line used to be that Reading was just as good.

Charles Indeed it was. And is. You were lucky to get into Oxford because you'd never have got through the interview at Reading. (*After a pause.*) Anyway, how dare you confuse my attitudes to sex with Mummy's? You wouldn't find a more enlightened attitude to masturbation than Headmaster's and mine at Amplesides. I'm not against sex, I'm very for it – good sex, that is. Which is what one has, lovingly, with those one loves.

Peter Such as oneself?

Charles Oh, ha ha. Anyway, this is all a waste of time – as I take it you haven't left Hilary because she won't allow you to masturbate. You know why you're a bloody fool, Peter? Not for moral reasons, or conventional or unconventional ones, as they are nowadays, to do with the sanctity of family life and the squalors of easy sex – not those. But simply that you're on your way to losing your wife and your son, both of whom you love. At bottom your nature is as affectionate as mine. So one day, probably very soon, you'll go back to Hilary, and it'll be too late. The damage will have been done. (*Pause.*) It's true, isn't it? You do love Hilary?

There is a ring at the doorbell, off.

Peter Ah, excuse me, Charlie, can we leave that question hanging while I open the door?

Goes to open door.

(*Off.*) Ah, here you are at last.

Joanna (*off*) Hello. Sorry I'm late.

Peter (*entering with Joanna*) Oh don't worry – I was in no danger of giving you up. This is my brother, Charlie.

Joanna Hello.

Peter Joanna's one of our freelance cover designers. I've asked her to accompany me to the party.

Joanna It'll be the first real publishing do I've ever wormed my way into.

Peter Then we mustn't miss a minute of it. Shall we go?

Charles Just a minute –

Takes a photograph out of his pocket, hands it to Peter.

Something I was going to leave for you if you weren't in.

Peter Ah, a memento mori. Well, as I was in, you can take it away again.

Charles It belongs to you.

Peter I don't want it, Charlie.

Charles Why not? Does it upset you?

Joanna God, what's it of, anyway?

Charles It's a photograph of my brother's wife and child.

He hands it to Joanna.

Joanna (*studies it*) Taken with an Instamatic, right?

Peter (*takes the photograph back, hands it to Charles*) It belongs to Alison, I believe we've established.

Holds the door open for Joanna. Joanna and Charles stare at each other. Charles coldly, Joanna puzzled.

(*To Joanna.*) Shall we go? Do stay, Charlie, if you want to and – (*gestures*) – help yourself to the soda water.

They exit. Charles stands trembling for a second, then goes to the soda syphon, squirts himself some.

Charles The little – the little –

He gulps down the soda water, pulls himself together, then goes over, places the photograph on the table, then changes mind and props it up in front of whisky. He exits through kitchen. Crashing sound.

(*Off.*) Blast!

Lights half down.

Lights up. Peter enters, followed by Joanna. They are both slightly drunk, and laughing.

Joanna Christ, no truly, you were devastating. I've never heard anyone put so many people down before. But then I've never seen so many intellectuals before. Are all publishing parties like that?

Peter (*who is lighting a cigarette*) It was a special occasion. We were launching a coffee-table book on Virginia Wade's six greatest defeats in our 'Back Britain to the Very Bottom' series.

Joanna Virginia Wade, the tennis player? Was she the woman that made the speech?

Peter No, that was the new Chairman of the Arts Council. He always wears drag for literary events, to give them a touch of style.

Joanna He doesn't!

Peter No, he doesn't. I'm just fantasising to distract our attention.

Joanna What from?

Peter The party.

Pours himself a Scotch, squirts in soda water.

Joanna (*laughs*) The way you put down that funny little specimen with the glasses and the baggy trousers and the sandals.

Peter Oh yes. Cyril. Our senior editor.

Joanna When he was praising up somebody or other's book.

Peter Was it Nuzek's?

Joanna That's right, Nuzek's book. He said one thing you could be sure of with Nuzek, anything he wrote was bound to be full of pith, and you said, 'Why Cyril, I didn't know you had a lisp.'

Peter (*puzzled*) But he hasn't got a lisp, old Cyril. Has he?

Joanna No, he hasn't, that's why you said it. Because he said full of pith and you –

Peter Got it, got it, got it.

Joanna It took me two minutes to get it at the time.

Peter Then Cyril was a mite quicker than you, if memory serves. Which it suddenly insists on doing, now you've set it in motion. Rather like some uncontrollably obsequious waiter . . . (*Sits down.*)

Joanna And who was the little creep with the goatee and the beady eyes –

Peter Oh, that was our chairman, his eyes aren't usually beady. They're usually twinkly. Famously twinkly, in fact.

Joanna Well, they were beady from the moment we arrived and you told that joke about Nu – Nude – what was it again?

Peter Nuzek. Nu-zek.

Joanna (*nods*) Nuzek. How the bottom copy was used to wipe a five-year-old bottom, so the paper hadn't been wasted after all. That one nearly brought the house down.

Peter It still might.

Joanna God, people really enjoyed you, except those two and that little roly-poly bloke – the one with the foreign accent standing next to me. He really hated you. Who was he?

Peter Mmmm?

Joanna That roly-poly bloke next to me.

Peter Oh yes. A roly Pole called Nuzek. Nu-zek. Oh Christ.

Joanna What's the matter?

Peter Nothing, nothing.

Joanna Hey, you're not sorry about those things you said or anything, are you?

Peter Sorry! Why should I be sorry? (*Laughs.*) No, no, it's only that it is a long time since I struck out without making sure of hitting only air. Or a loved one.

> *Goes over to her, whispers in her ear, then looks at her, attempts a little laugh.*

Look, we've got far better things to do – (*lurches slightly*) than reminisce over my past before it's properly begun. I did say please this time. I don't know if you heard it.

Joanna (*smiling*) I'd really like that. I really would.

Peter Right.

> *Straightens up and takes jacket off. Joanna begins to undress as well.*

Joanna (*who has been staring at the picture as she undresses*) How old's your wife anyway?

Peter What? (*Sees the picture.*) Oh. Um, thirty-one and a half.

Joanna Your boy's what, five?

Peter Nearly six. That was taken a year ago.

Joanna (*picks up the picture*) What's she look like? It's hard to tell because she's out of focus.

Peter (*going over in trousers and shirt*) Can we keep her that way, do you mind?

Taking the picture from Joanna.

To avoid pre- and even post-coital depression.

Comes back with the picture, drops it on the floor.

I'm free now, you know. Absolutely free.

They go on undressing, on opposite sides of the room.

Lights.

Act Two

SCENE ONE

The sitting room. Some time later.
  Joanna is sitting on the bed in her underpants, doing up her bra. Peter is on the chair, in vest and trousers, pulling on his socks. He stops, sits staring blankly ahead, then fumbles in his jacket pocket (which is slung over the back of the chair) for his cigarettes. Takes one out.

Joanna (*who has been watching him*) I've got some pot, if you want. (*Taking a small box out of handbag, beside the bed.*)

Peter What? (*Sitting down, not looking at her.*)

Joanna Do you want a joint?

Peter No, thanks. I find these altogether more exciting. (*Lights up, drags deeply, coughs.*) Don't need the police to be frightened of them.

Joanna (*putting a joint between her lips*) Can I have a light, then?

Peter What? Oh, sorry.

  He half turns, tosses her the lighter without looking at her. It falls to one side.

Sorry.

  Joanna lights up, also drags deeply into her lungs. They sit smoking for a short while. Peter coughs once or twice.

Joanna You've had a bad scene going recently, haven't you? I could tell that first time you brought me back and you were so desperate. And now it's got even worse, hasn't it? You're moving out, aren't you, or you've been thrown out. Is that it?

Peter grunts.

Look, if it helps, I am just getting over something too. (*Pause.*) But I've learnt it's just a matter of time, that's all. I've got to the stage, you know, where I can tell myself it's over without even weeping. Dead. Terminado, finito. Finished. Not that anything ever finishes, right? Christ, we were even going to get married!

Peter That would have finished it.

Joanna His name was Josh. Whitby.

Peter Look, you really don't have to talk about it if you don't want to.

Joanna No, I want to.

Peter Then I suppose it's irrelevant that you don't have to.

Joanna Thank you. You can't even bring yourself to look at me, can you?

Peter Sorry. (*Turns, looks at her, looks away again.*) I am sorry. It must be that pre-coital depression I was worried about. It's struck.

Joanna But truly it doesn't matter. I don't mind.

Peter Good. Unfortunately I do.

Joanna (*comes over to him*) But you don't have to sit around like a sick dog. I mean the way you got out of bed and into your knickers – it was almost as bad as the way you got out of them – all doubled up and walking across the room in a crouch. You were ashamed before we even started – what of?

Peter I think it must have been my paunch.

Joanna You know what you did while you were – I mean, you actually proposed to me.

Peter Oh, you heard that, did you? I tried to make it sound like a love-cry. (*Pause.*) If you'd accepted on a pro-tem basis, things might have ended differently.

Joanna Perhaps, if you hadn't drunk so much, you'd have done it.

Peter Perhaps if I hadn't drunk so much, I wouldn't have tried.

Joanna Thank you. Thank you. (*Grinds out her joint.*) Oh Christ, whatever has gone wrong between you and your wife isn't my fault, this is all a lot of balls.

Peter You don't need a lot, actually one will do. Bull-fighters manage on even less, so they say.

Joanna This hasn't happened to you before then, never?

Peter No.

Joanna Never with your wife, even?

Peter Not even. Except in Paris on our honeymoon when I pretended for a fatal fraction of a thrust that we were on a dirty weekend.

Joanna Look, am I the only girl since you were married, apart from your wife?

Peter says nothing.

Well, am I? (*Little pause.*) I am, aren't I? Right?

Peter Right, right. You're the only girl I've had apart from my wife. Right?

Joanna Wrong. You didn't have me. Right?

Peter Right. Thank you. I'd forgotten your gift for instant recall. Perhaps because I try so hard to lack it myself.

Joanna What were you doing, practising? Christ! (*Goes to the rest of her clothes, begins to put them on.*) You know what you are, you're the type . . .

Peter Don't bother. I know the type. (*Gets up, puts on shirt, etc.*) I gather all the other married men you've slept with managed to come good.

Joanna But then they enjoyed it too.

Peter Even the guilt?

Joanna Even the sex. You know, there was a time today when I truly liked you – at the party, I thought you had something then, but it was just words, wasn't it, just showing off, and then only because you'd got yourself drunk.

Peter Yes, I think that's a pretty accurate summing up. Well done.

Joanna I just hope you haven't given me anything catching, that's all.

Peter What? Oh, you mean my inhibitions? But they don't get passed on by casual contact, only through an intimacy that digs deep into tissues you seem to have been born without. No, don't you worry, dear, you'll still be able to sleep around, smoke pot, promote your new jargons, bury our old language, and generally see our dying culture underground, where my son . . . my son . . .

Joanna (*looks at him, laughs*) And I was only talking about your dandruff. (*Goes out.*)

Peter (*after a moment*) So was I.

*Looks at shoulders, left and right, brushes futilely at
them. He goes over to suitcase, closes it. Picks it up,
exits.*

Lights down. Lights up.

SCENE TWO

*The same. Several days later. It is evening, about eight
o'clock. Lights on.*
Hilary enters, left. Jeremy, off, left, calls out something.

Hilary (*at the door*) No more cuddles tonight, you don't
mean it anyway, sleep now. And no sneaking into my
bed.

> *Listens, sounds of Jeremy off, complaining. Hilary
> smiles, goes across to the desk, picks up her briefcase,
> sits down at the desk, opens it. Takes out some
> papers, begins to look through them. Stops. Sits
> staring ahead.*
> *There is a sudden rap on the window.*
> *Hilary lets out a little scream. There is a crashing
> at the kitchen, and as Hilary rises in alarm, Charles
> enters.*

Charles Hello, I thought I'd come this way so as not to
disturb.

Hilary Thank you.

Charles In case Jeremy was asleep.

Hilary Yes.

Charles Actually it's the pot. Nindy's pot. We left it here
that Sunday – and Nindy's suddenly taken against the
new one, after using it the last week. I don't know why,
but she wants her old one back. Alison's had to use the

128

sink ploy with the tap running – anyway I thought I'd just pop over and get it. You know? (*Little pause.*) I should have phoned.

Hilary It's very nice to see you. I'll go and get it.

Goes off, left. Charles goes to the drinks table. Makes to squirt some soda water into a glass. The syphon farts emptily. Charles studies the bottom of the syphon, then raises the syphon, bending slightly at the knees, puts the tube into his mouth, and squirts and sucks. Hilary re-enters with the pot, watches him. Charles not seeing, puts the syphon down.

Hilary Here you are. (*Hands him the pot.*)

Charles Thanks.

Hilary (*after a pause*) Would you like a drink?

Charles No, no thanks. Well, just some soda water, if there is any.

Hilary I think it's empty.

Charles There isn't another one in the cupboard? Peter – sometimes there's a spare in the cupboard.

Hilary (*goes to the cupboard, looks*) No.

Charles Oh.

Hilary Something else perhaps? There's some lime, or squash or Ribena . . . ?

Charles No, no thanks. I like soda water, you see. Its taste.

Hilary But surely it hasn't got any taste.

Charles Yes, that's what I like. And the way the bubbles shoot up against the roof of the mouth –

Hilary Well, some coffee – or something to eat?

Charles No, I had a nut and spinach cutlet before coming out. With boiled potatoes and blackberries. The blackberries were for pudding.

Hilary Charlie – are we having this awkward conversation because you can't get into another awkward conversation you feel we should be having?

Charles Well, I suppose I was wondering whether you'd heard from Peter yet.

Hilary No.

Charles But it's been almost a week now. Do you mean to say he hasn't even bothered to let you know where he's gone?

Hilary I told you, Charlie, I don't want to talk about it.

Charles goes and sits down, evidently depressed.

It's very sweet of you to take it all so badly, but really I think it would be more helpful if you tried to take it well.

Charles (*nods*) But I think he's a little – (*Checks himself.*) Sorry, Hilary. (*Sits in a sort of stupor.*)

Hilary Is there something else the matter? Alison's all right . . . ?

Charles Oh yes, yes. She's fine. (*Little pause.*) Perhaps a touch of pre-natal depression.

Hilary Oh dear. But that's unusual, isn't it? She's generally so exuberant just before.

Charles No, I meant me. I always get a bit low – but I don't let Alison see, of course. Or anyone. But this time it's worse than usual – what with you and Pete – a double touch really. Appropriate as we're going to have twins.

Hilary Twins! Why, Charlie, that's marvellous, twins! How wonderful.

Charles I thought you knew.

Hilary Yes, Alison did tell me, as a matter of fact. But she said she wasn't going to tell you. She wanted it to be a surprise.

Charles Well, she couldn't resist after all. She told me this evening. I think to cheer me up over Pete and everything.

Hilary But Charlie, you don't mind, do you? Twins, just *think*!

Charles Oh, I'm sure once they're here. I wish she'd kept the surprise as a surprise though. Then I wouldn't have had time to prepare for it. Anyway I just used the pot as an excuse – I had to get away for a little, in case I couldn't cope. (*Little pause.*) It's monstrous of me to burden you with myself, isn't it?

Hilary No, it isn't. I'm glad you came. It would be far more monstrous if Alison suspected – Charlie, you don't think a little whisky would help?

Charles No, only a lot would. Sorry, Hil. I suppose really it's an inevitable progression. We've been turning them out in singles for eight years, we were bound to advance. Recently in class I've taken to saying everything twice. Perhaps it was an early warning –

Hilary Is it a matter of economics, your depression?

Charles Well, I have got used to pacing them out in my mind and planning ahead. But if they're going to start coming in clusters –? What can I do?

Hilary Couldn't you count this as two goes worth? Oh, of course, how silly of me. I'd forgotten Alison's Catholicism.

Charles Her Catholicism's just a blind, Hilary. Lots of practising Catholics also practise contraception these days, while Alison scarcely bothers to practise Catholicism, except in her attitude to contraceptives. When it comes down to it, the Pope's just her fertility symbol. She likes babies, lots and lots of babies. She likes cuddling them, burping them, changing them, feeding them, preferably while bearing them. (*Pause.*) Oh, I don't blame her, of course. I always knew she was a natural homemaker, it's one of the reasons I wanted to marry her. It's just that the house I'm paying the mortgage on isn't big enough for the home she's making. I haven't dared tell her yet – (*Stops.*)

Hilary What?

Charles Well, there was a chance of getting a house that belongs to the school – much larger than ours and the rent would be nominal. Bursar was sure it could be arranged, but Headmaster said no.

Hilary Why?

Charles Oh, he was very nice about it, of course. He wants to start a new school house for boarders – perfectly sensible, really. But it's always a bit of a shock being turned down. (*Little pause.*) Especially – (*Lets out a little laugh.*)

Hilary Charlie?

Charles Can I tell you something? In great confidence.

Hilary If you're sure I ought to know.

Charles It's something ridiculous. Something very ridiculous. On the other hand it's not. You must try not to laugh, but I shan't blame you if you do. You see – I asked Headmaster about the house at lunch, but at tea I suddenly thought I'd look in on him, just for a cup and – well, I often do, you know, to talk about co-education or scholarships – but this time I also wanted him to see that I perfectly understood about not getting the house. Well, we had a very affable chat together, his wife was there and we always get along very well – it was very pleasant, I thought, very pleasant.

Hilary Well, it sounds very pleasant.

Charles Yes, it was. And when I left I decided to walk back to the car through their garden. I often go that way, especially if it's a fine evening. I wasn't at all depressed then, you know, of course I didn't know about the twins – well, perhaps I was a little depressed about Pete, thinking what a fool he was and why he couldn't count his blessings – and then I began to count my own, you know, the way one does, miscounting as it turned out. But I began to feel rather happy. Rather happy, that's my point.

Hilary And why shouldn't you be? You've got a great deal to be happy about.

Charles Exactly, I know. And I wished I had Pete there because I was sure I could persuade him – when suddenly I heard Headmaster's voice. He was talking to his wife. They didn't see me – in fact, they must have thought I was long gone. I was just about to squeeze through some shrubs to let them know where I was, I didn't want them to think I was eavesdropping – when I heard Headmaster say, 'But there must be some way of keeping the pest out of my house.'

Hilary (*after a pause*) Oh Charlie!

Charles And his wife said, 'Oh, I know he's an appalling nuisance, but I can't help having a soft spot for him.'

Hilary Oh Charles!

Charles 'That's because he grovels whenever he sees you!' And then he said –

Hilary Oh Charlie, don't go on. Please. I can't bear it.

Charles Said, 'The other day I saw him peeing over the roses. He's always squatting in the path and fouling it. He leaves fleas over the carpet, you've said so yourself.'

Hilary They were talking about that stray – Alfonso! At least I hope they were.

Charles So what it comes to is this. You don't think I have the physical habits of a dog, just the moral temperament of one.

Hilary I think no such thing!

Charles Oh God, I admired him though, for a moment.

Hilary Headmaster?

Charles Alfonso. I wished I could pee over his roses, drop turds on his path and shake fleas over his carpet. But I wouldn't grovel to his wife, I'd bite her ankles.

Hilary I thought you liked them!

Charles So did I. Until I thought I heard them talking about me like that.

Hilary But they weren't talking about you. They were talking about Alfonso.

Charles I know, I know. But you see, the fact that I thought they were talking about me like that must mean there's something in my idea of them that expects them to talk like that about me. And something in me that expects to be talked about like that. It's just the sort of thing I know Pete's always – (*Stops.*) Well anyway. But you know, almost the most shameful thing, Hil – when I was in my car and well, trembling a little – a muddle of feelings, hate and anger for them, oh quite irrational, I realised it even at the time – but in the middle of all that I had this sudden very clear thought. Do you know what it was? Something really shameful?

Hilary (*after a moment*) I think so. That you'd better stop feeding Alfonso, now you know what Headmaster thinks of him.

Charles (*nods, despairingly*) And a second later I imagined myself making some casual reference to the effect – that perhaps we ought to have something done about him.

Hilary Put down, you mean? Oh Charlie!

Charles If you met me now, for the first time, you wouldn't dream of asking me back to your house for dinner, would you?

Hilary Of course I would.

Charles No you wouldn't. Alison's very attached to you, you know.

Hilary Yes, I do know.

Charles Still, she thinks you're a conceited little turnip.

Hilary Turnip?

Charles Sometimes parsnip. She hates the way you prattle boastfully on about your job. That's the sort of thing she says about you, although she loves you. So what sort of things do you say about her, although you love her, if you do? About her constant pregnancies, for example, or her earth-mother laugh – or her unattractiveness.

Hilary I think she's *very* attractive!

Charles What's so attractive about her?

Hilary She's got a lovely, open face, a marvellous complexion.

Charles And a dreadful figure.

Hilary She has not!

Charles Yes, she has. What isn't dreadful about it?

Hilary (*thinks desperately*) Well, for one thing, she's got absolutely beautiful breasts. So full.

Charles Yes, well, they usually are, aren't they? (*Little pause.*) What about her bottom?

Hilary Charlie, this has gone on quite long enough.

Charles Actually, her bottom isn't as baggy as it looks when she's wearing those pregnancy trousers she usually wears. (*Little pause.*) You don't think I hate her, do you?

Hilary No. I know you love her.

Charles But you hate hearing me say things like this about her.

Hilary Yes. But I'd rather you said them to me than to her.

Charles I'll stop in a minute. Honestly. But do you know what would make it all right for me, absolutely? If I could just go to bed some evenings, and stretch, and turn on the reading light, and sigh luxuriously, and open a book. An Arthur Ransome. I long to re-read all the Arthur Ransomes.

Hilary Surely you can manage that?

Charles Alison always goes up before me. Then when I come in she stretches, turns off the reading light, gives a luxurious sigh, and opens her legs. (*Little pause.*) No, that's not true. We have a long cuddle first, which I need. But that's how it ends. Every night. We have this joke, that she can't get to sleep without it. And recently since we've gone macrobiotic there's been a joke about not being able to get up without it, either.

Hilary But not every night, Charlie, it's not possible.

Charles Yes, every night. Even when there are bottles to warm up, nappies to be changed, midnight wee-wees and six-week colic. Every night, Hilary. You see, she loves everything to do with babies, but especially the way they're made.

Hilary But couldn't you, well, just hint that you need a rest sometimes?

Charles Of course I can't. Our marriage is constructed on our triumphant sex-life, as you know. That, and our shared love of children.

Hilary But you do like children. Don't you?

Charles Nobody likes children these days. Why should I? They don't even like each other. But I love them, if that's what perpetually counting them and fretting for them and planning because of them amounts to. But I don't want to look at them, or hear them, let alone watch them eat, empty their pots and nappies –

Hilary You sound just like Peter.

Charles Oh God, I wish I were just like him, or even better, be him! (*Little pause.*) Sorry, Hilary, I wasn't referring to – to his current behaviour. But you see he's always been the younger one, the brighter one, the indulged one – the anarchic one. While I've just been the conventional one, the slow and loving and responsible one. The one-girl one. All those affairs he had before you –

Hilary What? What affairs?

Charles But surely he told you about them?

Hilary No.

Charles I shouldn't have spoken.

Hilary No, I want to hear.

Charles Are you sure?

Hilary I want to hear.

Charles But how could he have not confessed! The German ballerina, the Italian painter, Gide's daughter –

Hilary Gide's daughter!

Charles No, it wasn't Gide's, it was – I can't remember, a French writer. His daughter. The affair of his life until he met you. And he never said a word?

Hilary I'd forgotten. It was all so long ago.

Charles I suppose it was. But it still makes me angry to think of them. Because, you see, secretly, I wanted them, and if I couldn't have them, I wanted him to. Just as – just as – well, although I've always loved Alison, but was never actually in love with her, so I've – I've always been in love with you. Though now I love you too as my sister-in-law. From the first moment he showed you off to me. But you know that, don't you?

   Hilary nods.

But you belonged to Pete, of course. Just as I did to Alison. All four of us were perfectly matched. You had lots of affairs too, didn't you, before you married Pete?

Hilary Lots?

Charles Well, quite a few.

Hilary I suppose quite a few, yes.

Charles How many?

Hilary (*after a pause*) Five, actually.

Charles (*whistles*) Five! Alison's always said – (*Pause.*)
So you see, you were perfectly matched. Almost
mathematically. While I was always the sort of chap
to meet the sort of chap that Alison is, without having
anything before – and that was that. (*Little pause.*)
You've never been the slightest bit in love with me,
have you?

Hilary shakes her head.

And perhaps that's why I can't help being a little glad
that you and Pete have broken up. Oh, not only because
of being in love with you, but also – this is my very last
confession, Hil.

Hilary Thank God!

Charles Because it's easier for me to bear being what
I am – a loving family man, an obsequious Assistant
Headmaster in a minor public school, a bit of an old-
fashioned Puritan – if he's behaving despicably. I want
him to live my destructive life for me, while I go on living
my decent life, for myself. Oh God, how shameful! I do
want him to come back, I do, I do.

Hilary puts her face to one side. She is in tears.

Hil – Hil – oh, I am sorry, I've been selfish. I'd no right –
oh, don't cry, please. (*Comes over, puts an arm around
her.*) Did I make you?

Hilary shakes her head.

Because of Pete and you?

Hilary No, not especially, a little.

Charles Because of Alison and me.

Hilary A little, but not only.

Charles Ah, *lacrimae rerum*. Tears within things. I felt them rising in me when Alison was laughing over the twins, and I was trying to laugh with her. Pete will come back to you, Hil. I know he loves you.

Hilary So do I.

Charles So you know he'll come back to you?

Hilary Yes, I know it.

Charles Then nothing's really too bad, is it?

Lights down.

Lights up. Muswell Hill. Charles is sitting on the sofa, eating a carrot and holding the pot. There is the sound of the front door closing, left, then Peter enters. He is carrying his suitcase, has a monstrous haircut, is neatly and newly suited. He is also carrying flowers and chocolates. He puts down suitcase and presents himself to Charles with a flourish.

Peter Well, Charlie, I'm back. Where's Hilary?

Charles Gone to have a bath.

Peter Ah! What are you doing here?

Charles I came to collect the pot. I was just leaving.

There is a pause.

And how's your girl?

Peter Did you mention her to Hilary?

Charles No.

Peter Thank you.

Charles For Hilary's sake, not yours.

Peter Naturally. (*Looks towards the door, then at Charles.*) Oh, for God's sake don't look so censorious. My tail is back between my legs, where it belongs. Isn't that what you wanted?

Charles But should you be smirking?

Peter Am I? Well, it's a family trait in moments of embarrassment. As you should know.

Charles Embarrassment? Is that what you call this mess? You walk out on your wife and son after weeks of the most repellent behaviour all for the sake of some heartless little creature – and then you turn up with a haircut and in a new suit and refer smirkingly to embarrassment. Well, let me tell you, Peter –

Peter No, please don't, Charlie. Please don't tell me anything. I know.

Charles (*biting angrily at the carrot*) What do you know?

Peter Well, for one thing, I know that you couldn't just go off, could you, and have a casual affair with some heartless little creature, just like that, after weeks of the most repellent behaviour. Could you?

Charles No, I damn well could not!

Peter Well, nor could I. (*Sinks into the chair.*) I could manage the repellent behaviour, but not the heartless little creature.

Charles You mean nothing happened?

Peter Nothing to speak of. Although I expect she'll speak of it, all right.

Charles So you haven't betrayed Hilary after all?

Peter Oh yes. I betrayed them both, given their different expectations. But incompetently. Neither a successful adulterer nor a faithful husband. Something between the two.

Charles I did warn you that you couldn't go back.

Peter To what?

Charles To your old promiscuity. Your Gertas, your Friedas, your – (*Gestures.*)

Peter My André Gide's daughters. (*Laughs.*)

Charles Oh, I've remembered since. It was Cocteau's daughter.

Peter You can't honestly believe Cocteau had a daughter either?

Charles I don't honestly care whose daughter it was. Whose was it anyway?

Peter Cocteau's.

Charles You just said he didn't have a daughter.

Peter Exactly.

Charles (*after a long pause, tensely*) What do you mean?

Peter Isn't it perfectly obvious?

Charles There isn't any famous French writer's daughter?

Peter I'm sure there are lots. But I've never slept with them.

Charles And the Gertas, the Friedas, the Italian painters, the ballet dancer who was old enough to be your mother?

Peter I think it was the Italian painter who was old enough to be my mother. Unless it was a retired ballet dancer.

Charles You made them all up?

Peter We made them all up, really, Charlie. The two of us. Your indignation gave substance to my fantasies. Without your help they'd never have existed for me – and they seem to have gone on existing for you. They died for me years ago, isn't that funny?

Charles So Hilary was the first girl you went all the way with.

Peter The only anything I've ever been all the way with, except of course for that old sock.

Charles (*sits staring ahead*) You lied to me, all these years.

Peter You seemed to expect that sort of thing from me. It seemed a shame to go on letting you down. Besides, you were so righteously convinced that I wasn't at all like you, it helped me to believe the same thing. I knew that we were both sheep, but my seeming a black one added a bit of colour to our joint self. (*Pause.*) But aren't you glad that underneath we're both such decent chaps? I've never done anything of which you'd really disapprove – at least not until after I left Hilary and even that . . . Well, here I am after all.

Charles We're not the same. We're not.

Peter In what are we different then, except in Alison's fecundity? And I've frequently longed for more children. It's Hilary who's against that – since she started going back to work.

Charles Well – well, you and Hilary, you made love long before you were married. Before you were engaged, even. Or was that a lie too?

Peter Not quite. The first time we went to bed we didn't manage to get quite all the way. The second time we

143

weren't engaged for most of the way, but we were by the time we'd gone all of it. It was a package deal. She insisted.

Charles On your getting engaged?

Peter On my going all the way. The engagement was my solution for getting there. Brothers, Charlie, you see, under the skin. (*Gets up, shows his hands to Charles.*) What do you see?

Charles Your hands. (*Studies them.*) Nicotine stains, otherwise – (*shakes his head*) just your hands.

Peter Not mine any longer. Daddy's. I never noticed them while he was alive but I recognise them now he's dead. Living heirlooms, without the liver spots. Doubtless they'll come.

Charles looks at his own hands.

You have Mummy's, to the very cuticle. As you don't smoke either. The rest of us, of course, the usual hodge-podge of inherited characteristics, some too far back to be traceable. I wonder whose hands Jeremy will recognise when he gets to our age . . . (*Pause.*) Anyway, we're on our way, you and I.

Charles On our way where?

Peter Just on. And on. Through these early-middle into the late-middle, the late-late-middle or the early-late – and so on and on, until pegging out. If not before. Somebody's father, somebody's husband, somebody's editor in my case, some Headmaster's Assistant in yours, somebody's brother in both our cases, eh, Charlie? All relationships and no self. Not even our own hands.

Charles (*after a pause*) But we're not the same in our attitudes to our work, are we? The way you've always sneered at my getting ahead. Virtually accused me of ingratiating myself –

Peter Now there it's true I thought there was a difference. I really despised some of your ploys, Charlie. But not any longer. I've since found out that in a crisis we're identical there, too.

Charles Identical in what?

Peter At that party – the six-simultaneous-publications party – I made some remarks. At the top of my voice. Which I subsequently regretted. Actually I regretted them a second before I made them.

Charles Then why did you make them?

Peter So as not to waste the regret. Anyway, my job hung in the balance, and I thought, as I set out to save it, that if you could do it with Headmaster and wife, I could do it with my lot.

Charles Do what?

Peter Grovel. With telegrams at first – I thought I might get a cheap deal with the Post Office. Apology cables on the lines of greeting cables. But I had to stop after the first two, I couldn't bear the operator's tone as he read them back to me. In the end I used taxis and grovelled direct. It was surprisingly easy.

Charles (*goes over to the drinks table*) You found it so, did you?

Peter Absolutely. Thanks to you, Charlie. At first I pretended to myself I was you, you see, and in no time at all I was grovelling happily away in my own identity. You'd have been proud of me. You know, I think that with a little bit of luck we're going to make it to the top together, just as Mummy would have wished, on all fours so to speak, and side by side. As you consult oilily with Headmaster over your next raise or house move, I'll be fawning my way up the publishing ladder.

Charles Did you know you were out of soda water?

Peter Then I shall order some more. (*Pause.*) Now I'd better go up and do some grovelling to my wife, eh? (*Looks at Charles.*) Charlie, what is it? You don't look yourself, and I've given you such a chance to be, only more so. You've skimped dreadfully on the I-told-you-sos. Haven't I earned them? (*Pause.*) Is everything all right at home? (*Pause.*) Alison all right? The kids?

Peter Fine. Fine.

Charles (*hesitates, then brightly*) By the way, something occurred to me about that dog.

Charles Dog?

Peter Dog. Your adopted dog. Alfonso, wasn't it? Hadn't you better make sure that Headmaster really doesn't mind him hanging about the garden before feeding him? Some people hate strays –

> *Charles leaps across the room, seizes Peter by the lapels, shakes him vigorously.*

Hey – hey –

> *Charles lets him go.*

Christ, what was that for? Haven't I grovelled enough, even for you?

Charles (*hits him on the upper arm, sharply and spitefully*) You little –

Peter Ow, you sod!

Charles Bastard!

> *Turns, walks off, stage left. Sound of door slamming.*

146

Peter Christ!

Rubs his arm, goes across to the flowers and chocolates. Picks them up. Turns to the door, left. Hilary enters in a bathrobe. Looks at Peter. Peter turns. After a moment:

Good evening.

Hilary Charlie's left, then?

Peter Well, first he shook me half senseless, clouted me on the arm, and called me little bastard. *Then* he left. What was interesting is that he chose the place where he used to get me, day in and day out, up to twenty years ago. It's soft and painful, doesn't do permanent damage, and leaves no bruise for a parental eye.

Hilary Were you baiting him?

Peter On the contrary. I was simply pointing out that we were brothers under the skin, and offering him some practical advice. Perhaps that's it – now I've shown him how my life is run, I've released all his sibling rivalry. (*Laughs nervously. There is a pause.*) Anyway, I've come – (*hesitates*) home. Groomed for the occasion. What do you think of my haircut, by the way? Executed by a great traditionalist in Holborn. He was so delighted to get back to old-fashioned hair-shearing that he tried to do it for nothing. I had to insist. (*Pause.*) But I didn't charge him much. (*Laughs.*) Well, the last time we spoke, you seemed to be hankering for what I'd once been. No other part of me is so immediately susceptible to backwards change. And look – (*Holds out chocolates and flowers.*) More memorabilia from our wooing past.

Hilary makes no move.

Am I smirking?

Hilary Not noticeably.

Peter Oh, well I ought to be. I'm very embarrassed. Not to say frightened even. (*Little pause.*) Surely you knew I'd come back.

Hilary Yes.

Peter And that I'd apologise for – well, you know.

Hilary Yes.

Peter Well – (*Puts the flowers and chocolates on the table.*) How's Jeremy?

Hilary He's asleep.

Peter Oh good. And how's school? His, I mean?

Hilary All right.

Peter Still not reading, I suppose?

Hilary Since the weekend he's moved on to the second *Janet and John*.

Peter Well, let's hope the narrative is beginning to gather pace. And how are you?

Hilary Perfectly well, thank you.

Peter Look, Hil, I've missed you and him and everything – perhaps it was worth my going to find that out – not that I didn't know it. But now the fact is it makes me happy, as it did when we first lived together. (*Pause.*) I know the fault was mine, entirely mine. I was taking my frustrations out on you and was being altogether childish. I had no right to do it, no right to walk out – (*This very quickly.*)

Hilary But I asked you to really – didn't I?

Peter Well, because I forced you to, didn't I? A fairly familiar marital ploy, I expect, so that when one gets tired of playing the role of culprit one can have a go at being the victim. I promise I shan't do that anyway. I abjectly admit that it was all my fault.

Hilary No, it wasn't.

Peter Oh yes it was, Hil, I drove you past the point of tolerance, I know that. But now what I desperately want is to put this whole mess behind us, with the understanding of course that you can put it in front of me during any healthy little marital spat of the future. (*Smiles.*) I've brought you something else, by the way.

    Takes a sheet of paper out of his pocket, hands it to Hilary.

The first items I've already had a go at putting into effect. The haircut is, I admit, a little excessive, but at least it takes care of the dandruff, for which there's no longer any room. I've also gargled my throat raw, my present huskiness isn't all emotion, you know, and as for items two and three, I haven't smoked since three this afternoon, and the Scotch I needed before facing you I didn't actually swallow. Now you'll see that I've been able to give a firm commitment on Sainsbury's shopping for Saturday mornings but that any weekday treks would, of course, be subject to various career responsibilities. (*Little pause.*) Both our careers, that is. I admit that the way I've shared the business of taking Jeremy to school seems a trifle inequitable on a quick glance, but then I had to take into account that you drive and I'll have to walk. Three mornings for you and two for me therefore seems reasonable, but I am, you'll note, prepared to renegotiate as particular weeks make particular demands. (*Pause.*) The clause on sex at the end was, of course, the trickiest and required several draftings, but you'll see that the only emphatic stipulation is a shared bed. The declaration with which I precede my signature is true.

149

Where it says I love you and always will. (*Pause.*) I've kept a second copy for myself as a memento mori – I mean, aide-memoire – but I thought of doing a third and circulating it to the Registry Office. They may feel it's worth incorporating into the official exchange of vows. Thus bridegrooms could make an immediate start on inflating into husbands. Of eight years standing.

Hilary finishes reading the paper.

You don't seem very interested. Have I left something out?

Hilary Nothing really.

Peter But you don't want to make a fresh start?

Hilary But we're not very fresh any more, Pete. Either of us.

Peter Well, what about an advance then, from where we used to be at our best? (*Pause.*) Hil, I'm not asking you for anything except the most precious thing in the world for me. To say that it's all right really.

Hilary But it isn't.

Peter But surely you can say – well, you know. That you love, and always will, whatever.

Hilary That's for children, not grown-ups.

Peter (*after a pause*) That's Jeremy taken care of. Oh, Hil – (*Steps towards her.*)

Hilary Don't! (*Crying out.*)

Peter (*stops*) Because – just because – Charlie has been talking, has he?

Hilary Almost non-stop. But not about you.

Peter But then what is it? I mean, all right, all right, I've conceded that I deserve punishing –

Hilary That's for children too.

Peter Surely not these days. I thought that was why adults had to settle for punishing each other. (*Pause.*) All right, let me put it another way, I'm back in my own maisonette, what are you going to do about it?

Hilary Ask you to leave.

Peter Are you going to explain?

Hilary I'm trying to avoid an ugly scene.

Peter This is your idea of a pretty one, is it?

Hilary Would you please leave, Peter? I'll tell you everything in a letter.

Peter In a letter! (*Incredulously.*) A letter! Well, darling, I promise you I shall receive it at my own front door. Because I'm bloody well not going. I've discovered I'm too young to leave home. I'm sticking, upstairs, downstairs, in the kitchen, in your way. I'm your husband, Jeremy's father. And what are you going to do about that? Call in the lawyers and the policemen?

Hilary If I have to. (*Pause.*) Anyway, now you know I really want you to go, and that I shall go on wanting you to go. And until you do – you stay down here. I'm going to bed.

Peter No, you're not. (*Takes her arm.*) Do you really think you can get out of it after eight years of my love and devotion because I've given you a few bad times recently? Well, what about my bad times, the ones I can't escape from though I've just tried – and I'm not talking about your neglect of me for your work, your increasing frigidity and those calculated little aloofnesses that you started practising even before I started practising going to seed.

Hilary Is that why you did it? So that I'd take a little notice of you?

Peter I'm talking about the real – the true – bad times, the ones that have come every day of my life since I first began to love you. When the telephone rings in my office and before I answer it I think of you in a car crash or of Jeremy ill or maimed in some idiotic accident at school or the sudden hopeless questions, such as, 'But what should I do if anything happened to either of you?' As I know it's bound to, to both of you in the end, and that all I can really pray for is that it happens to me first, after a decent interval, and then that there are further decent intervals between your going and his. Except that life doesn't work according to decent intervals, which are anyway formulated by types like you and me out here in Muswell Hill.

Hilary Shut up, shut up, this isn't fair.

Peter Precisely my point. But it's true.

Hilary Of course it's true. Do you think I haven't thought the same about Jeremy?

Peter But not about me?

Hilary Yes. But it doesn't matter.

Peter Doesn't matter!

Hilary Because I'm still going to live my own life. (*Pause.*) Oh God, Peter, it's not the beginning when we were in love with each other. Or the end, when we could have cried over each other, and probably still will, both those parts are easy, anyone can do those. It's the stretch in between, that's our married life, that I can't stand.

Peter Because for a short time, a matter of months, what, three months –

Hilary Oh, longer. Much longer.

Peter Four then, at the most. Before that I was a model husband, father, the lot! Second only to Charlie.

Hilary I wouldn't want to be married to Charlie either. But he's found himself an Alison, why couldn't you?

Peter What!

Hilary Did you sleep with anyone, while you were away?

Peter Is that what you think?

Hilary Well, did you?

Peter I certainly did not!

Hilary Why not?

Peter Because I couldn't – it's not in my nature. Perhaps I tried, I won't deny it – we went to bed together, yes, all right – but we didn't make love! You know I couldn't!

Hilary Why not?

Peter You wouldn't let me! When it came to it I didn't want a foreign body next to mine in bed. I felt clumsy and awkward and dirty, and that's the truth too. So you can't make anything out of that, Hilary. I may not be so in law, but you know I'm a faithful husband.

Hilary Yes, I know. And that's what I can't stand.

Peter stares at her.

Pete – you're married to a faithless wife. (*There is a pause.*) Oh, why didn't you come back as you left – drunken and sneering. You look so – so clean!

Peter You mean there's somebody else?

Hilary nods.

In ten days you found a replacement – well, send him back.

Hilary Not in ten days. A long time ago! I wanted you to go, I wanted you to go, I want you to go. I can't bear your wretched innocence, your oppressive faithfulness. It's been like deceiving a child.

Peter It's not . . . (*blankly, after a second*) fair. At that bloody school of yours, is he?

Hilary Yes.

Peter Well, what is he – some damned . . . foreigner? What? A Turk, an Arab, a Spanish monk, a Frenchman – how low have you sunk?

Hilary He's a teacher.

Peter To the very bottom then! What's his name?

Hilary What does it matter?

Peter What's his name!

Hilary Please, you'll wake Jeremy. George Green.

Peter George Green. You've never mentioned any George Green. Nothing. Nothing. No passing references to any George Green, no murmurings in your sleep of George Green, no smiling by-the-ways-have-I-told-you-about-George-Green. Nothing, I don't believe it.

Hilary It's true, Peter, I love him.

Peter Love George Green! Well, come on, come on, what is he? Married, widowed, divorced, one of these fashionably converting homosexuals – he can't be single unless he's a mere boy, is he a mere boy, George Green?

Hilary No. He's older than us, actually.

Peter How much older?

Hilary By ten years.

Peter Divorced, eh? How many times?

Hilary Twice.

Peter A bit of a specialist then, but not versatile. Or has he just been practising until the right married woman, my wife, came along? How many children?

Hilary Two by his first wife, one by his second.

Peter But is he trained in children over five? Or does he pass them on at an early age? I'm speaking for Jeremy now.

Hilary He sees a great deal of them.

Peter And he sees a great deal of mine?

Hilary Not yet. (*Pause.*) Peter, I –

Peter Shut up!

Hilary At least he's a grown-up. I want you to move out straight away.

Peter Oh, but just a minute, darling, isn't it slightly unconventional to see me from our bedroom to the drawing-room sofa to the pavement, back again and out again all within ten days? Most marriages conclude at a slightly more leisurely pace. We're skimping on the niceties. After all, we've been complacent witnesses to a lot of break-ups in our time, we must owe returns to newly re-weds and divorcees all over London. So for God's sake let's stick to form. By your own admission we haven't even begun to make Jeremy miserable. What about the heart-searchings followed by the heart-rendings, yours and mine . . .

He sits, shaking, on the arm of the sofa. Hilary makes to leave the room, stops, comes back. Makes to put a hand on his head.

Don't do that! (*Sharply, then:*) They still stock period Brylcreem in Holborn. My period anyway. (*Pause.*) Go to bed, Hilary, leave me alone.

Hilary hesitates, then turns, goes to the door, left.

After all, you'll have another of your hard days tomorrow, won't you, with all its explanations, caresses, half-plans, avowals and pronunciation classes, not to speak of collecting Jeremy from school.

Hilary goes out.

Then buying me a Chinese throwaway and facing me over it –

Looks, sees Hilary has gone, remains sitting on the arm of the sofa. Takes out cigarettes from pocket, studies government warning on package, takes cigarette out, lights up.
There is a crashing noise from the kitchen. Charles enters. He is carrying a syphon of soda water.

Charles I got you some. (*Holds up the syphon.*)

Peter Thanks.

Charles Well, I do drink so much of it –

Carries it across to the table, puts it down.

Um, may I –?

Peter Help yourself.

Charles (*squirts some into a glass*) I'm sorry about before. Drink?

Peter Please.

Charles (*pours him a very small Scotch, brings it over*)
That's the first time in twenty years I've hit you.

Peter (*looking at the Scotch in dismay*) At least it was
evocative.

Charles No hard feelings.

Peter No. But I don't know why you did it.

Charles Nor do I really. (*Pause.*) By the way, I don't
know if Hilary told you, we're going to have twins.

Peter You and Hilary?

Charles (*laughs*) Alison is, I should say.

Peter Twins, Charlie. Congratulations.

Charles Thanks. (*Little pause.*) Is everything all right
between you two?

Peter Oh yes.

Charles Well, you said it would be. You told her
everything, did you?

Peter I think we're much clearer about each other,
Charlie, thanks.

Charles Even about that girl, eh, and going to bed with
her, even though you didn't –

Peter She knows everything, even about Cocteau's
daughter.

Charles But I realised afterwards that she'd never known
about her. Them. I mean, how could you tell her about
affairs you've never had?

Peter I didn't have to tell her, she always knew I didn't
have them. After all, she virtually had to give me
directions on our engagement night.

Charles She's very understanding. (*Little pause.*) You know, I'm sorry they didn't exist.

Peter So am I. So, probably, is she. But then if they had, I'd have been a different sort of person and –

Charles And she wouldn't have wanted to marry you.

Peter Yes, a bit of a conundrum, that. (*He smiles.*)

Charles Anyway, I'm glad you're back, Pete. I missed you. I mean, the great thing is, isn't it, to love one another in spite.

Peter In spite? Yes, I'll drink to that. (*Raises his glass.*)

Charles *and* **Peter** (*toasting each other*) In spite.

Charles Goodnight, old Pete.

Peter Goodnight, old Charlie.

Charles exits. Crash. 'Drat.'
　　Peter picks up bags, looks around, exits. Door slams.

Curtain.

MOLLY

Introduction

Molly is an adaptation for the stage of the earliest of my television plays – *Death of a Teddy Bear* – which was written for BBC's Wednesday Play about ten years ago. Brenda Bruce, Hywel Bennet, Rachel Kempson and the late Kenneth J. Warren played the original Molly, Oliver, Eve and Teddy; Warris Hussein was our director; Kenith Trodd the producer; and Gerald Savory wiped the tape.

The source of *Death of a Teddy Bear* was the Alma Rattenbury case, an account of which I came across in a paperback called (I think) *Ten Famous Trials*, left discarded in a railway compartment. I was on my way from London to Cambridge to supervise Trinity undergraduates in (probably) Hobbes, or Hume, or Aeschylus or some such, and had a briefcase full of essays to mark. I flicked through the pages of the paperback – it was stained and swollen as if a dog had urinated over it – in the cursory manner of one who has something of more consequence on his mind, plucked out a handful of essays, and settled down to the book. When I arrived at Cambridge I left the book where I'd found it, but for the rest of that day, and for many subsequent days and (especially) nights, I was haunted by Mrs Rattenbury's story – or what of it I could perceive behind the dozen pages or so in which her trial had been described. So when Kenith Trodd asked me if I'd like to try my hand at a full-length television play the subject was already fully there, and at least partially shaped, even though unwritten. Which is perhaps why I didn't go back to Mrs Rattenbury herself, neither to her trial nor to reconstructions of the crime. I based my play on the effect that the dozen pages had had on me (the specifics being pretty well forgotten), changed the names, and hoped that my sense of the drama would find its own form. *Death of a Teddy Bear* was not, therefore, *about* Mrs Rattenbury and the murder in which she was involved, although of course without her it would never have been written.

I felt strongly enough about *Death of a Teddy Bear* not to want to lose it to television – not realising then that the BBC, after showing it twice, was simply going to chuck it away (see *The New Review*, Vol. 3, No. 27) – and about five years ago I wrote the first stage draft. I followed as closely as I could the emotional line and basic structure of the original, extending some scenes and subtracting those that depended on the mobility of the camera, and so inevitably, and against my intentions, altered the tone of the whole. Further drafts altered further, and I might have left the final draft in a drawer if it hadn't been for the discovery that the television version no longer exists. So in a sense its recent production (at the new Spoleto Festival, in Charleston, last Spring) and its present slightly different (slightly rewritten) production (at the Watford Palace Theatre) and its publication in *The New Review* must be attributed to 'Wiper' Savory, who left me with no alternative but to preserve the play in the only form now left.

N.B. Terrence Rattigan's play, *Cause Célèbre,* now on in the West End, is also based on the Rattenbury case. I haven't seen it, but gather that it started life as a radio play a couple of years back, and unlike *Molly*, concentrates on the trial. I believe there have been other Rattenbury plays, but have no details of them.

Programme note for the original production at the Watford Palace Theatre, November 1977.

Molly was first performed in England at the Palace Theatre, Watford, in November 1977. The cast was as follows:

Molly Mary Miller
Teddy Raymond Francis
Oliver Anthony Allen
Eve Barbara Atkinson
Greaves Arthur Cox
Police Constable Stephen Enns

Director Stephen Hollis
Set Designer Christopher Morley
Costume Designer Ann Curtis
Lighting Brian Harris

Characters

Molly

Teddy

Oliver

Eve

Greaves

Police Constable

The play is set in the 1930s

Act One

SCENE ONE

Living room of a house. It has three doors: one stage right, which leads into the conservatory, part of which is visible on the stage; one back, that leads into the kitchen, dining room etc.; and one left, that leads to the hall, front door, and other offices and stairs. In the room is a cocktail cabinet, new and of the thirties, amply stocked; an armchair; a large sofa; tables, chairs, all in the style of the twenties and thirties. The curtain rises on the room, empty. Light beginning to fade. There is a pause, and then Molly, wearing a light coat, a silk scarf, enters slowly through the conservatory. She takes off her scarf, drops it onto the sofa. She stands listless, then takes from her coat pocket her cigarettes and a lighter. She lights a cigarette, draws on it deeply, then stares around her with an air of desperation, goes to radio, turns it on, listens for a moment to music, makes an irritated expression, turns the radio off, goes to drinks table, pours herself a drink, takes a sip as, above, sound of door opening.

Teddy (*off, up*) Moll! (*Calling.*) Molly!

Molly (*hesitates*) In here, darling.

There is another call of 'Moll', then a door slams. The sound of footsteps, coming down. Molly puts down glass, walks swiftly out through the conservatory, vanishing exactly as the door, left, opens and Teddy enters, saying irritably 'Moll' as he does so. Sees the room empty, makes an irritable exclamation, goes over to the conservatory, shouts 'Moll!' He is in his

167

mid-sixties, has a deaf aid, elaborate and visible and of the thirties, and an air of slightly bogus physicality. Shouts again: 'Moll—ly'.

Eve enters from the back. Looks towards the conservatory. She is a woman in her mid-fifties, severely dressed and severe of expression; spectacles; and an air of brisk efficiency.

Teddy (*off*) Damn it!

He comes back from the conservatory, sees Eve.

Oh, hello Evie, where's Moll?

Eve (*speaking loudly*) She's gone for a walk.

Teddy When?

Eve About an hour ago.

Teddy Then why didn't she ask me? (*Goes to cocktail cabinet.*) I could have just done with a walk.

Eve You were taking a nap.

Teddy But I didn't want to. I wanted to go for a walk. I spend the whole afternoon waiting for her to make up her mind whether she wants to go or not –

Pours himself a large Scotch. Eve sees Molly's scarf, goes over to it, deftly and surreptitiously picks it up, and puts it on one of the tables, where it is unlikely to be noticed.

– and then I go upstairs to get a book and sit down on the bed with it for a moment and – (*Adds soda water to his Scotch, splashes it.*) Damn, damn! (*Looks at Eve.*)

Eve I'll get a cloth –

Teddy Oh sit down, Evie, sit down. I can manage – (*Mops up the soda with a handkerchief.*) Sorry, Eve, I'm always a grump if I doze through the afternoon – like a bear with a headache. What'll you have, one of your dry-as-dust sherrys?

Eve Oh, no thank you, Teddy, I really ought to get back to the kitchen –

Teddy (*pouring Eve a sherry*) Tell me, Evie, do you think Moll wants to stay? We've been here a month now, but she makes me feel as if we only just moved in yesterday, or we're going to be moved out tomorrow, but we're never going to have the part in between. Has she said anything to you?

He brings her the sherry.

Eve Thank you. Well, she's said she likes it here.

Teddy What about you?

Eve Oh yes. Very much.

Teddy That's good, because we need you, Evie. Your hitching on to us was real luck, you keep us orderly. Don't you think of abandoning us.

Eve That's very kind of you, Teddy.

Teddy Well, it's her England, that's what she said she wanted. And it'd do for me if she settles for it. Wish I didn't sleep so much, that's the only thing. Never slept like this in Canada. Never had time to. But then I had a business to run, bills of lading to get out, had to meet the ships at sometimes two in the morning, did you know that, Evie? (*Pause.*) Funny thing is, I miss the smell of fish. The whole town smelt of it, the uptown streets, it got into the stores. I didn't notice it until I'd left. Hey, it's getting dark. That's something else I'm not used to, your English springs. We don't have springs in Canada, just a sort of wink between winter and summer. But then we have our falls, you don't have falls, do you?

Eve No, we only have autumns, I'm afraid.

Teddy What? Well, I don't like her out in the dark. Wandering about. She used to tell me England's got the best climate in the world, you know what I think now I've seen it, it may be the best climate, but the weather's terrible. (*Laughs.*) Not my idea of friendly either. (*Goes back to cocktail cabinet.*) Now in Nova Scotia, move into a village, they'd be right round asking what they could do to help, inviting us over, but we've been here two whole weeks, and who do we know? Dr Gracey, when I need him to look after my ears.

Eve More people know Tom Fool than Tom Fool knows people.

Teddy Who?

Eve Tom Fool.

Teddy Tom who?

Eve Fool.

Teddy Well I don't know him, somebody in the village?

Eve It's a saying.

Teddy (*not having understood*) Oh. Ready for another? (*Coming across with the bottle.*)

Eve No, I won't, thanks –

    Teddy pours sherry. Eve just manages to catch it.

Teddy You know what woke me up? I thought I heard her singing, that one about the seals of Nanaimo, and playing the piano – I heard it quite clear, every note, so it must have been a dream – she was going to try and write more songs once she got back here, that's why she wanted a place with a piano in it, but she hasn't played it yet – I'm going to get on to her about that, this

evening. Did you know I got that seal song played over
Station RCVX – knew the owner – he put it out across
the whole of Nova Scotia. Bob Hoskins. He was a good
friend of mine. In hardware. You ever been married,
Evie?

Eve No.

Teddy Why not?

Eve I'm afraid no one ever asked me.

Teddy That's the girl. (*Laughs.*) Hey, Evie, mind if I ask
you a delicate question?

Eve No.

Teddy You sure?

Eve Well, as I'm living in your house, you have a perfect
right to know anything about me you want. Within
reason, of course.

Teddy Am I paying you enough?

Eve Yes, quite enough, thank you, Teddy. No thank you.
You're more than generous. Now if you'll excuse me,
I really must go and have a look at the dinner. (*Gets up
and goes out.*)

Teddy Oh.

> *Sits for a moment, then gets up, goes to the cocktail
> cabinet, adds a dash of Scotch, squirts soda water,
> splashes it slightly, makes as if to mop it, gestures
> irritably, goes over to the conservatory, stands looking
> through.*

What the hell's she playing at?

> *There is a ring at the doorbell, left. Teddy makes no
> move.*

Eve (*appears from back*) Somebody at the door.

Teddy still makes no move. Eve makes to speak again, instead goes off, left. Teddy turns, walks to the door, back, stands at it.

Teddy Hey, Evie, I'm getting really worried –

Eve re-enters from left, accompanied by Oliver.
Oliver is a boy of about seventeen, awkward and not particularly attractive. Dressed in his Sunday clothes, as for an interview. Teddy turns away from the door, sees Oliver and Eve.

Eve (*coming over to Teddy*) It's a boy from the village.

Teddy What? Is Moll all right?

Eve He says something about a job.

Teddy What job?

Eve I've no idea.

Teddy (*goes over to Oliver*) Well, hello, boy, what can we do for you?

Oliver Sir. They said at Sprinkley's there was a job.

Eve That's the garage in the village.

Teddy What's your name, boy?

Oliver Oliver, sir.

Teddy What?

Oliver Oliver, sir. Oliver Treefe.

Teddy Oliver?

Oliver Yes, sir.

Teddy Oliver what, Oliver?

Oliver Oliver Treefe, sir.

Eve You'll have to speak up please, Oliver.

Teddy Sorry, Oliver, I'm not picking you up.

Oliver (*realising*) OLIVER TREEFE, SIR. (*In a bellow.*)

Teddy Oliver Treefsir, well, Oliver Treefsir, what can we do for you?

Oliver (*in a bellow*) They said at Sprinkley's Garage a lady had been in to inquire about a boy, sir.

Eve (*to Teddy*) It must have been Molly. (*To Oliver*) When did she come in?

Oliver (*bellowing at Eve*) This afternoon, they said. They said she said there was a car needed looking after. Mr Goldberg's Alvis.

Teddy What?

Eve Mr Goldberg's Alvis, Teddy.

Teddy Mr Goldberg hasn't got an Alvis. I've got it. Part of the deal for the house. He left it for me for what he called a consideration, he's probably bought himself a new car out of the consideration, eh, boy? Quite a businessman, your Mr Goldberg. (*Laughs.*)

    Oliver laughs.

Quite a businessman. It doesn't go, boy. Needs a lot of tinkering. Can you tinker?

Oliver Yes, sir.

Teddy Can, eh? That's right, don't undersell yourself, what about a drink, we got some of that stuff you English call beer somewhere and you look to be at the beer-guzzling age, eh, Evie? Like one? (*Goes to cocktail cabinet.*)

Oliver Well, no thank you very much, sir.

Teddy begins to wrestle with a bottle of beer.

Eve Did the lady mention any special time to call, Oliver?

Oliver They said she said the evening would be best, Missus.

Eve I see. And was it only about the car?

Oliver Well, they said she said it would be a bit of driving and helping about the garden and odd jobs. They said it was a proper job, Missus.

Eve Well, I'm afraid Mrs Treadley isn't here at the moment, but I'll take down your details and let her have them. Who can give you references, Oliver?

Oliver Well, there's Sprinkley's.

Eve And anyone else?

Teddy pours beer, which foams up over cabinet.

Teddy Damn! (*Mops at it with handkerchief.*) First thing you've got to do is make her go, second thing is to break me into her ways. I'm not used to cars like your Mr Goldberg's Alvises, especially now my balance's gone, so you'll have to show me how to handle her, whether she needs coaxing or bullying, a car's like any machine, a man's made her so she's going to have something wrong with her. I used to do a lot of driving – ever heard of the Breton Trail? That's in Nova Scotia.

He brings Oliver his beer.

Here, get yourself outside of that –

Oliver Thank you, sir.

Teddy That's in Nova Scotia, where the roads go straight ten yards before they turn around and go back five. In a

Manson. By God I loved that car. Always knew where to tinker when she gave me trouble. Think I could get to love a car that used to belong to your Mr Goldberg, eh, that he left to rot and rust for a consideration? Eh?

Eve I was just getting down some references, Teddy.

Teddy Oh.

Eve Now who else besides Sprinkley's, Oliver?

Oliver I done some gardening with my dad –

Teddy Who?

Oliver My dad, sir.

Teddy Your dad – a reference from your dad? We could all get references from our dads, boy. (*Laughs.*)

Oliver No, I only meant –

Eve Where else have you worked, Oliver?

Molly enters the conservatory, stands watching for a moment, unseen by the others.

Where else have you worked, Oliver?

Oliver Well – (*Pauses.*) Well, I did some for Mrs Shepherd, Missus, but I stopped after a bit.

Eve Indeed, why?

Molly (*enters*) Of course, you're the boy, aren't you, that Sprinkley's promised to send. I'm so sorry I wasn't here when you arrived, please forgive me.

Oliver That's all right, Miss.

Molly (*to Teddy and Eve*) I popped in as I was passing the garage, when the thought struck, and then it slipped my mind, sorry, darlings.

Teddy Where you been, Moll? Old Evie was getting worried about you, out there in the dark.

Molly (*to Eve*) Were you, darling? There was no need, it was all quite friendly and above board. Well, what have you fixed up, between the three of you?

Eve We're just sorting out the question of references.

Teddy Drink, Moll. (*Going to cocktail cabinet.*)

Molly Thank you, darling, I'd love one.

Teddy We've just been trying to make out from your Oliver Treefsir here whether he's the sort that kills us.

Molly (*smiling at Oliver*) Are you the sort to kill us, Oliver?

Oliver No, Miss.

Molly There we are, what more could we ask? You see, my husband's the sort that likes to drive very fast himself, but when he's being driven he likes it to be by the sort that drives very slow, don't you, darling? But I can't drive at all, so I like everybody to drive fast, even the people in other cars.

Teddy comes over, hands Molly a drink.

Thank you, darling. Now what about the gardening, are you going to do that for us too?

Oliver Well, yes, Miss, I mean if you want –

Molly Because we need a gardener to garden for us as well as a driver who won't kill us, Oliver, it's all in the most terrible tangle out there, some of the spring whatsits look quite alarming. What are your fingers like, can we see them?

Oliver Miss?

176

Molly Can we see your fingers?

Oliver shows his fingers.

Mmmm – yes, they look as if they could be green. You see we met a lady on the boat coming over from Canada who talked every lunchtime and dinnertime about gardening, and she said – do you remember, darling . . .?

Teddy What?

Molly The herbaceous-border lady, darling, she said that for gardens green fingers were quite essential, of course, and that the best way to make flowers grow was to talk to them and sing to them and even to recite to them, now would you be willing to talk and sing and recite poems to our flowers, Oliver? (*Looks at him seriously.*)

Oliver Um, well – (*Gives a little laugh.*)

Molly (*smiling*) Oh well. What about pulling up weeds and mowing the lawn instead?

Oliver Oh yes, Miss. I could do that. I mean, my dad does the gardening for some of them in the village in the evenings, and I've helped him.

Molly There you are then. You meet our requirements exactly, doesn't he, darling?

Teddy What?

Eve Excuse me, Moll, but I haven't quite found out how you can get hold of Mrs Shepherd.

Molly Why do I want to get hold of Mrs Shepherd?

Teddy Hey, that boy's been standing there with a mitt full of beer and you ladies haven't let him take a sip of it. You have your drink, boy. Go on.

Oliver hesitates, then raises his glass, drinks.

Eve (*to Molly*) Oliver used to work for Mrs Shepherd until she let him go.

Oliver finishes his drink.

Teddy That's the boy!

Molly Why did Mrs Shepherd let you go, Oliver?

Oliver She – well, she just said she didn't need me any more, that's all.

Molly Oh. And if she had needed you any more we wouldn't be able to have you now, would we, so you see, Evie, Mrs Shepherd was only acting for the best, wasn't she, Oliver, if we *can* have you now, that is? But omigod, how much are we to pay you?

Oliver Well, Miss, whatever – I don't know.

Molly How much did Mrs Shepherd pay you?

Oliver Two pound a week, Miss.

Molly Two pounds a week!

Eve That would be the normal rate.

Molly But it seems a mere trifle for chauffeuring us about and not killing us and keeping our weeds down and our flowers up and general handymanning – you would do a little handymanning wouldn't you, Oliver? I really think a minimum of four pounds a week, wouldn't you, darling?

Eve Four pounds!

Teddy What?

Molly Four pounds a week for Oliver, darling, includes handymanning.

Teddy Give him four and a half.

Molly Four pounds ten, Oliver, there we are. Will you come to us for that?

Oliver Yes, Miss! I mean, I'll have to talk it over with my dad –

Molly Of course you will. But even so, I think we've got you, haven't we?

Oliver Yes, Miss.

Molly Well then, Dad willing, when can you start – tomorrow?

Eve Tomorrow's Sunday.

Molly Monday then.

Oliver Yes, Miss.

Molly All settled, darling. I had to use my wiles but I've brought him to it.

Teddy Another beer, boy?

Oliver Um, no thanks –

Molly Oh, we mustn't keep him any longer.

She takes the glass from Oliver, winks at him.

He's got important matters to discuss with his dad. Haven't you?

Oliver Yes, Miss.

Eve I'll see you out, Oliver. (*Leads him to the door.*)

Molly See you Monday, Oliver.

Teddy Bye there, boy.

Oliver (*shouting*) Sir.

Teddy I like the look of him.

Molly Did you really, darling? Can't say I did, pale, spotty and slightly furtive, I thought. But just the sort to know all about engines and lawnmowers and things – (*Taking off her coat.*) And one never does know how to turn people down – (*Drops coat in chair.*)

Teddy Where did you go?

Molly Further than I meant.

Teddy (*sits down, looks at her*) Why didn't you take me with you?

Molly (*goes over to him, rumples his hair*) You were snoozing, my sweet, I hadn't the heart to wake you.

Kisses the top of his head, goes over to the cocktail cabinet with his glass, pours them both a drink.

And it really wasn't very nice anyway, you'd have found me a terrible bore. I kept thinking I heard a tune I could write down and make into one of my silly songs, it was as if I were following it, through one field, then another, right to the river where the bridge is, I was sure it was there somewhere, like a person I was going to meet, but nobody came.

Brings him his drink back.

Nobody at all.

Teddy What? I missed all that.

Molly I was just chattering.

Eve enters, from left.

Well, darling, you got it all out of him, I take it.

Eve What?

Molly Mrs Whatsit's address and the rest of it.

Eve Mrs Shepherd's. Yes, I did. I hope you don't mind. I think she might be that lady we saw in the post office the other day, having a parcel weighed.

Molly With a ridiculous hat and false teeth?

Eve I didn't really notice her teeth.

Molly What about her ankles, did you notice those?

Eve Notice what?

Molly Weren't they very thick?

Eve I'm afraid I didn't notice her ankles, either.

Molly Then it can't have been Mrs Whatsit, darling, in the post office.

Eve You've met her then?

Molly Who?

Eve Mrs Shepherd.

Teddy Who are you two nattering about?

Molly Mrs Shepherd, darling.

Teddy Who's she?

Molly We haven't the slightest idea, but Eve's got her address and she's determined to find out, aren't you, darling?

Eve I'm sorry, Molly, I know it wasn't my place to interfere –

Molly Oh Eve!

Eve It's just that I don't think you should take people on without knowing anything about them, except what they tell you themselves.

Molly Really, darling? I don't agree, we took you on without knowing anything about you except what you told us yourself, and that's worked out quite well.

Eve I gave you three references!

Molly Yes, darling, but you don't think I read them? They were far too long, and bound to be flattering, which wouldn't have been fun, so I hired you in lieu.

Eve picks up Molly's coat and scarf, takes them out to hall, left.

Omigod! (*Sinks into a chair.*)

Teddy What?

Molly I've offended Eve again.

Teddy What?

Molly She really is the most humourless –

Eve enters, from left.

Teddy (*not seeing her*) When's she going to feed us, that's what I want to know.

Eve I'm on my way to the kitchen now.

Molly Oh darling – (*To Eve,*) I was only teasing, of course I read your references, they were divine, one from the two ladies in Richmond, one from the doctor in Kingston and one from – from – wherever, but I remember it quite well, said you were scrupulous in violet ink and couldn't manage without you and no more could we, and you were right to insist on Mr Whatsit's address, and I did rush us into the youth quite fecklessly, it was just that I felt funny about having forgotten him entirely, but I know he won't get away with anything, darling, with you to keep an eye on him, and if you ever bump into Mrs Shepherd again you can quiz her to your heart's content, all right, darling, all forgiven? Please. Pretty please with sugar on it?

Eve (*smiles*) Oh Moll. Now you're teasing me again.

Molly No, I'm not, darling. I mean it. Every word almost.

Eve (*still smiling*) It'll just be a few minutes, Teddy.

Teddy No rush, Evie, have another drink!

Eve Then you'll never eat. (*Goes out back.*)

Molly (*wearily*) Omigod!

She lights a cigarette. Teddy watches her. There is a pause.

Teddy Hey, you, come here! (*Pause.*) Come on, come here, I said.

Molly, concealing irritation, clearly knows what is to happen, gets up, goes over to Teddy.

Molly Sir?

Teddy Now my girl, how many's that since lunch?

Molly Only one, sir.

Teddy Come on, Moll, the truth now. All the time you were gadding about out there.

Molly Well, three. (*Pause.*) Four. (*Pause. Holds up five fingers.*) Ten. Twenty.

Teddy (*not hearing*) Five, eh? Well, add on another four and one on top of that makes – one – two – three – four – five – six – seven – eight – nine –

He slaps Molly on the bottom, laughing. Molly giggles, cries 'Ouch'.

Now get us another drink, girl.

Molly My Lord.

*Makes a little curtsy, takes his glass, pours him a
drink and one for herself.*

Teddy And another thing, girl, what about getting to the
piano? All your talk about your songs and you haven't
touched a key since we moved in, that was another of
Mr Goldberg's considerations – he can hire himself a
whole band out of that one – I was telling Eve all about
your seal song and Bob Hoskins transmitting it over
RCVX –

He takes her hand as she brings him the drink.

Play it now, eh, Moll?

Molly But darling, she's getting the dinner on the table.

Teddy What? Don't want to?

Molly Not very much, darling. For one thing the piano's
out of tune. And so am I. (*Looks at him from above,
sadly.*) You come and sit here then.

*Takes him by the hand, leads him to the chair nearest
the piano, then goes to the piano, begins to play
uncertainly. The piano is out of tune.*
  *Molly makes a face. After a moment she begins to
sing, very loudly, but nicely, 'And Did Those Feet'.*
  Eve enters from the back, stands listening.
  *Teddy is evidently straining to hear, his foot beating
out of time to the music.*

Teddy (*as Molly is fading out*) There. There, Evie. She
wrote it herself. What do you think of it?

Eve I think it's lovely.

Molly Why Evie, you're tone deaf!

184

Eve Perhaps I am. But I know a nice voice when I hear one. Dinner's ready.

Molly comes over, takes Teddy's hand; they go through back, and as Eve closes the door behind them: lights.

SCENE TWO

A week or so later. Mid-afternoon. The room is full of sunlight, the conservatory door is open.

Oliver enters through the conservatory, furtively. He is wearing an open-necked shirt, baggy gardening trousers. He looks towards the kitchen, back, then towards the door, left, then goes to the sofa, on which is Molly's handbag. Opens the handbag, takes out a package of cigarettes and the lighter. Quickly extracts a cigarette, puts it in his pocket, then another, which he lights. Puts the lighter back in the handbag, closes it. Stands smoking, looking around.

Eve enters from the back. Stands watching Oliver.

Oliver, suddenly conscious of another presence, turns. They stare at each other.

Oliver I've finished digging up them weeds around the garage, Missus.

Eve And have you done the hedge?

Oliver No, Missus, I – I don't know where the shears is.

Eve We don't keep them in the sitting room, Oliver. Perhaps they're under the potato sacking on the second shelf in the conservatory where I told you to put them the last time you used them, have you looked?

Oliver No, Missus.

Eve Have you put the weeds in the compost?

Oliver No, Miss.

Eve Then do that first. Then the hedge. And oh, Oliver –

Eve gets an ashtray, comes towards Oliver, holds it out.

In here, please.

Oliver stubs out the cigarette.

Now here are two things for you to understand, Oliver. Firstly, we don't like you wandering into the house whenever you feel like it, and secondly we don't like you smoking in the house. You left a saucer full of stubs in my kitchen after your lunch today. All right?

Oliver (*sulkily*) Yes, Missus.

Eve And by the way, I'm not Missus, I'm Miss. Miss Mace. (*Attempts a more friendly tone. Little pause.*) Is anything the matter?

Oliver Well, Missus – Miss. The only thing . . . Well, I mean, I was told it was going to be fixing the Alvis and driving it mainly, that was my work, and there was a bit of gardening on the side, but I mean I've got the Alvis fixed, but I've only got to drive it twice in two weeks, it's been gardening all the time, and even painting the inside of the garage.

Eve I see. Well, Oliver, if you're not satisfied with the conditions of your employment, you're quite at liberty to leave. Is that what you want to do?

Oliver No, Missus.

Eve Miss.

Oliver No, Miss.

Eve I'm sure you don't. So you'd better get on with it, hadn't you?

Oliver (*after a pause*) Yes, Miss. (*Turns to go.*)

Eve (*looks into the ashtray*) Oliver. What cigarettes do you smoke?

Oliver Any sort, Missus. Miss.

Eve Including the sort that Mrs Treadley smokes?

Eve (*shrugs*) I don't know what sort she smokes.

Eve She smokes this sort. (*Holding up stub.*) Did you take one of hers?

Oliver No, Miss!

Eve I think you did, Oliver. That's what you were doing in here, wasn't it?

Oliver No, Miss, I never!

Eve Please don't lie, Oliver.

Oliver (*as Molly enters*) I'm not lying, Miss!

Molly (*looking from one to the other*) What's going on, it sounds thrilling!

Eve I'm just trying to find out whether Oliver's been helping himself to your cigarettes.

Oliver I didn't, Miss.

Molly Oh, I do hope you didn't, Oliver, I'm terribly low and I do hate to be caught without one. Shall I check and see how I'm off? (*Goes over to handbag, opens it, looks into the cigarette package.*) About a dozen, I suppose that'll do, could you remember some, Evie, if you're going shopping? (*Little pause.*) Are you doing something in the garden, Oliver?

Oliver I've got to put weeds in the compost and then clip the hedge, Miss.

Molly Such a nice day for being outside.

Oliver Yes, Miss. (*Smirks at Eve, goes out.*)

Eve Molly, I know he helped himself.

Molly (*lighting a cigarette*) Yes, darling, I expect you're right.

Eve Well, if there's one thing I hate it's a pilferer. And a liar.

Molly Well, we all have our pet aversions, I detest ghastly scenes and boys getting shrill all over something extremely trivial, darling.

Eve I see. (*Turns, goes out, back.*)

Molly I see. I see. Pretty please with sugar on it. (*Imitating first Eve, then herself.*) Oh God – (*She gets up.*) Evie! (*Makes to go back.*)

Teddy (*enters, left*) Hey, Moll, you nearly let me fall asleep again – you ready?

Molly What? What for, darling?

Teddy Our walk.

Molly What walk?

Teddy Aren't you coming for a walk?

Molly But darling, we worked it all out at lunch, now we've got the piano tuned at last I was going to try and settle to some song writing, and you were going to go for a walk.

Teddy We're going to Gwyllup, it's five miles.

Molly No, darling, we were going to *drive* to Gwyllup another day –

188

Teddy No, no, walk.

Molly Anyway, not this afternoon –

Teddy You're smoking again.

Molly So I am, I am.

Teddy If you don't want to, you'd better not.

Molly But I do. I do.

Teddy Then we'd better get started.

Molly No, I mean smoke – (*Stubs the cigarette out irritably.*)

Teddy Do you or don't you, I can't make it out.

Eve (*enters back*) I'm just going to do the shopping.

Teddy What?

Eve I've got down tomatoes, oranges, cauliflower, the beef to be collected, four skewers –

Molly Oh darling, do come in properly, it can't be any good for your throat – baying at me from over there.

Teddy I'm going to walk to Gwyllup. The question is whether you are.

Eve (*frostily*) I'm sorry. I didn't mean to bay at you.

Teddy I can perfectly well go by myself.

Eve I just wanted to know if you wanted to add anything.

Molly Add anything? To the skewers and the four cauliflowers?

Eve To the shopping list.

Teddy When you two have sorted it out, whatever it is that's so important to you, I'll be upstairs in my room.

I don't want to keep interrupting you ladies when you're nattering about something important –

Going out, he slams the door, left. There is a pause.

Molly Omigod! We go to all the trouble of getting that little man over from Guildford so that I can play the piano properly at last, and perhaps even, who knows, compose a song, and when I actually at last arrange to spend an afternoon at the piano, I find myself harassed with tales about youths stealing cigarettes, and grown men demanding to be taken for walks – it's too much, it's too, too much!

She takes out a cigarette, lights it.
  Eve turns away, her face working.
  Molly looks at Eve, looks away angrily, draws on her cigarette.

Sorry, darling. Didn't mean to be ratty. Forgive please. (*Little pause.*) Pretty please, with sugar on it.

Eve I expect it *is* all my fault. *I'm* sorry, Molly. The truth is, I've got a bit of a headache, this weather's a little close for me. (*Attempts a little laugh.*) That always means it's going to rain. Sorry, Moll.

Molly Oh poor darling, can I get you an aspirin?

Eve No – nothing does any good until it rains.

Molly Anyway, you mustn't think of going to the shops. Why don't you have a nice lie-down?

Eve Oh, I'll be all right. Really. I shouldn't have made such a fuss over Oliver.

Molly Someone's got to make fusses for us, darling, and as you're the only grown-up in the house, it'd better be you. We are childish, aren't we, Teddy and I?

Eve Of course you're not.

Molly Yes we are.

Eve Well – I've always liked children.

Molly Really, darling? I wouldn't have thought you'd much to do with them before.

Eve Oh yes. I helped to look after some once. A long time ago.

Molly Did you? (*Abruptly.*) I'd like a child. Do you think it's too late for me?

Little pause. Eve looks embarrassed.

I mean adopt one, of course. Now that I'm back in England – home again. One could easily adopt one, couldn't one? What do you think?

Eve I think it's the most marvellous idea!

Molly After all, if we keep this place on, we've lots of room. He could have the small room as a bedroom, and the room opposite as a playroom and I could move across the hall to be next to him – and even if we don't stay here we could find somewhere else just as big. You see how I've been working it out?

Eve Oh Moll!

Molly And you wouldn't run away if we did?

Eve I'd love it! And what does Teddy think?

Molly Oh, I haven't mentioned it to him yet. One thing at a time for the poor darling – first England, then a child, then if we get on with that one perhaps another to go with it and so on, we may end up with a flock of them – (*Laughing.*) We'd have to keep some out in the fields!

Eve (*laughs*) Oh Moll!

Teddy (*enters left*) I'm not going to doze through the afternoon, have you two fixed it all up between yourselves, yet?

Molly Oh yes, darling, completely. Haven't we, Evie?

Eve (*smiling*) Yes.

Teddy Then you're ready to hike to Gwyllup? Or do I go on my own?

Molly Oh darling, do you mind if I try out the lovely piano you've had fixed up for me? Do you?

Teddy You're saying no?

Molly Darling, I will, if you like.

Teddy I'm going anyway, as that's what we arranged.

Molly Besides, Evie says it's going to rain, and you know how bad that can be for your ears – why don't you take a little local stroll?

Teddy I'm going to Gwyllup. (*Pause.*) I'm going to Gwyllup.

Molly (*hesitates*) Then at least take your raincoat and your mackintosh hat.

Teddy What?

Molly Your raincoat and mackintosh hat.

Teddy What for? It's not going to rain. Bye. (*Stamps out through the conservatory.*)

Molly Oh damn, damn, what shall I do, if it rains into his ears – and he *will* go to Gwyllup too, he's so stubborn – and if I go after him now he'll just stump angrily along –

Eve (*getting up*) I'll take them to him.

Runs to door, left, returns at once with hat and coat.

Molly Oh thank you, darling. But really somebody ought to go with him, I know it's a lot to ask – will you?

Eve (*hesitates, then smiles*) Of course, Moll.

Molly You are a darling – and they say Gwyllup's very beautiful.

Eve runs through the conservatory, with hat and coat. As she does so, she calls:

Eve Oliver – Oliver – run after Mr Treadley, tell him to wait a minute, hurry, hurry!

Molly stands listening for a moment, then goes into the conservatory, stands watching, still visible to the audience, then returns. Goes to the cigarettes, picks one out, lights it, puffs on it. Sits down to smoke. After a moment gets up, stands uncertainly, kicks off her shoes, then wanders over to the piano, picks out a tune, tries to play, then crashes a discord, sits puffing on her cigarette. Gets up, paces about restlessly, then goes to the cocktail cabinet, pours herself a gin, walks determinedly back to the piano, sits down, gets up, goes over, lights another cigarette, sits down with the drink.

Molly Alone at last. (*Pause, then in a desolate voice.*) Omigod! (*Pause, suddenly shakes her head from side to side, stops, puts her fingers to her forehead.*) Omigod!

Collapses back into the sofa.
 Oliver appears in the conservatory. He is carrying the coat and the mackintosh hat. Molly doesn't notice him. Oliver clears his throat.

(*Looks at him.*) Oh hello. He sent them back, did he?

Oliver Yes, Miss. He said to say he doesn't need them. And he says thank you, um, for –

Molly What?

Oliver Well, Evie, Miss.

Molly (*smiles wryly*) Thank you. Well, sling them – sling them over there somewhere, would you?

Oliver puts them on the end of the sofa.

And how's everything in the garden?

Oliver I got the weeds on the compost, I'm going to start on the hedge.

Molly How lucky – to have something you've got to do.

Oliver Yes, Miss.

Slight pause. Oliver goes into the conservatory, clatters about, just in sight. Molly looks towards the conservatory, watches.

Just getting the shears, Miss. (*Holds them up.*)

Molly (*with authority*) Come in for a moment, Oliver, please.

Oliver enters, carrying the shears.

Two, Oliver.

Oliver Miss?

Molly (*holds up two fingers*) You took two of my cigarettes, Oliver.

Oliver I didn't! Miss, I swear –

Molly Oh, Oliver, don't, please. It makes you sound like a goose when you protest – you honk.

Oliver But – (*Stops.*)

Molly (*gets cigarettes, holds package out to Oliver*) Here, have another one.

Oliver No thank you, Miss.

Molly Oh, go on. You mustn't mind my knowing about you being a liar, I lie all the time, all the time, about lots of things, about cigarettes too. I promise I won't smoke more than five a day, my husband thinks it's bad for my health, but of course I sneak extra ones, like now with you, he'd have a fit if he could see me puffing away. Do you know what he'd do? He'd put me across his knee and spank me, Oliver. Yes, he would. What do you think of that?

Oliver Well Miss – (*Gives a strange half-laugh.*)

Molly Now I've told you all that, you've got to take one, haven't you?

Oliver hesitates, then takes one.

I bet your dad doesn't put you across his knee and spank you, at least not any more, does he?

Oliver No, Miss. (*Laughs again.*)

Molly You did take them, didn't you?

Oliver Yes, Miss.

Molly There, now we've both confessed. But I'm very sorry, Oliver, now I shall have to punish you. You do realise that, you can't pinch my cigarettes and then lie and bluster about it and not expect punishment, can you? (*She allows a long pause.*) Sit down please, Oliver.

Oliver, after a moment, sits.

Do you know what I'm going to do to you?

Oliver shakes his head.

I'm going to teach you a lesson, Oliver. I'm going to make you sit here and talk to me. (*Laughs.*) Just for a little, do you mind?

Oliver (*smiles*) No, Miss. Except there's the hedge and she goes on at me.

Molly Oh, *her*! Don't worry about her, Oliver, I'll protect you from her! (*Pause.*) Tell me, do you think it's going to rain?

Oliver Yes, Miss.

Molly Oh, don't say that, why?

Oliver Because it feels like rain. And my dad said it would.

Molly And is your dad always right?

Oliver Usually, Miss.

Molly About everything, or just about the weather?

Oliver Well, about the weather, anyway, Miss.

Molly How does he know, by sniffing the air, or holding his finger up or rising at six for shepherds' warning?

Oliver No, Miss.

Molly How then?

Oliver He listen to the radio, Miss, at breakfast. (*There is a pause.*)

Molly Well, clever old Dad. (*Laughing.*) I bet you don't dare lie to him.

Oliver Oh no, Miss.

Molly What about?

Oliver Miss?

Molly What do you lie to him about?

Oliver I said I didn't, Miss.

Molly Yes, that was a lie to me. What do you lie to him about? Come on, Oliver, do tell me. Please, pretty please. Because I know you do.

Oliver How, Miss?

Molly Because if we didn't lie to people we love and live with, we wouldn't be able to love and live with them. See.

Gets up, goes to cocktail cabinet, pours herself a gin, studies Oliver.

Oliver (*after a pause*) Well, only about Guildford. What I do over at Guildford. That's all.

Molly And what *do* you do over at Guildford?

During this scene, and by imperceptible degrees, the stage darkens to suggest the sky darkening.

Oh, of course, you've got a girl there. (*Drinks.*)

Oliver Well – (*Shrugs.*)

Molly Haven't you?

Oliver Not any more. There was a girl. I used to have tea with her sometimes.

Molly Only tea?

Oliver Yes. She worked in a tea shop.

Molly (*drinks again*) And is that all you did with her?

Oliver We went to the films sometimes.

Molly Were you lovers?

Oliver What?

Molly Lovers.

There is a pause.

Here –

She pours a drink of gin, brings it to Oliver.

Have a sip of this.

Oliver What is it?

Molly A truth drink. To help you tell me whether you were lovers. It's all right, I swear I won't tell your dad if you promise not to tell mine. Husband. Sip and tell, Oliver.

Oliver (*sips*) Well – (*Sips again.*) No, Miss.

Molly No, won't tell, or no, weren't lovers?

Oliver Weren't – um, lovers.

Molly Oh dear, oh dear, why not?

Oliver (*laughs, embarrassed*) Don't know anything about any of that.

Molly Any of what?

She goes over to him, takes the shears off his lap, puts them on the floor.

There. Any of what?

Oliver My dad wouldn't stand for any of that. He'd kill me if I did anything like that.

Molly (*standing close to him*) Then what happened between yourself and this girl, what was her name?

Oliver Rosie. Rosie Hitchens. Well – just one day she turned around when I went over and said her mum didn't want her to see me any more.

Molly And she didn't?

Oliver (*after a pause*) No.

Molly (*after a pause*) Poor Oliver. Poor Rosie Hutchings, come to that.

Oliver Hitchens. Her name was.

Molly Is your mother dead?

Oliver Yes, Miss. When I was born.

Molly You're terribly fond of your dad, aren't you? Tell me, what do you do together? I mean in the evenings, or the weekends?

Oliver Well – we go shooting.

Molly Do you, oh, dear, what do you shoot?

Oliver Only rabbits.

Molly *Only* rabbits? Oh, Oliver. And do you kill many of them?

Oliver Quite a few. My dad's a good shot. I'm not bad.

Molly What do you think, when you see them dead?

Oliver That they're dead, Miss. Dead rabbits. For pie.

Molly Have you got a dog?

Oliver We had one once, Miss.

Molly What happened to it?

Oliver It got run over.

Molly And what did you think, when you saw it dead?

Oliver It was in the middle of the Guildford road, where all the lorries run. My dad took me down to see it, lying there squashed, I was only six about.

Molly Why did he do that?

Oliver To show me what happened if I was careless on the road.

Molly Omigod, Oliver! And what did you say, when you saw it there?

Oliver I said – (*thinks*) were we going to have it for lunch?

Molly You didn't!

Oliver No, Miss. We had it for supper.

Molly (*after a moment, laughing*) You're making fun of me! That's nice. (*Pours more gin into Oliver's glass.*) There! You see how it helps. And me. (*Pours some into her own.*) Because now I'm going to tell you why I hate to think of shooting only rabbits even, and you mustn't laugh at me, promise?

Oliver Miss.

Molly You see, I hate anything being killed by people. Ever since I heard about something very dreadful – about how these great Canadian men with their red necks and tartan caps on their heads drive down to the beach in the trucks and they catch the seals, the mother seals and the baby seals, and they beat their heads in with clubs and hammers. (*Sits down beside him.*) Yes, they do, Oliver, and sometimes the mothers stay a little way out in the sea, watching, while these – these men! – skin their babies while they're still alive often, skin them for their furs. Dreadful. Dreadful. They have such big eyes and they stare at their babies – D'you see, Oliver? (*Looks at him intently.*) I wrote a song about it. It was broadcast on the radio over there, and played right across Novia Scotia. But it didn't stop them. That's when I knew I couldn't live in Canada any more, amongst people like that. So don't shoot any rabbits ever again. Please don't, Oliver. Pretty please. With sugar on it. (*There is a pause.*) Oh I know, you've got to, for your dad's sake. You'll just have to try to miss them, that's all. For my sake. Aim – (*raises her arm at Oliver, jerks at the last second*) sideways. (*Laughs.*) But don't hit your dad. For his sake. Are you happy with us?

Oliver Oh yes, Miss.

Molly I watch you sometimes, Oliver. Did you know that? When you're in the garden. As busy as bees. Mowing the lawn yesterday. I watched you from an upstairs window. And then on your knees weeding this morning. But I haven't seen you recite poetry to the flowers. No. And sometimes you even look a trifle – sulky. There. I've said it. As if you weren't truly and really deeply happy with us. Why not, Oliver?

Oliver I am, Miss. (*Pause.*) Well.

Molly No, go on. On.

Oliver She gets at me a lot, Miss.

Molly Oh, she gets at us all a lot, pay her no mind, we don't. When she gets at me I pay her out my very best smile and say forgive me, Evie, pretty please, with sugar on it. You can try that. Because then you can ignore her and be rude to her or whatever you want. What else is wrong?

Oliver Nothing, Miss. Well.

Molly Oh, Oliver. On.

Oliver Well, only about the car, that's all. I mean I was taken on to do the car, but now I've got it fixed up I've only taken it out twice, the rest of it's been gardening and painting the garage, and the other day it was sash cords even she made me do.

Molly I'm so glad you've told me this, Oliver. I'll have a word with Teddy when he gets back. (*Pours herself another drink.*) I promise you more outings in the car. I never break my promises you know.

Oliver Oh, I don't really mind. It's just that that's what I thought I was being taken on to do mainly and, well, they make jokes about it at Sprinkley's and up at the pub, because my dad told them all I was going to be a chauffeur and they say if you're a chauffeur where's your uniform. My dad doesn't like that.

Molly If your dad doesn't like it, that settles it. Although I don't know about a uniform – I don't know if I'd like you so much in a uniform. Will you teach me to drive, Oliver, and keep it a secret from Dad? Will you?

Oliver Yes, Miss.

Molly And then when you've taught me I'll show him I can. Eh? Oliver? (*Laughs.*) If you promise to teach me then you shall have a uniform – even though I like you just as you are, Oliver. I like you very much. You do know that, don't you?

They stare at each other.

Do you like him?

Oliver Who?

Molly Teddy.

Oliver Yes, Miss.

Molly So do I. Even though he calls you boy and Ollie and Oliver Treefsir?

Oliver Oh, I don't mind that. It's just his way.

Molly Because he's deaf, you see. It's so sad. Because people when they're deaf can't have normal friendly conversations with each other, as we're having, so they have to find little tricks of their own to show normal friendliness, and to hide their deafness too. And he's very friendly. More than, normally.

Oliver He doesn't really –

Molly What?

Oliver (*hesitates*) Put you over his knee, does he?

Molly (*stares at Oliver*) D'you mind?

Oliver Miss. (*Laughs.*) He doesn't! Does he?

Molly I'm so worried, Oliver, about his getting his ears wet. And your saying it's going to rain – (*Goes over to the window, looks out.*) It's darker, getting darker. It *is* raining a little. Oh damn! Oh, poor Teddy. But it's delicious, too, isn't it, the two of us snug inside, talking and drinking, while outside – (*Shivers.*) Delicious. (*Takes a gulp of gin.*) Do you like me, Oliver?

Oliver Miss?

Molly Or do you think I'm just a silly old vamp, do you?

Oliver No, Miss.

Molly What then? Say it. You must say it. I said it to you.

Oliver Like you, Miss.

Molly But I don't frighten you, do I?

Oliver No, Miss.

Molly We'll have another cigarette, shall we?

Goes with cigarettes, offers one to Oliver, lights it for him. She is staring at him. Takes a step around the

side of the sofa, puts her foot on the shears, stumbles,
cries out.

Oliver (*gets to his feet*) What is it, Miss, what is it?

Molly I've cut myself – my foot – (*Tries to see the sole*
of her foot.) Can you see?

Oliver, bending some yards away, stares.

Look properly – take it – (*Stretches out her leg.*)

Oliver (*takes her foot gingerly*) I can't see any cut, Miss.

Molly But it's wet – I can feel the bleeding.

Oliver No, Miss – that's your drink – I can smell it –
that's all.

Molly But it hurts, oh God, it hurts – (*Loses balance,*
hops.)

Oliver Miss – Miss –

He lets go of Molly's leg. Molly stumbles towards
Oliver, who puts out his arms to catch her.

Molly Oh, Oliver – (*Clinging to him.*) It did hurt – it did –

Oliver (*in alarm*) Miss.

Molly Oliver – don't be frightened. Don't be.

Oliver Miss?

Molly begins to kiss Oliver, ravenously. Oliver clumsily
responds. Lights down to sound of rain. Rain continues
through the darkness.

SCENE THREE

About an hour later. Lights up to greyness. Still raining heavily. Oliver is sitting on the sofa, putting on his socks. He has already put on his underpants. The raincoat is spread under him, across the sofa, the waterproof side up, there are cushions on the floor. Molly is in her underpants, doing up her bra. She is standing some way from Oliver. She is dressing quickly. Oliver stops dressing, watches Molly. His face works. He turns, rolls into the sofa, puts his arm over his face.

Molly (*not noticing*) Oh that rain, that bloody rain – but they'll have found somewhere in the village – or a tree – the poor man – next time I'll check the weather with your dad or the wireless. (*Dressing through this, turns, looks at Oliver.*) Oliver – (*Goes over to him.*) Oliver, darling, what is it?

She sits down on the sofa next to him, tries to remove Oliver's arm from his face.

Oliver – don't – you mustn't – here, here – (*Pulls his arm away.*) Why are you? Is it because you're unhappy? Are you unhappy?

Oliver (*shakes his head*) No, Miss.

Molly Because you're happy then?

Oliver, crying, turns his face away.

(*Taking his face in her hands.*) Because you're happy?

Oliver Miss. I don't know, Miss.

Molly (*cuddles him*) There, Oliver, nothing to cry for, nothing to cry for. I'm glad, I am, yes, I am, and I want you to be happy, but you mustn't cry –

Oliver (*embraces her with sudden and desperate passion*)
Please Miss please Miss please Miss –

Molly What, darling? What?

Oliver You won't send me away, Miss?

Molly No, no – of course not – just for now – just for a
little while – but there'll be other times. I promise you.
Lots of other times, but we mustn't let them find out,
must we? They wouldn't understand, and I wouldn't
want to hurt Teddy, he loves me, you know, and I must
care for him too, mustn't I, and not let him be hurt, so
now I've got to put everything right and you must finish
getting dressed, darling, and help me by being as quick
as you can, darling, before they come back – do you
understand, darling? Do you?

Oliver nods.

Go on then. Go on, my darling –

*She gets up, finishes dressing. Oliver goes on dressing,
sniffing. Molly comes over, buttons his shirt.*

Now you go now, my darling –

Leads him to the door, left.

There's a good boy –

Kisses him.
    *Oliver goes out left. There is a pause. He comes
back, rushes over to Molly, throws his arms around
her. Molly strokes his head.*

I'll see you soon. I promise. And I never break my
promises.

They separate. Oliver stands looking at Molly.

Go, Oliver.

*She gently leads him out, left. Sounds of her saying
goodbye quickly at the front door. Front door closes,
off, Molly enters left as Teddy, followed by Eve, enters
the conservatory, right. Teddy is soaking, mud-stained.
Followed by Eve, also soaking. Molly stares, shocked.*

Omigod – darling, what happened?

Teddy Well, here I am, Moll, back from a stroll in your
nice quiet countryside, right in the middle of the fields –
eh, Evie? – then wham, right from out of your nice quiet
clouds, wham, wham, wham! (*Laughs.*)

Molly (*getting up, going to him*) Darling, you must get
into some dry clothes.

Eve And a hot bath!

*Teddy has gone to cocktail cabinet, pours himself an
enormous Scotch.*

Teddy And there we were, Evie and me – (*gulping the
Scotch*) licking across the field in the dark, sheets of it
coming down, and there was this tree Evie saw, on a
bank and a ditch running under it, anyway wouldn't
pass in Novia Scotia for a river. (*Laughs.*) And I swayed
on the edge, eh, Evie?

Molly Darling, tell me afterwards, get changed now!

Teddy Felt like minutes, rocking and swaying, and Evie
had hold of my arm pulling me back, but a hand shot
out of nowhere and down I went.

Molly A hand?

Teddy And down I went – right, Evie?

Molly You were pushed?

Teddy And down I went – right, Evie? – Evie almost
coming with me. (*Laughs.*) So don't you two talk to me

about your friendly English countryside again, we've got bob-cat, bear and skunk in Nova Scotia but we don't have anything you can't see or hear or understand come up behind you and tumble you into the mud for no damn reason – (*gulps again*) raining inside my skull – (*Pulls out the hearing aid.*) Damn thing, damned thing, battery soaking – get it fixed, fixed tomorrow – (*Takes another gulp, stands staring at Molly.*) Hey, Moll!

Molly He's trembling – darling! He's feverish – come on, darling, we must get you to a bath and bed – come along.

She pulls Teddy towards the door.

Teddy I'm all right – I'm all right. (*Goes out.*)

Molly (*before she closes the door, turns, stares at Eve*) I told you to make him take his raincoat and his mackintosh hat! I *told* you! (*Goes out.*)

Eve stands for a moment. Then bends, automatically. Picks up Teddy's hat.

Eve (*in an emotional voice*) It's jolly well not fair!

Suddenly takes in the chaos of the room, glasses, cushions, etc.

Lights. Curtain.

Act Two

A week or so later. The sun is shining. It is mid-afternoon.
    Eve is sitting with some knitting on her lap. She is
staring ahead. There is the sound of a door closing, off,
up left. Then quick footsteps. Eve starts knitting.

Molly Hello. darling, seen my handbag?

Eve On the sofa.

Molly You are clever. (*Going to the handbag.*)

Eve You usually leave it on the sofa. Have you got
Teddy's drops?

Molly Oh yes, here they are.

   Fishes them out of the handbag, puts them on the
   table.

Eve He always needs them first thing, when he wakes.

Molly I know, poor darling. Isn't that growing – Teddy'll
be so thrilled. I wish I could knit.

Eve Do you? It's not difficult.

Molly No, I suppose it can't be, as so many dolts can.
It's one of those activities I always thought I'd find
myself doing when I grew up – like putting on grey hair
and wrinkles.

Eve Indeed?

Molly Oh, darling, I didn't mean – (*Laughs.*)

Eve (*smiles coldly*) Are you going out?

Molly Yes, I've got an appointment with Oliver for a driving lesson. What about you?

Eve Oh no. I don't think Teddy should be left alone at the moment.

Molly But darling, he's asleep, I've just checked.

Eve Yesterday when you were having a driving lesson and I was down here he woke up and thought he was alone in the house. He was quite fretful for a good half-hour.

Molly I must say, darling, that doesn't sound like a good half-hour to me. (*Hesitates.*) In that case why don't you go out and I'll stay in, it's your turn.

Eve No. I'd as soon get on with this. Besides, Oliver will be expecting you.

Molly Oh, I can always find something else for him to do.

Eve I'm glad he's settling down so well. Since you moved him into the house.

Molly Hasn't he been a godsend?

Eve Yes. Mrs Shepherd says he's funny in the head. She came around yesterday morning. She'd heard he was living in so she came around especially to warn us. She said he was funny in the head. That's why they dismissed him. Her husband caught him in their bedroom, going through her underwear drawer.

Molly Oh, don't worry, darling. Your underwear drawer is quite safe. Oliver's told me all about it.

Eve I see. You don't think it peculiar even, then?

Molly Nothing like as peculiar as Mrs Shepherd, trekking all the way up here to tell us about it.

Eve Oh well, as long as *you* don't mind –

Molly No, I don't mind, darling. Not at all. And if you're not keen to go out I'll get some fresh air.

Gets up, goes towards the conservatory. Eve watches her, and as Molly gets to the conservatory door:

Eve Oh, by the way, Molly, as soon as Teddy's better I shall be leaving. (*Little pause.*) I thought I should tell you now, so you'd have time to find someone more suitable.

Molly (*takes out a cigarette, lights it*) More suitable to what, darling?

Eve To what's going on in this house.

Molly What *is* going on in this house?

Eve Wasn't Oliver in your room last night?

Molly Yes, he did look in to say goodnight and to ask how Teddy was.

Eve He stayed the whole night.

Molly makes to exclaim.

Please don't lie to me, Moll, I couldn't bear it. I heard Teddy stumbling down the hall at midnight. It was only by the grace of God that I managed to stop him opening the door on the two of you. He'd had a nightmare, and wanted comforting. Thank God *he* couldn't hear what I heard.

There is a honk from outside, right.

Molly Omigod! Thank you, Evie!

Eve Oh, it wasn't you I was thinking of, it was Teddy.

Molly I know. Thank you. Teddy and I don't sleep together, surely you've realised that.

Eve But – but he's still your husband. You married him.

Molly Yes. And I do my best to make him happy, haven't you noticed? I get drunk with him, and cuddle him, and let him slap me on the bottom – all – all that. It's enough for Teddy. It's not always enough for me.

Eve You mean – you've done this before?

Molly From time to time. Though not as often as I want to.

Eve Oh, you sound so hard – so hard.

Molly Do I, darling? Sorry. You've been companion-housekeeper to a wicked woman, darling, you see. I need my sex. There. I've said it.

Eve Then you had no right to marry Teddy.

Molly Hadn't I? He wanted me to.

Eve But what did you marry him for? His money?

Molly I admit I wouldn't have if he'd been an impoverished – (*Gestures.*)

Eve Garage hand. Like Oliver Treefe, you mean?

Molly Well, unlike Oliver, Teddy would have been a sixty-year-old impoverished garage hand when I married him, so I probably wouldn't have married him, no.

Eve I don't understand.

Molly What, darling? What don't you understand?

Eve You who could have married anybody –

Molly Not when I married Teddy. Don't forget he *was* sixty, and I was *all* of thirty – and he was quite a dynamic Halifax businessman and I was one of those, you know, glamorous English divorcees that end up in countries like Canada on spec.

Eve I didn't know you'd been married before.

Molly Gets worse and worse, doesn't it, darling. Yes. Married before. Sorry. There were no children though, other than the two of us. Then he began to grow up, and left me for someone who would look after him properly. I've never been very good at getting meals on tables and organising homes and curtains and housekeeping – all the things you're so good at doing. He's a solicitor in Harrow now, I think it is, with no doubt children and all the rest of the things – (*gestures*) he couldn't imagine me providing him with. (*Pause.*) Actually, I did almost manage a child, but it miscarried. He blamed me for that – my fecklessness – because we'd been to a party and I drank a mite too much and slipped and fell down the stairs. He rather hated me – (*Pause.*) So after I'd set him free I took a plunge, and went off to Canada, where I just managed to keep my head above water doing ladylike little jobs and being glamorous and English – all the right things to be if one wanted one of those ghastly Canadian men as a lover, you know, balding and fattening, but no good for husbands, because they were already. Until Teddy came along. I was working as a part-time receptionist sort of person who did a little piano playing and drinking in the hotel and he was the first eligible male I've infatuated. Except there is just this little thing wrong with him, I don't know what, but he doesn't have sex, I don't believe he ever has. But apart from that and already beginning to deafen, he was quite dynamic and infatuated. There. Now do you understand, Eve?

Eve I suppose I might – oh I wouldn't approve, but I might understand if it were some – some man you'd – you'd – but Oliver Treefe! Can't you see what he is?

Molly What is he, darling? Other than peculiar in the head?

Eve Well, for one thing he's – he's twenty years younger than you.

Molly Is that worse than being almost thirty years older?

Eve But he's – he's completely uneducated. He's not even particularly nice to look at. Even I can see that. He's a common, loutish –

Molly Stop it, Evie. Please. The truth is, Ollie and I –

Eve Ollie and you! Ollie and you! No, I can't – stop it. I jolly well think it's disgusting. Disgusting!

Molly (*in a sudden scream*) We're all disgusting! (*There is a pause.*)

Eve (*gets up*) Well *I'm* not, Molly Treadley. No, *I'm* not!

> *Oliver enters through the conservatory. He is wearing a chauffeur's uniform, carrying a cap and gauntlets.*

Oliver Oh, excuse me, Miss, I've been honking for you outside.

Molly Honking for me?

> *Eve exits, left.*

Oliver She in one of her bad moods?

Molly A touch edgy, perhaps. (*Little pause.*) Look, darling, I'm sorry, but I'd better not come this afternoon, after all.

Oliver Why not?

Molly Why don't you give your dad that ride you've been promising him? He's scarcely seen you this last ten days.

Oliver He's working.

Molly Well, darling, anything you want to do – do. (*Smiles at him.*)

Oliver I want to go out with you. You promised me, Moll. To make up for all that hanging about outside Gracey's this morning.

Molly I know, darling, I'm sorry, but really I can't.

Oliver It *is* because of her, isn't it?

Molly I suppose so. Because of her and him and you and me – it's all very complicated and I'm not up to explaining it and you wouldn't like it if I did, darling, but what it comes down to is that it would make everything worse if we skipped off right now.

Oliver It's not fair. I've been sitting out there, honking and waiting and honking and waiting and I've changed the oil even, and now you tell me you can't come out and won't tell me why, but it's because of her and him – I know it is.

Molly Oliver!

Oliver makes to say something else.

No, don't say another word, Ollie. Not now. Just go. For your sake, darling.

Oliver looks at her, turns, makes as if to exit through the conservatory, stops.

Oliver It's true what they say, isn't it? That you hooked him for his money and car and that. That's what Sprinkley said from the beginning, the first time he saw you, and my dad said something about you and him, he thinks it's wrong, and Bob Howells making jokes in the pub, if he pays you for every go or how many times a week you have to let him do it. They were all laughing at his jokes

in the pub about him and you. All of them. That's what
I have to sit and listen to.

Molly (*goes to Oliver*) Who is Bob Howells, darling?

Oliver He's Sprinkley's cousin, he –

*Molly slaps Oliver across the face. Oliver stands for a
moment, then runs over to the sofa, falls onto it.*

Molly (*looks at him, goes over to him*) If you ever –
ever – talk to me like that again, it's back to Bob Howells
and Sprinkley's for you, my boy.

Oliver (*in a whisper*) You wouldn't.

Molly Yes, I would, my lad. You can add some jokes of
your own and lead the laughter, but you'll never see me
again, except from a great distance.

There is a pause. Oliver sits upright, staring at Molly.

Oh Oliver, why do you get like this?

Oliver But I love you, I love you.

Molly That's all right, darling. You may love me. I want
you to.

Oliver But I can't stand it when I'm not with you, when
you're in here talking to her, or go into his room to talk
to him, and I don't know what's going on, but I think of
you and him touching you and I don't know, what am
I to do, Moll? You see, before it was like – it was like I
was stuck somewhere underground and – and you took
me out – and now I want to be out all the time, but when
you're not there it's like being stuck back down again.
(*Little pause.*) Last night you said I was your husband
even. But I'm not, am I? He is, isn't he? He has you most.

Molly But you have far more of me, especially now. He
doesn't kiss me where you kiss me, he doesn't hold me as

you hold me – we mustn't grudge him anything, Ollie. Not anything. (*Little pause.*) Darling.

Oliver (*looks at her*) I'm sorry for what I said. I didn't mean it.

Molly I know. (*Puts her arms around him.*) Oh my Ollie.

Oliver You still love me then, don't you?

Molly Of course I do.

Oliver You won't ever send me away, will you?

Molly When Rosie Hitchens from Guildford comes to claim you back.

Oliver Never!

Molly Well, not if I can help it.

Oliver Then I've got you, then, haven't I? (*Jubilant.*) Got you!

> *They embrace. Molly kisses him tenderly, as if he were a child. She wipes his cheeks with her fingers, then kisses him again. The kiss becomes passionate. Oliver puts his hands on Molly's breasts, sighs. Molly responds.*

Please, Moll. Come out.

Molly (*steps away*) You're quite impossible, Oliver Treefe. (*Laughs.*)

Oliver You will, won't you?

Molly (*hesitates*) Oh why not – yes – let's –

> *There is a knock on the door, left. Molly looks at the door. Another knock.*

Come in.

Eve (*enters*) Excuse me. I wasn't sure whether you'd gone.

Molly Oh, that's all right, darling. We're just off.

Eve I wondered if I could have a few words with you.

Molly Of course. Oliver, wait in the car, would you. I won't be a minute.

> *Oliver glances suspiciously at Eve, exits.*

Eve I think it would be better if I left as soon as possible. So I'd be grateful if you got back by five. I'd like to catch the six o'clock train.

Molly Would you like Oliver to drive you to the station?

Eve No, thank you. I'll call for a taxi, if I may.

Molly Where are you going?

Eve To Gosport.

Molly I didn't know you had anyone in Gosport.

Eve A niece.

Molly And does she have children?

Eve Yes.

Molly You'll be able to help her with them, I suppose.

Eve They're quite grown up.

Molly Those are the ones that really need your help. (*Smiles.*)

Eve If Teddy wakes I shan't say anything, I'd rather you explained.

Molly He'll miss you dreadfully. So will I, of course.

Eve I'll pack now. (*Goes towards the door, left.*)

Molly (*hesitates, then*) Evie.

Eve stops, turns.

Evie, please don't go! (*Runs across to her, embraces her.*) I need you so. I do.

Eve stands stiffly for a moment, then turns, embraces Molly.

Eve Oh Moll!

Molly You won't leave me, Evie. Will you?

Eve (*after a moment*) No, Moll. Not if you really need me.

Molly Oh thank you, darling. Thank you. Thank you.

There is a sudden thumping from above. There is a pause. There is a honk from off, right.

Teddy (*off, above*) Hey, Mollie, Eve – hey!

Molly looks at Eve appealingly.

Eve You'd better go. But I can't tell lies for you, Molly Treadley. I can't do that.

Molly No, darling. I know.

She goes out through the conservatory. Eve watches her go through conservatory, stands for a moment. Puts her hand to her forehead. Teddy enters, left. He is wearing dressing gown, slippers, but is without a hearing aid.

Eve (*turning*) Teddy – you shouldn't be up.

Teddy Where's Moll?

Eve (*slowly and loudly*) She's gone out.

Sound of the car screeching down the drive.

Teddy She went out this moming – where's she gone to this time?

Eve (*hesitates*) Oh, just for a drive.

Teddy What?

Eve To get your drops. Teddy, you mustn't stay down here. (*Goes over to him.*)

Teddy What? (*Irritably, pulling his arm away.*) Did she forget them this morning, then?

Eve They had to make up a fresh batch – it's too cold for you down here, Teddy.

Teddy Not going back to bed with a stuffed nose – like being in a damned prison.

> Goes over, pours himself a Scotch, slops the drink, pays no attention, takes a gulp.

Can't taste the taste, only the heat. (*Sits down.*) Go in the car?

Eve Yes. (*Goes back, sits down.*)

Teddy (*after a pause*) Saw them coming around the side of the house the other afternoon. Looked out of my window and there they were, around my side of the house, right beneath me. Like a pair of ghosts. (*Attempts to sniff.*) Don't worry, not delirious, Evie. Like ghosts because I couldn't hear them. Couldn't have smelt them either, come to that. Lost my hearing, now I lost my smelling, what goes next, eh? (*Laughs.*) She was laughing. He had his mouth open. Maybe shouting a joke or something. Anyway, his mouth was open.

Eve I think he has adenoids.

Teddy Great sense of humour?

Eve No, adenoids.

Teddy Knocked on my window, but they didn't hear. Went right on round. A moment later they were back

again, on the other side, gravel showering every which
way. Too damned fast. (*Pause.*) Too damned fast. God
knows what he gets up to when I can't see him. (*Pause,
sniffs.*) Why didn't you tell her yesterday I was running
out, you could see I was, couldn't you?

Eve I'm sorry.

Teddy What you knitting there, a coloured ladder?

Eve A scarf.

Teddy What?

Eve (*explosively*) A *scarf*! It's going to be a scarf.

Teddy Like having him around the house all the time?

Eve Who?

Teddy What's he like?

Eve Oh, I expect he's a normal boy.

Teddy What?

Eve A normal boy.

Teddy (*after a pause*) Hey, Evie – (*Pause.*) Last night –
(*Sniffs.*) You tuck me up in bed? Or was it a dream?

Eve I made your bed comfortable for you. The covers
had slipped.

Teddy Oh. (*Little pause, then vaguely.*) What? (*Attempts
to blow his nose.*) Damn! Damn! (*Sits, sunken in misery.*)

*Eve looks at Teddy, goes on with her knitting, looks
at Teddy, then suddenly:*

Eve Get rid of him, Teddy!

Teddy (*looks at her. Pause*) What?

Eve gets up, goes over to him, takes out the bottle of drops, hands it to Teddy.

Eve I can't bear to see you suffering like this.

Teddy That's all right, Evie, anyone can make a mistake.

Takes the bottle, administers the drops, two to each nostril. Eve goes back, sits down.

Tell me something, Evie – that scarf. Is it for me?

Eve Yes.

Teddy Thank you, Evie.

There is a pause. Teddy sits staring ahead. Eve goes on with her knitting.

(*Dimly.*) What?

Lights.

SCENE TWO

A couple of hours later. Teddy is sitting, staring ahead, as before. Eve is knitting. Teddy gets up, goes with his glass over to the cocktail cabinet, pours himself another large Scotch. Eve looks up towards him then goes on with her knitting.

Molly enters through the conservatory, followed by Oliver. She stops, stares at Teddy, looks at Eve.

Molly Darling, should you be up? Gracey said a few more days in bed –

Teddy Got tired of being stuck up there in bed – thought I'd come down, I'm fine – Hello there, boy, how are you?

Oliver Sir.

Teddy What?

Oliver All right, thank you, sir.

Teddy What about a drink? Moll?

Dashes some gin into a glass, hands it to her.

Molly But darling –

Teddy Where you been?

Molly Oh, just out for a little drive.

Teddy What?

Molly For a little drive.

Teddy Get my drops?

Molly No, I got you a fresh bottle this morning –

Teddy Don't need them anyway, Evie had a bottle all the time. Nice drive?

Molly Except for a horrid little scene on the way back.

Teddy What?

Molly A horrid little scene.

Teddy You and him?

Molly No darling, two louts shooting in the field past the bridge. I made Oliver stop the car and when we went over there was a rabbit, they'd only wounded it and tied its legs, can you believe? And a beastly little dog –

Oliver A terrier.

Teddy What?

Oliver A terrier, sir.

Teddy No good, boy, yours is the voice I'll never catch.

Molly Anyway, they just stood there while Oliver had to kill it with a stick.

Teddy Killed the dog with a stick.

Molly No, a rabbit, darling –

Teddy Rabbit, eh? Bet she didn't like that – eh, boy?

Oliver No, sir.

Teddy Doesn't like animals being hurt, do you, Moll? Ever told you about the seals at Nanaimo? She wrote a song about it, got done across Nova Scotia because Bob Hoskins was a friend of mine, I asked him to do it for her. A good friend. (*Laughs.*) Eh Moll? But she'd never ever been to Nanaimo – eh, Moll? – but somebody told her about the seals and she made up a song out of her head, and that's how it got heard right across Nova Scotia. Nanaimo's in British Columbia, four thousand miles away – What do you think of that, eh Ollie – these ladies, seals, rabbits, songs – all the same to them, hey, boy? Out in Nova Scotia we only shoot rabbits when we can't find any Catholics. We like to shoot Catholics. (*Laughs.*) Ever told you about that, Moll? When some damned fool out hunting saw the bushes move, fired into them, wounded another damned fool hunting. Nova Scotia paper headlined the story, 'Father of Nine Shot. Mistaken for Rabbit.' Hey. Nine kids, that's how we knew he was a Catholic. (*Laughs.*) Wish we'd had you around, boy, to beat him to death with a stick.

    Molly has lit a cigarette.

Hey, girl, come over here. Come on.

    Molly looks at him.

Come on, girl. Here, I say.

    Molly goes over to Teddy.

How many's it been, eh? How many seen her smoke, boy? Two hundred, three hundred, since I was laid up – say five, let you off with five, Molly, eh – one – two – three – four – five – (*Smacking at her bottom.*) There, letting you off lightly, eh, girl.

Oliver's face is set.

Molly (*seeing Oliver's face*) Evie, is there some tea for Oliver?

Eve (*gets up*) Come with me, Oliver. (*Goes out, back.*)

Teddy Hey, boy, something I've been meaning to ask you – that hedge you started, remember seeing you at it on my way to the ditch I fell into – how's it going, got it level?

Oliver Well, I've been doing a lot of driving. Haven't had a chance to get back to it yet.

Teddy Don't know what you're saying, boy, but I can see from your face it's an excuse, where's Mr Goldberg's Alvis, put it away?

Oliver Sir.

Teddy Where?

Oliver In the garage, sir.

Teddy Give me the keys, boy.

Molly Darling, I did say Oliver could give his dad a run later this evening –

Teddy The keys. (*Holds out his hand.*)

Oliver takes the keys out of his pocket, glaring at Teddy.

That's the boy. Now why don't you go trim the hedge until the sun sets – eh? (*Gives him a friendly cuff on the shoulder.*)

Molly But he hasn't had tea –

Teddy What?

Turns around, gives her a malevolent stare.

Molly He hasn't – (*Stops.*)

Teddy Well? (*Looks at Oliver.*)

Oliver turns, blunders into the conservatory.

Hey, just a minute –

Oliver picking up shears.

There's another thing, don't need you around the house at night any more, you can go back to your daddy now, best if you move out this evening, eh?

Oliver stands staring at Teddy, then turns, goes off.

(*Turns.*) Tell you the truth, Moll, don't like him. Foxy little face. Have you noticed his foxy little face?

Molly No.

Teddy Just what you said when we took him on – furtive, pasty, crooked –

Eve (*appears at the back*) Oliver's tea is ready.

There is a pause.

Teddy Oh, hey, Eve, that boy, he's not going to be around at night – just told him to go home to his daddy.

Eve Oh.

Teddy Come and have one of your dry-as-dust sherries, Evie. (*Goes to the cocktail cabinet.*) Things are getting back to rights here, going to get Moll to play us one of her tunes in a minute –

Eve That'll be nice – (*Advancing.*)

Molly (*low, to Eve*) Would you please leave us.

Teddy What?

Eve goes towards door, left.

Hey, Evie, where are you going?

Eve exits.

What's the matter with her? (*There is a pause.*) Hey, Moll? Hey?

They stare at each other.

Molly Why did you do that?

Teddy What?

Molly I've never known you humiliate a child before.

Teddy What?

Molly (*loudly, fiercely*) Never known you humiliate a child before.

Teddy Oh. (*Pause.*) Never had one to humiliate before.

He laughs, then turns, goes and sits down. Molly watches him, then runs to him.

Molly Oh Teddy – what is it, what is it?

Teddy looks at her, turns his head away, mutters something. Molly kneels, takes his hand.

You're still not well, you shouldn't be up, darling – please come to bed –

Teddy What? What? What? (*Pause.*) Faces are different when they shout at the deaf. Ever thought of that, what I have to see in your faces – swelling, with effort and – contempt. And a little trickle of noise comes out I have to make sense of. Most often I get it wrong. I can see that in your faces too. Bellowing, contempt and

boredom. That's all I see on your faces, all there is to
see, isn't anything else, I see what's there. Everything.
All I have of my own is – is the smell of fish. Fish. Know
what's ahead of me – think I don't? I've seen old men.
Hate this country of yours. Small and damp like a
prison. Shambling, shambling about – cocktail cabinet to
armchair, armchair to cocktail cabinet, pyjamas bagging
out around the arse, crutch stained with pee dribble,
cocktail cabinet to lavatory to armchair, to – to – Eve
tucking me in, like I was a kid – teeth out in a glass –
and all the time your faces swelling and bellowing,
boredom and contempt, hate it, hate it, hate you all –
what you've done to me – why didn't you leave me
alone, never needed you, don't need you, natter, natter,
natter – (*Sits staring ahead.*) Brought me here to die.
Know you. Know what you are.

Sits staring ahead, shrunken and malevolent.

Molly Omigod!

Teddy What? (*Laughs.*) Ha! Look – there he is – back –
look at him – little – (*Gets up, goes over to the
conservatory.*) Get up!

Oliver rises. He is holding the shears.

Hah! You're fired, boy! Fired! Mine. Belongs to me. Mr
Goldberg's Alvis too – do what I like with her –
everything – you're fired, fired –

*He spits into Oliver's face, laughs, turns, goes to chair,
sits down with his back to Oliver, looks at Molly,
laughs. Oliver stumbles towards Teddy.*

Molly Don't, don't, omigod – don't – don't –

*Oliver thrusts the shears into Teddy's neck, again and
again. Teddy lurches back, blood spouting.*

Omigod – omigod – (*Goes to Teddy.*)

Oliver Didn't mean it, didn't mean it, Miss – he made me – made me – what'll I do? (*Pause.*) Miss!

Oliver drops the shears, turns, runs out through conservatory.

Molly (*looks at Teddy*) Poor Teddy. Poor old man. (*Pause.*) Omigod! Omigod!

Goes to him, puts her arms around him.

Eve! Eeee-eeve! Eee-ve!

After a pause, Eve enters.

Eee-eeve! (*Sees her.*) He's alive, he's still alive, get help, you fool! Get help!

Lights.

SCENE THREE

About an hour later. Teddy's body has been removed. Greaves and a Police Constable are standing, whispering.

Eve (*enters, left*) It's just as I said. She's asleep. Dr Gracey gave her a very strong sedative. There's not the slightest chance you'll be able to see her until the morning.

Greaves Then perhaps you'll answer a few questions, Miss Mace.

Eve I'm afraid I can't. I must get back to Mrs Treadley.

Greaves But if she's asleep?

Eve Dr Gracey asked me to sit by her. She was in a state of shock. And if she wakes –

Greaves Miss Mace, I don't quite understand your position in the household.

Eve I'm – the companion-housekeeper.

Greaves I see. And are you the only staff?

Eve Well, there's a boy from the village, to help with the gardening and drive the car from time to time.

Greaves And was he here when the accident happened?

Eve No. He'd gone home.

Greaves So there was just you, and Mr and Mrs Treadley?

Eve Yes.

Greaves And did you see the accident?

Eve No. I was in the kitchen.

Greaves So Mr and Mrs Treadley were alone in here?

Eve Yes. Now I really must –

Greaves Where are the shears?

Eve The shears?

Greaves Dr Gracey said the wound had been caused by gardening shears.

Eve Oh. Oh yes – they're in there. On the second shelf under the potato sacking.

Greaves Why?

Eve Because that's where they belong.

Greaves But they must have been covered in blood.

Eve Of course they were. I washed it off.

Greaves But that was important evidence.

Eve Evidence of what? It was an accident. Now I really must go to Mrs Treadley – you can come back tomorrow.

Molly enters, in nightdress and dressing gown.

Molly Ee-eeve – (*Stops.*) Oh, who are you?

Eve (*crosses to her*) Molly – you shouldn't be up, you must get back to bed.

Molly Who are they?

Greaves Police, Mrs Treadley, I wonder if we could –

Eve They were just leaving. Now come along –

Molly The police. Oh I'm so glad you've come, I want to make a complaint.

Eve Molly –

Molly No, darling, I'm going to. About those ambulance men. They were rough – far too rough – I told them to be careful, but one of them pushed me away, yes, actually *pushed* me, didn't he, Evie, when I was trying to help them lift him – and then they said he was dead but he wasn't, not until they came and heaved him about and wouldn't let me – He was alive, wasn't he, Evie? I know because I held him to see, and I could feel something pumping under his blood, quite strongly, there was life in him and then they came – it must have been them, something they did – and they were very rude too, weren't they, Evie, do you know they refused to let me ride to the hospital with him, my own husband, and they refused – so I want to report them, will you report them for me?

Greaves I shall certainly question them, Mrs Treadley.

Molly Will you? Oh thank you – thank you, you're very – Would you like a drink?

Greaves No, thank you, Mrs Treadley.

Molly What about you, I'm sure you'd like one, wouldn't you?

Greaves We're not allowed to drink on duty, Mrs Treadley.

Eve Now come, my dear – back to bed –

Molly No, no, just a minute, Evie, I'd like a – I can't sleep, you know – it's no good – I've tried and tried – you're sure you're not allowed – Will you excuse me if I just have a little, teeny-weeny – (*Goes to drink.*)

Eve You really mustn't drink – Dr Gracey gave you a sedative –

Molly Well, it hasn't worked, darling, has it? I mean here I am full of beans, God knows what he gave me, unless it was beans of course – (*Laughs.*) And wasn't he so incompetent, he really was, not that I want to get him into trouble, he's old and easily upset, all he could do was shake those dreadful wattles of his, he had no idea, no idea at all. I can't help thinking if we'd got a younger man Teddy might still be someone who could stand up to those ambulance bullies and – but all poor Gracey could do was shake his wattles and try to get me to bed. Oh – (*Laughs.*) I don't mean – of course not – (*Stops.*) But I don't want to get him into trouble. Certainly not. He was very good to Teddy's ears. (*There is a pause.*) Oh, I do feel – feel – drinking by myself – do excuse me, but it's been a bit of a – a bit of a –

Greaves Would you mind telling me how it happened, Mrs Treadley?

Molly What?

Eve You can't possibly ask her questions – you can see the state she's in. Now come, Molly, I insist –

Molly Oh tush tush, Eve, tush, I'm perfectly all right, perfectly. And I want to – to help these men. Now what is it you –?

Greaves How did it happen, Mrs Treadley?

Molly What?

Greaves How was Mr Treadley killed?

Eve Molly, don't –

Molly But it was an accident. Surely you know – haven't you told them, Evie? It was nobody's fault – except those men who were rough and poor old Gracey, it just – just happened you see, didn't it, Evie?

Greaves But Miss Mace wasn't in the room at the time.

Molly What? Oh – no, no, you weren't, were you, darling, she generally comes in later, to clean up our messes for us, don't you, darling? (*Laughs.*)

Greaves You and Mr Treadley were alone.

Molly What?

Greaves There was just you and Mr Treadley.

Molly Oh, yes. Yes, that's right. Me and Mr – Teddy. And the cocktail cabinet, of course, that's always there, to make a third.

Eve Molly – (*Goes to her.*) Don't talk now. Don't talk now.

Molly What, why. darling, there's nothing to be afraid of, is there?

Greaves No, Mrs Treadley.

Molly You see, it was just an accident. They understand that. That's all there is to it.

She turns on the radio. There is music playing.

Eve Now Molly, you're going to come with me –

Greaves (*goes to Eve, and very quietly*) Miss Mace! Mrs Treadley has offered to help us in our enquiries. If you persist in interrupting, I shall have to ask you to leave the room.

Molly What? (*Looks at Eve.*)

Greaves You were telling us what happened, Mrs Treadley.

Molly Well, it was – something ghastly happened, you see. He had an accident. I – I didn't really see it, my back must have been turned or I was looking away for a moment, but – but then there he was. Spurting – spurting – do you see?

Greaves One moment he was alive, and the next he was dying?

Molly Yes – well, he had these sudden changes of mood recently, didn't he, Evie? (*Laughs.*)

> *Greaves looks at Molly. There is a pause.*

Just a minute – need to – another little – a truth drink so you'll know I –

> *She laughs, going to pour herself another drink, unsteady on her feet. Eve goes over.*

Eve No, Molly – no –

> *Attempts to take the bottle from her. There is a short, absurd wrestle.*

Molly Bugger off, bitch!

> *Eve recoils.*

Sorry, Evie – sorry. Forgive please. Pretty please with sugar on it. (*Laughs, pours, then to Greaves.*) That's all I have to say –

Eve (*to Greaves*) This is disgraceful, disgraceful. I'm going to phone Dr Gracey and tell him –

Greaves That's your privilege, Miss.

Molly What? She's got a pash on me, haven't you, Evie?

Eve exits, left.

Yes, she has, do you know about the pashes ladies have on ladies, ladies like her on ladies like me. Are you married?

Greaves Yes.

Molly Is she pretty, your wife?

Greaves crosses to the radio, turns it off. Silence, then intimately:

Greaves You were going to tell me the truth, Mrs Treadley.

Molly What?

Greaves The truth.

Molly What about?

Greaves Your husband's death. He was murdered, wasn't he?

Molly Murdered? (*Pause. She yawns.*) I'm sorry – sorry – what?

Greaves Did you do it?

Molly What?

Greaves You did, didn't you?

Molly What – what do you do to people, when you – you catch them?

Greaves That's for the courts to decide.

Molly But if they're children?

Greaves But there aren't any children, are there, Mrs Treadley?

Molly Oh yes. Yes. We're all children in this house, all of us. That's what caused it, you see. But nobody meant – oh, please believe – it wasn't meant. He – he brought it on himself! He did! He did! An old man, come to the end, he wanted to die, he wanted to – full of hate – I couldn't bear his hate – and he knew – you see he knew – he was right, about his old man's smells, his deafness and the boredom, the boredom and the bellowing and the contempt and the pee-dribble and his pyjamas arsing – and – and –

Greaves And is that why you killed him, Mrs Treadley?

Molly What?

Greaves Did you kill him?

Molly I –

Pause.

Eve (*enters*) I've spoken to Dr Gracey. He's coming over.

Molly It was her! She did it! She did it! (*Pause.*) No, no, sorry, Evie, sorry, darling – it was me. Yes. I killed him. I killed him. I took the things and I – I – (*Makes thrusting movements, stops abruptly.*) And now you all hate me, don't you, like the ambulance and Gracey and all – all hate me – well, here I am, look at me you – you – (*Runs to the Constable.*) What do you see, an old vamp, is that what you see? But you'd roger me, too, wouldn't you? I could make you love – I'm still – look – look –

Makes to lift her nightdress to him. Eve strides across, grips Molly by the arm, pulls her away. Molly collapses against Eve.

Bed now, Evie, bed please. Bed, darling.

Lights.

SCENE FOUR

Some months later. Afternoon. The room fills with light, steadily, to bright sunlight. There are dust sheets over the sofa, the chairs. On the sofa, Molly's scarf, handbag. The door, left, is open.
  Eve enters from the left, wearing a light raincoat. She goes to the handbag, begins to go through it. Molly appears at the door, back. She is also wearing a light coat. She stands watching Eve, then comes across, takes the handbag from her.

Molly Thank you, darling. I do wish people would stop rummaging through it, it's been emptied and refilled by so many different ladies recently, police ladies, prison ladies, hospital ladies – (*Takes out a cigarette.*) It doesn't feel mine any more. (*Lights cigarette.*) What were you looking for, darling? The sleeping pills?

Eve I couldn't remember whether we'd brought them.

Molly Do you need them, though? Surely we don't mind being awake on an August afternoon? (*Takes a bottle out of the pocket.*) Do you want to look after them?

Eve No, of course not, Moll.

Molly Oh, you might as well, darling. I'm not going to try again. For one thing, I don't seem to be very good at it, and I do hate the way they drag one back, with stomach pumps and sermons. Do take them, darling. There.

Eve (*takes them*) I'll make up a bed if you still want to lie down.

Molly Lie down?

Eve You said you had a headache.

Molly Did I? Well then it's gone.

Eve Oh. Oh good! Well, what about our walk then?

Molly Our walk?

Eve You were looking forward to a walk.

Molly I think I'll leave it until tomorrow. (*Pause.*) To tell you the truth, darling, I'm a bit confused at finding everything so familiar.

Eve It's my fault. I shouldn't have agreed to let you come back – at least so soon.

Molly So soon? But I haven't been here for a long time. After such an eventful spring, and a summer wasted in – in institutions – I'd have hated to have missed the old haunts in their autumn colours. I long to see them.

Eve You do want a walk then?

Molly What do you want, Evie?

Eve (*intensely*) I want our old Moll back again.

Molly Do you really? Our old judge found the old Moll a trifle too degenerate for his taste. Quite disgusting, in fact. Quite disgusting. Disgusting.

Eve He had no right – no right to say those things. They had no right to make you go through that trial, not after – after the truth had come out. I shall never believe in British justice again.

Molly Poor Eve! Still, think what we would have lost. The sight of old Treefe, for example, touching his forelock to thank everyone for all the trouble they were putting themselves to, to hang his son. Who's only just come of hangable age. (*Pause.*) Can I have a drink? No – no more drinks for me.

Eve You must stop blaming yourself, Molly. You stood by him right to the bitter end.

Molly Not quite, darling. His bitter end comes on Monday week, at six in the morning, isn't it? He's going to that without me. (*Pause.*) Looking across as if he believed I could just come out of my box and into his, and cuddle him through it. His peaky face, and the spot blooming on his nose. Do you think he'll expect me on Monday week, too, right to the very last, as a child expects his mummy to come and take him away? (*Turns away.*) I'd have made a good mother, wouldn't I?

Eve He did do it, Moll.

Molly Of course he did. (*Pause, makes a violent gesture.*) So hang the little beggar! By the way, darling, I haven't thanked you properly for bringing him to book. Thank you. If it hadn't been for you –

Eve I couldn't let you sacrifice yourself. I couldn't, Moll.

Molly No. No. I don't suppose you could.

Eve We have to do right by those we care about.

Molly Yes. Yes, we do. You love me, Evie, don't you?

Eve Yes.

Molly Thank you.

Eve Oh Moll – (*Gives a sudden shy smile.*)

Molly It *is* a lovely afternoon, isn't it? Would you like a walk?

Eve I'd love one.

Molly Right. Off you go then.

They stare at each other.

Darling, we really must start doing our separate wants, or how shall we two live together? Please go, darling. (*Pause.*) Please.

Eve exits through conservatory.

(*After a pause.*) Pretty please. (*Pause.*) With sugar on it.

Lights. Curtain.

PIG IN A POKE

Author's Note

I wrote *Pig in a Poke* such a long time ago that I can scarcely remember the circumstances. It was my first play with the late James MacTaggart, and I do remember admiring his part in the production. I only hope it works as well on the page as he made it work on the screen.

From the Eyre Methuen edition of *Close of Play* and *Pig in a Poke*, 1979.

Pig in a Poke was first transmitted on London Weekend Television in 1969. The cast was as follows:

Grieg Colin Blakely
Wendy Jennifer Hilary
Stephen John Steiner
Mrs Wycherley Joan Benham
Mr Wycherley John Harvey
Amanda Jane Bond
Leary Donald Sumpter
Mr Huggle Clifford Cox
Veronica Meg Ritchie
McGonnigal David Engers

Director James McTaggart
Designer John Clements
Producer Kenith Trodd

Characters

Grieg

Wendy

Stephen

Mrs Wycherley

Mr Wycherley

Amanda

Leary

Mr Huggle

Veronica

Gwen

McGonnigal

EXT. HOUSE

Shots of house in various stages of being for sale and then sold. Credits.

INT. THE BEDROOM

Wendy, fully dressed, goes to the chest of drawers, opens one drawer. It is piled strikingly high with underwear. She shuts the drawer, opens the one underneath it. It is piled high with gloves. Takes out a pair, goes towards the door, stops, goes back to the chest of drawers, puts first pair back in, takes out another pair, goes out, down the stairs to the living room. Picks up a letter from the desk, on down the stairs. The kitchen door is open; get a glimpse into it. She hesitates for a moment, then goes to the door facing it. Opens it. In contrast to the rest of the house, it is just as it was when it was being inspected. She hesitates a second before Grieg's door, then knocks, calls out:

Wendy Hello, Mr Grieg?

The door opens. Grieg is standing in vest and jeans, a mug of tea in his hand. He nods, holds the door wider for Wendy to pass.

Um, we phoned the builders yesterday, it seems that they can come back next week to – (*glances around*) put the finishing touches . . .

Grieg (*nods, holds up his mug*) Would you like some tea?

Wendy Um, no thank you. Really. (*Smiles.*) So we were just wondering what your plans were? (*Puts her hand on the table.*)

Grieg (*blandly*) Thank you.

Wendy Um, I mean, you said something about leaving?

Grieg Yes?

Wendy Do you know when exactly? Because then we could tell the men when they could come in, precisely.

Grieg Soon. (*Takes a gulp of tea.*)

Wendy (*more sharply*) But you don't know more definitely than that?

She lifts her hand up, blinks, looks quickly down at her glove, which is covered with a stain.

Grieg No. I haven't finished here yet.

Wendy Finished what?

Grieg shrugs. After a pause:

Only you *did* say that you'd be gone. (*Laughs pointedly.*) And we were rather banking . . . (*Stops, looks at him.*) But it will be soon?

Grieg smiles, little pause, then turns, goes into the kitchen. Wendy watches in confusion. He comes out holding a pair of secateurs and a cloth, puts the mug down and begins to wipe at the secateurs.

It will be soon?

Grieg Soon, yes.

Wendy Well, thank you, Mr Grieg.

She turns, goes out. Grieg stands by the door, staring after her. Sound of Wendy on the stairs, then a stumbling noise, a sudden exclamation.

Grieg (*blandly*) All right?

Wendy It's so – (*extremely irritated*) dark out here.

Grieg Oh, it is.

Wendy Yes it is.

> *Grieg smiles. Sounds of Wendy going up the stairs, and cut to:*

EXT.

Front door opens, Wendy steps out, clearly still irritated. Slams the door, then looks down at her glove, then at her stocking, and cut to:

INT.

Grieg at the basement window, lifting back a soiled lace curtain and seeing Wendy, with her ankle raised, and then as she goes down the path, out on his face, and cut to:

EXT. A STREET IN HAMPSTEAD

Wendy passes a shop window display of lingerie, etc. She hesitates, makes to go by, then turns, goes in, looking at her watch as she does so. See Wendy through the window, buying. She comes out of the shop carrying her purchases in chic bags.

INT. PUB

The pub is fairly crowded, and cut to the packages, on a chair, and Stephen and Wendy at a table. Drinks in front of them.

Wendy I don't believe he's got the slightest intention of going.

Stephen (*vaguely, he is glancing around the pub*) I suppose we'll have to do something.

Wendy He's utterly filthy. He contaminates the whole house.

Stephen No, he's not very wholesome – which reminds me, it's going to be Amanda after all. Amanda and the up-and-come-and-shove-your-face-in-it Leary. (*Looking around again.*) They're meant to be meeting me here, all of them. What intrigues me is I'm sure I heard something recently about the two of them, Amanda and Leary. The question is whether it's something useful – (*In a low voice.*) Oh, here he is. (*Louder.*) There you are.

> *Wendy looks at him confused, then looks around. A man, young, bearded and scruffy, is standing in front of them, holding a script. He looks at Wendy.*

Leary (*North Country accent*) Hello.

Stephen Um, darling. This is Leo Leary. Wendy, my wife.

Leary I thought it must be, you look so alike.

Stephen Is Amanda with you?

Leary Not quite. She's showing herself off by the door. (*Looks over towards the door.*)

> *Cut to Amanda, who detaches herself from someone not clearly seen, drifts over to the table. She is also carrying a script.*

Amanda Hello. (*Smiles and nods at Wendy.*)

Stephen Darling, Amanda Gracely. What do you think of it?

Amanda rolls her eyes, pinches her nostrils.

Leary (*in a flat, expressionless voice, reading from script*) 'My dear lady, we ought to have exchanged teething rings in the registry office, or perhaps one of those ebony do-dahs in the shape of our respective throats, because that's what we spend our time sinking our respective bridge-work into.' Oh Christ. A kind of Glaswegian Noël Coward.

Amanda Oh Christ, especially as I've just left him. So he might be in hearing range.

Stephen Oh Christ, has he turned up? I'd better go and have a word. (*Gets up, goes over to the corner.*)

Leary (*to Wendy*) What do *you* do?

Wendy (*shrugs, smiles*) Exist.

Leary If you ask the housefly the meaning of its existence, it would soon cease to exist.

Amanda (*to Leary*) What's the meaning of your existence? (*Little pause, smiles.*) Now how long do I have to wait? (*To Wendy.*) We're all thanking God Stephen's on this.

Leary (*neutrally, looking at Wendy*) Yes, he seems to have got it all.

Wendy He thinks you're both going to be marvellous. Actually, um – (*Gets up, picks up her bags.*) I've got to go. (*Little pause.*) Goodbye.

Shot of her crossing the room with her bags, towards Stephen. Seen from Leary's point of view. Stephen is talking to a small man, carrying a briefcase. Then cut to the man – McGonnigal, the author, talking.

McGonnigal No, I've seen him once or twice in those North Country things, where he falls down drunk or gets into punch-ups, but I'm just wondering if he's going to catch the style. I mean, he looks a bit short on that.

Stephen Oh, he's thoroughly grotty, but it doesn't matter because – (*smiles*) I've got the style. And it's covered far worse than him. But you don't have to torment yourself by turning up at readings, rehearsals, etc. if you don't want – Oh, hello darling. You off?

As Wendy nods:

I'm just having a word with our author, the one man we can't do without.

Wendy nods, smiles. Stephen bends forward; slightly self-consciously, they kiss. Cut to Leary watching as Wendy goes to the door, and then to Stephen looking at Leary with a knowing little smile, and:

INT. OFFICE

A small, cramped office. Three desks. Telephone on one of the desks. Behind this desk a middle-aged man is sitting. He is plump and bearded. Come in on his face.

Mr Huggle (*tugs at his beard*) Um . . . have you done anything like it before?

Wendy (*voice-over, not yet seen, slight rustlings*) Well, you know, just standing on street corners – and shaking my tin. (*Laughs awkwardly.*) And then once at Oxford I was driven out in a, well, sort of bikini thing.

Long pause as Mr Huggle nods, waits.

Well, you know, standing on a taxi and saluting and – (*Laughs.*) I caught coins. (*Another pause.*) But still – (*Voice earnest.*) It was *for* something, I suppose . . .

Mr Huggle Well, we're for something. I expect Gwen's told you. (*Solicitously.*) Do you mind muck?

Cut to Wendy's face for the first time. She is sitting opposite the desk, her legs close together, the chic bags, from which the rustlings on her lap, and her hand pressed down on top of the bags.

Wendy No, really. (*Leans forward, more rustlings.*) I'd love to try it. (*Very intensely.*) I really want to, I mean, there are so many people who need, well, help.

Mr Huggle (*worried*) Yes, yes, there are.

Cut to:

INT. KITCHEN

Carry Wendy's face over immediately from the last scene, but bent, absorbed. Then down on various articles from the carrier bags spread out. Picks up a pair of knickers, the bra, her expression odd. The telephone rings. She gives a start, as if coming out of a trance, picks the telephone up. It is fastened to the wall.

Wendy Hello. (*Little pause.*) Sorry, who? Oh – (*Carefully.*) Hello. Yes, of course I do, we met at lunchtime, you're in Stephen's play. Stephen's not back yet. I'm afraid, the last time I saw him was with you and Amanda, shall I get him to – (*Pause.*) No, I'm afraid that's, um, I can't. (*Little pause.*) No, I'm sorry, I don't think it would be a good idea. Goodbye.

Puts the telephone down, looks at the underwear, picks up the bra and pants, suddenly turns her head sharply. Grieg's face at the door, as he passes. He smiles, goes on down the corridor. Wendy shoves the underwear into the carrier bag, turns determinedly to the stove, and stirs something in a saucepan.

INT. DINING ROOM ADJOINING THE KITCHEN

The table with the wine bottle on it, also the remains of a consumed meal. Wendy's father is at the head of the table. Wendy beside him. Wendy's mother sits opposite, but in fact closer to Stephen at the other end. There is a slight gap, in other words, between the two couples. Stephen is smoking a cheroot. Mr Wycherley has in his mouth a large, unlit cigar. But come in first on Stephen speaking.

Stephen The trick is to keep them on the boil for as long as I need them. For instance, I was telling Wendy, Leary had or might still be failing to have or would like to get out of something or other with Amanda and it's part of my job to find out exactly what and use it in the performances. The author on the other hand just haunts around hoping to be noticed, which he politely isn't, which is also part of my job, in other words it's a matter of oiling here and jarring there and hoping it'll turn into a – (*gestures*) something chemical.

> *Include in this exchange Mr Wycherley's handsome and cynical face.*

Mrs Wycherley Darling Stephen, you're terribly good at that, it must be nice to do it to such glam people.

Stephen They're the most boring people in the world, simply the most boring. Absolutely unreal.

Mrs Wycherley (*as Wendy and Stephen exchange little private smiles*) Oh, don't say that, just like everybody else you mean?

Stephen Oh worse, much worse, aren't they, darling?

Wendy (*innocently*) Are they, darling?

Stephen Yes, they really are.

Mrs Wycherley (*with an air of triumph*) But I thought they were all meant to be so camp. (*Daringly.*)

Wendy (*lights her father's cigar during this*) All right then? (*In a low voice.*)

Mr Wycherley (*pulling on cigar*) All right then. (*In a low voice.*)

Stephen Oh, some of them are. Camply boring. Which is worse than butchly boring.

Mrs Wycherley's eyes go to Wendy and Mr Wycherley, away again.

Mrs Wycherley The only thing is, Stephen, I do hope it's not going to be one of those grubby pieces about illegits, and disinfectants and hospitals and coloured what-nots, don't you, darling?

Mr Wycherley (*to Wendy*) I pass.

Wendy I should think you do.

Stephen Oh no, it's going to be terribly stylish. I've promised.

Mr Wycherley (*abruptly*) How's your sitting tenant?

Stephen What? (*Glances at Wendy.*) Grieg? Yes, well actually he's still sitting. (*Little pause.*) Really, he's quite a character, in his way.

Wendy He's an extremely filthy character, and so is his way.

Mrs Wycherley There you are, just like one of your plays.

Mr Wycherley (*with quiet authority*) I'd get rid of him, if I were you. You could always buy him out.

Stephen Yes. (*Nods, glances at Wendy.*) Anyway, we'll think of something.

There is a pause.

Mrs Wycherley What is exactly butch, darling?

Cut very directly to: Stephen full shot, in an apron, wiping a dish, and beside him Mrs Wycherley washing up, and then, through the open door, from Stephen's point of view, shot of Wendy and Mr Wycherley, Wendy's hand over Mr Wycherley's, her voice very low and intimate.

Wendy (*just heard*) You're looking very well.

Mr Wycherley Am I?

Come in on:

Wendy Pleasingly prosperous.

Mr Wycherley But I expect I'm due to lose a little weight. How much?

Wendy Terribly little, Daddy. Three hundred pounds? For the decorators and other thieves.

Mr Wycherley I'll make it four, on condition that this isn't the last time. It'll be in the post tomorrow. (*Stares at Wendy, smiles.*) All right, then.

Wendy All right, then. (*Smiles.*) Butch.

Stephen (*puts his head through the door*) Darling, is there another drying-up cloth?

INT. BEDROOM

Wendy comes into the bedroom, picks up the carrier bag, as from below sounds of Vivaldi. She opens the bag,

*peers in. Takes out a couple of garments, looks at herself
in the mirror over the bed. Suddenly the Vivaldi stops,
sounds of a door opening, closing, Wendy thrusts the
stuff back into the bag, puts it down by the bed, begins
to unbutton her blouse as Stephen comes in. He looks
at her.*

Stephen I didn't hear you come up.

*He is carrying his briefcase. He opens it, looks in.
Little pause.*

You haven't told me.

Wendy What?

Stephen What he said.

Wendy About what?

Stephen About the – you know – loan? (*Turns around.*)

Wendy Oh. (*Little pause.*) There'll be a cheque in the
post tomorrow.

Stephen Oh? How much.

Wendy Three hundred.

Stephen (*clearly slightly disappointed*) Great. (*Shuts the
briefcase.*) He's sending it to you?

Wendy I'll make another one out to you. Now, if you
want.

Stephen OK.

Stares at her, smiles, comes over, sits down at her feet.

Are you all right, then?

Wendy Perfectly.

Stephen (*smiling knowingly up at her*) And what about
Hump-them-as-soon-as-look-at-them Leary?

Wendy (*slight pause*) Leary?

Stephen He didn't phone?

Wendy Why should he?

Stephen It's his method – or so I gather, from bits of gossip and pieces of rumours.

Wendy Perhaps he doesn't fancy me.

Stephen Oh, he fancies you all right. The real problem, though, is does he still or did he ever fancy Amanda?

Wendy Wouldn't it be worse if the problem was me?

As Stephen puts his hand on her knee, then slides it up under her skirt.

Stephen Oh, I can handle you. At least, I'd know what was going on.

Wendy gets up, goes across the room.

(*Smiling.*) Where are you going?

Wendy To have a bath, of course.

Stephen Oh. (*Pulls out the bag, against which he has been pressing.*) What is in here? (*Fishes in, pulls out a pair of knickers.*) Mmmm.

Wendy (*turns, looks at them, him*) Be careful. (*Sharply.*) I don't want them crumpled.

INT. THE CHARITY OFFICE

Gwen, tall and dark, handsome, Australian accent, and Veronica, small girl, strained manner. Wendy at the end of the desk, writing down items in a book. Mr Huggle at the other desk, is on the telephone. But (having cut directly from Wendy's knickers) come in on an undefinable

*but filthy garment being held by Gwen. Then cut to
Veronica, and then to Wendy. She looks at the garment,
then looks quickly away.*

Veronica (*matter of factly*) Men's knickers.

*Gwen drops them on top of clothes pile at Wendy's
foot, which she moves.*

Gwen Men's knickers. 'C' column, darling, I think.

As Wendy writes:

We ought to send them back.

Veronica (*digging in again*) Who to? You don't think
they own up, do you?

Gwen (*as another object comes out*) It *can't* be!

Veronica Oh, we used to get masses of those, in Kilburn.

Wendy (*looking up*) What?

Gwen A nappy, my dear, straight, by the smell of it,
from baby's bum. There isn't a column for this one – put
it down under miscellaneous.

Cut to:

Mr Huggle (*his voice rising to audibility*) No, no, I do
see that and we *are* grateful for any interest, Mrs Jellybein,
but I think that a local jumble sale is the best place – a
church fete – (*Little pause.*) A synagogue fete then?
(*Laughs.*) Oh, I'm sorry, I didn't mean – I'll certainly try
and think of somewhere to place it. Goodbye.

Veronica What was it?

Mr Huggle A bone-china tea set. In shards, I suspect.

He watches as Veronica pulls out another garment.

Veronica Vest.

Gwen (*to Wendy*) You'll have gathered by now that we're the most chi-chi tip in town.

She takes the garment from Veronica, drops it in one of the piles at Wendy's foot.

Veronica They mean well.

Take in Mr Huggle, sitting with his hand to his forehead.

Gwen What would we get if they meant badly, then?

Mr Huggle (*stands up, clears his throat*) I've got to go and chat up a lady who's talking cash, um, Veronica, would you mind coming along?

Veronica gets up, slightly self-consciously, goes out, followed by Mr Huggle, who turns, nods at the other two, closes the door. There is a silence. Gwen picks up another piece of clothing, throws it onto one of the piles.

Gwen He's married, the poor sweeties.

Wendy Oh.

Gwen They probably have to make do with the back of his van.

INT. FIRST-FLOOR ROOMS

Furnished, decorated very elegantly. The hi-fi set is on. Stephen is sitting on a Barcelona chair, smoking a cheroot. He is wearing his dark glasses, perched on the end of his nose. He has his briefcase on his lap, and is doing some blocking on a square of paper. He puts the briefcase down, gets up, nodding his head slightly in time to the music. The camera follows him, across the hall, up a few

*stairs, goes into a door, glimpse of an extremely elegant
little lavatory with a rug on the floor, little stick of
deodorant, a stool beside the lavatory with a book on it.
Shuts the door, little pause to music, luxurious flushing
sound, comes out, nodding his head to the music, waits
as it comes to climax, conducts the last few bars, brings
arms down in a majestic sweep as the music stops, then
turns the handle of the bathroom door. Pushes. The door
doesn't open.*

Stephen Darling? (*Waits. No reply.*) Darling?

*Puts his ear to the keyhole, tries the door again, faint
gurgling water sounds from within. From below the
music starts again. He turns around, goes down,
enters the living room. Wendy is turning away from
the hi-fi.*

Oh, there you are.

*Slightly apprehensive, goes to his armchair, sits down,
picks up his briefcase and blocking paper.*

Where've you been?

Wendy (*sardonically*) Washing up.

Stephen Oh. (*Little pause.*) Sorry, I'm just working out
my campaign to keep Amanda's tits, Leary's profile and
McGonnigal's camera instructions off screen.

*Bends over the paper, and shot of him from Wendy's
point of view. She gives a little smile at him. Goes
over to the bookcase. Stephen looks up towards her.
Licks his lips slightly. She takes a book down, goes
towards the door, followed by Stephen.*

(*Slightly.*) Where are you going?

Wendy To have a bath.

They look at each other.

(*Calmly.*) You get on with your campaign in peace.

She goes out. Stephen stares at the door, then looks down at his paper, slowly begins to move his head to the music, and cut to:

INT. THE BATHROOM DOOR

Grieg comes out, fully dressed, his hair slicked back, looking unnaturally groomed. Hears a sound above, looks up. Wendy, in her pants and bra, comes down the stairs, as Grieg steps back into the bathroom. She goes past the door, into the living room.

INT. LIVING ROOM

Stephen looks up as Wendy comes in, smiles at her, pretends to look down at his paper again, then looks up covertly as Wendy goes to the bookcase, puts book back, runs her hand along the shelf. He stares at her, and cut to Grieg, at the door, staring impassively at Wendy. Wendy moves along, looking at book titles.

Stephen What are you looking for?

Wendy Nothing really.

This seen from Grieg's point of view, then cut to Wendy as she takes down a book, looks at Stephen, who stares back at her, transfixed. She turns, goes to the door, Stephen watches her, then frowns, runs the dark glasses up and down his nose, bends over the paper. Cut to Wendy going upstairs, from Grieg's point of view a few steps down the next flight.

(*Voice-over from above.*) Stephen! (*More shrilly.*) Stephen!

Stephen (*comes running out of the living room*) What? (*In a panic.*) What? (*Runs up to the bathroom.*)

Wendy Look at it. Just look at it!

Stephen (*also voice-over*) Christ!

Cut to Wendy coming out of the bathroom, her face set. She goes back upstairs to the bedroom, comes out again almost at once.

Wendy Go down and have it out with him. The pig.

Stephen (*comes out of the bathroom, hesitates*) He's gone out.

Wendy How do you know?

Stephen I heard him.

Wendy turns, goes back to the bedroom. Stephen goes into the bathroom. She comes out again almost at once.

Wendy That's the limit, when he starts leaving his scum in our bath for me to sit in.

Stephen, unseen, mutters something.

(*Shrilly.*) What?

Stephen comes to the door, holding package of Vim. Wendy turns, stubs her toe.

Ooooh! Christ!

Limps into the bedroom, muttering viciously.

Stephen You all right, darling?

Stands for a moment, then goes back into the bathroom.
    Cut to Grieg. He turns, goes down the stairs. Then cut to Wendy; she is sitting on the edge of the bed, her

*hands clasped between her knees. Stephen comes into
the room. She looks up at him blankly.*

I've got it all off.

Wendy I spend the day among filthy garments worn by
filthy people, and I come back home to find I'm expected
to sit in a filthy bath.

Stephen Darling, don't be depressed.

Goes over to her, kneels down in front of her.

Wendy Why not?

Stephen (*shrugs, smiles*) It makes *me* depressed when
you're depressed.

Wendy Does it?

Stephen Yes, it does.

Wendy (*smiles, a ghastly radiant smile*) Does it make
you radiant, when I'm radiant?

Stephen (*stares up at her, gets up*) Thank you. (*Coldly.*)

Wendy That's all right. (*Little pause.*) Daddy warned us.

Stephen (*after a little pause*) That's true. And very
constructive. He didn't actually tell us how to go about
it, though, did he? Except to buy him off with money we
haven't got.

Wendy (*sarcastically*) We could always borrow it from
him, couldn't we?

Stephen (*slightly shrill*) What the hell's the matter with
you?

Wendy (*looks at him*) Is it really so hard for you to
understand? I just don't like the way that pig is turning
our house into his personal trough. He makes me feel
sick. Can't you understand that? Can't you really? Can't

you really understand that? (*Glares at Stephen.*) Also you didn't hear him go out. You were just fobbing me off because you're too nice or something to go down and do anything about it.

Stephen I *did* hear him go out, excuse me.

Wendy (*suddenly calm, shakes her head*) You did not.

Stephen (*slaps his arm against his side, shakes his head*) I *did* hear him go out.

Wendy stares at him, smiles, shrugs. Stephen turns, goes to the door, flings it open. Follow him down the stairs, running. Come to the bottom hall as Grieg advances up it, dressed to go out. Stephen does a sort of jig backwards and to the side, to let Grieg pass. Grieg waits calmly.

Ooops, sorry. (*Gives a little laugh.*)

Grieg That's all right. (*Goes on down the hall.*)

Stephen goes into the kitchen, Grieg goes out, Stephen reappears, goes up the stairs and cut to Wendy sitting on the edge of the bed. Stephen stands at the bedroom door, then comes in.

Stephen (*triumphantly*) I told you. He's gone out.

INT. MORNING

Wendy comes down the stairs, into the hall, dressed to go out. She stands before Grieg's door, hesitates, then opens the door, looks down the stairs, shuts the door, turns. Grieg is just coming through the front door. She glances at him quickly, then goes into the kitchen, as if she hadn't seen him. Goes to the sink. Stiffens slightly, turns around. Grieg is standing at the kitchen door.

Grieg Looking for me?

Wendy (*slight hesitation*) Um, oh, Mr Grieg, good morning, yes, I was just wondering, did my husband speak to you before he went this morning?

Grieg shakes his head.

Oh. (*Little pause.*) I know he wanted to. (*Little pause.*) About the bath, actually.

Grieg tilts his head enquiringly.

Yes, my husband and I – (*Stops in recognition.*) We just feel that the bath isn't in your part of the house, frankly.

Grieg (*nods*) You feel that?

Wendy (*very sharply*) So *if* you don't mind, could you *not* use it in future without at least asking us first and would you also do us the favour of cleaning it out afterwards *if* it *is* all right for you to use it, please. (*Long pause.*) Is that understood?

Grieg (*nods*) Yes, I understand that.

Wendy Good. Thank you.

> *Turns to the sink, turns on the tap; come in on her face, the tap running. She picks up a cup and saucer, holds them under the tap, on her face an expression of tension. She turns the tap off; as she does so she gives a jump, her eyes widen. Continues to stare ahead as sound of footsteps crossing the floor.*

INT. REHEARSAL ROOM

Come in immediately on Stephen, observed from the door, back to camera. He is making gestures with his arms and hips, very effeminate. Leary and Amanda are in front of him, making them back to him. Various people scattered about, drinking coffee, reading. McGonnigal is seated at a large table by the wall, writing into an exercise book. Then Wendy moves forward into camera, uncertainly. Steps sideways, sits down some distance from McGonnigal. He looks at her, nods and smiles in recognition. She nods back, watches intensely. Stephen has taken Amanda by her shoulders and is doing his effeminate dance with her. Leary comes over to Wendy, sits down beside her.

Leary (*in a low voice*) I suppose Stephen asked you if I'd phoned?

Wendy (*staring straight ahead*) Yes.

Leary (*in a low voice*) And did you tell him?

Pause. Wendy remains staring ahead.

Don't you think I've got enough style for you? (*Little pause.*) Well, Stephen's going to give me some of his.

Wendy turns, looks at Stephen, cut to him. He circles effeminately around Amanda, sees her, stops, says something to Amanda, comes over.

Stephen Darling, what are you doing here?

Wendy Can I speak to you for a minute, please?

Amanda (*coming behind Stephen*) Now we can get the real story about Mr Grieg's bath.

Wendy looks at Stephen, who smiles fleetingly, embarrassed.

Leary Apparently you think some people don't rate baths.

Wendy What? (*Looks at Stephen again.*)

Amanda The talcum powder bit's gorgeous.

Wendy Talcum powder?

Amanda (*to Stephen*) I knew you were lying. *His* version is that your Grieg or whatever was poncing about the house in your talc and a fingertip or two of your best scent behind the ears.

Stephen (*smiles falsely*) What I *actually* said was . . .

Amanda And Leary's furious because Yorkshire coal-miners don't get talc and scents on the National Health, or their sons don't. Or he doesn't. Or someone doesn't; anyway he's furious about it. It seems they're betraying the working classes again, and RADA boys with surly faces.

Leans over Leary, puts her arm around his neck.

Doesn't it, darling?

Leary straightens, tries to look up into her face, says something that makes Amanda tighten her expression and then, smiling, her grip around his throat. Leary attempts to break free with his shoulders. After a second Amanda steps away.
Wendy gets up, Stephen walks beside her towards the door.

Wendy Why did you tell them about the bath?

Stephen What? No reason. It was just coffee and camping-up time before we started, one invents these things, you know. (*Little pause.*) What's the matter? I mean, why aren't you at work?

Wendy (*after a pause, shrugs*) I just wanted to see you.

Stephen (*blankly*) Oh. Great. You all right?

Wendy Perfectly.

Stephen Actually there's so much strange sex in the atmosphere here, I'd better not walk you to the Tube. I'm beginning to think the key to a sane life is to go in for charity work.

Looking past her to McGonnigal, who is approaching rapidly.

Oh Christ. Our bloody author, he's never been to bed with – (*points a finger*) Tim. Hello.

McGonnigal Could you spare me a moment, Stephen? There are a few notes I've jotted down.

Cut to:

EXT. SHOP

Wendy in lingerie shop.

INT. THE HALL

Wendy comes through the front door, packages clasped tight to her chest as she struggles to get the key back into her handbag. Suddenly stares ahead. Grieg is bearing down on her. She strives to move out of the way, packages slip, a few pieces of underwear (white) scatter to the floor. She tries to crouch to pick them up. Grieg watches, looking down at her, and cut to her face, frantic, embarrassed, as she scrambles the pieces together, stands up. Grieg steps past her, smiles into her face, goes out. Wendy stands for a moment, then hurries blindly along to the kitchen, drops the packages on the table, still clinging unconsciously to a pair of white knickers. Stands for a moment, then goes to the telephone, dials. A little pause. The knickers still in her hand.

Wendy Daddy?

EXT. GARDEN

Shot of Grieg working in the garden, taken from the living room. The hi-fi set is playing. Wendy at the window (Grieg from her point of view, in fact). Suddenly she looks to her left. Mr Wycherley saunters easily into the garden, a cigar in his mouth. Stephen and Mrs Wycherley follow, Mrs Wycherley with a hand across her nose. They stand for a moment, talking, then Stephen gestures to the tree at the end of the garden. Mrs Wycherley looks towards Grieg, who is still crouching, then goes towards the tree, Stephen in attendance. Mr Wycherley stands smoking his cigar, then glances up at Wendy, smiles, saunters easily over to Grieg, his hands in his pockets, stands above him. Wendy gives a little smile, and cut to:

Mr Wycherley *(after a moment, takes cigar out of his mouth)* You're Grieg? *(Smoothly.)*

Grieg looks up, nods, goes on with his trowelling.

And you're what is known as the sitting tenant.

Grieg pays no attention. Mr Wycherley smiles calmly.

You're a good gardener, aren't you?

Grieg That's right.

Mr Wycherley To tell you the truth, I didn't expect to find you here. There seemed to be a general impression that you were leaving.

Grieg *(looks up at him)* And is there a general impression that I'm still here?

Mr Wycherley *(smiles suavely)* You taking the micky?

Grieg goes back to his trowelling. Mr Wycherley glances up at Wendy, still at the window. The music should, of course, sound in the garden throughout this.

Or possibly conducting a piece of business. Shrewdly, eh? (*Little pause.*) For example, being unprepared to settle for less than a hundred and fifty pounds.

Grieg (*looks up at him*) What'd I want a hundred and fifty pounds for? (*In genuine disbelief.*)

Mr Wycherley (*pulls on his cigar*) What *do* you want?

Grieg I can get anything I need.

Mr Wycherley Very well. Two –

Mrs Wycherley (*coming up with Stephen*) What have *you* found?

Mr Wycherley Um, I've found Mr Grieg, digging – what the dickens is that you're digging up?

He squats down, Mrs Wycherley and Stephen now standing around the two of them. Cut to Wendy still watching from the window as Stephen, and then Mrs Wycherley, also crouch. As the music achieves a superbly royal flourish Grieg rises, and from Wendy's point of view, looks up at Wendy as her family remains squatting in various accidentally worshipping postures around him.

INT. BEDROOM

Stephen, in his pyjamas, is going through the contents of his briefcase. Takes out his dark glasses, puts them on the dresser.

Stephen Um, it was all right, was it?

Wendy (*voice-over*) What?

Stephen Letting the three hundred run over a bit?

Wendy (*voice-over*) Don't worry, no money's going to change hands.

Stephen That's very decent.

He shuts the briefcase, turns, looks for his dark glasses, puts them on, takes them off.

Wendy (*voice-over*) You're a very pretty man, very very pretty. Gwen says you're the prettiest man she ever met. Do you know you're pretty, Stephen?

Stephen (*after a pause, staring at her – straight into the camera, in fact*) Yes.

Wendy (*voice still over*) Are you pleased you're so pretty?

Stephen (*after another pause*) Yes.

Little pause, goes over to the bed. Wendy is sitting on the edge of the bed, in pale pyjamas. He sits down beside her.

Are you?

Wendy Mostly.

Stephen puts the dark glasses down on the bedside table.

Stephen But you're prettier. (*Little pause, then thickly.*) You know I love you.

Pushes her tentatively down on the bed.

I do.

Smiles pleadingly into her eyes. Wendy looks up at him, then slowly shakes her head.

Please, darling. (*In a whisper.*) Please.

> *Wendy shakes her head again. Fade out, and in on Wendy face up on the pillow, naked, pyjamas lying across the bed.*

(*Voice off.*) A sort of therapy party. For the whole cast-cum-ladies-and-gentlemen, my idea being to get all the noise and nastiness in one place for an evening, you know? Turn it into a collective experience – a purification rite or a ritual murder for mainly, frankly, Amanda and Leary. I shall be the observer of all observed, if Leary makes a lunge at you I'll have to rethink my strategy, but if he chases Amanda all evening I'll know I've got them taped until the taping. (*Little chuckle.*)

Wendy Why do men do that?

Stephen (*complacently, voice-over*) What?

Wendy Come wheedling for a bit of love or body or whatever it is they think they need and have a right to and when they've had it they lie there like – I don't know – men.

Stephen (*after a pause*) What do you mean?

Wendy What I've said.

Stephen (*rolls over, looks at her*) Oh darling, come on.

Wendy (*in camera, staring up*) Come on where, darling?

> *Stephen stares at her, aghast, then rolls back again, stares up, tight-lipped.*

Stephen (*tautly*) Thank you very much.

Wendy You're welcome.

Stephen (*after a little pause*) I thought you loved me.

Wendy I do.

Turns her head, looks at him, then with her finger traces the line of his nose, smiles, says flatly:

Because you're so pretty.

INT. LIVING ROOM

Party in progress. About forty guests. The hi-fi set playing some cool modern stuff, very low, and over it the row of voices. Visible among the guests several members of Stephen's production group; take them in generally, then transfer to a man talking to Wendy. Gwen talking to Stephen, Amanda standing aloof, with McGonnigal unhappily beside her. She is watching Leary. Then cut briefly and tantalisingly to a shaggy head and back, to give just an impression of Grieg in a corner. Come back to Wendy and her man.

Stephen is laughing boyishly, sweeping his hair out of his eyes. There should be a little play from Gwen, intensification of expression.

Stephen Well, actually I don't think he intends to join us this evening.

Gwen You should have asked him up. Then we could have occupied his basement, which would have been much nicer.

Leary How's Stephen?

Wendy Don't you know?

Leary Well, I don't suppose he handles you like the ladies and gentlemen of the cast, does he? Wouldn't the strain show in a bit of wife-beating, or sommat?

Wendy (*licks her lips, then with a tight smile*) Wrong class, I think.

Leary Is it husband-beating down in the stylish South?

Wendy Or sommat. (*Nods.*)

Wendy looks from Amanda, who is smiling pleasantly, to Leary, whose face is suddenly set, then looks vaguely around, sees Stephen, back with Gwen but smiling knowingly towards her, then on, past more guests, standing with a drink, looking around, puzzled, then on, seeing Grieg by the door, his back to her and stooping slightly.

Wendy Excuse me, there's somebody there I have to, um . . .

She walks towards Grieg, determined.

Amanda (*to Leary, who is watching her go*) Well, what is it with Mrs Cool-Knickers, class or sex? Or both?

Leary (*savagely*) It's what you haven't got. What is it?

And cut to: Wendy a few feet away from Grieg's back. Veronica suddenly brushes around from in front, her face tremulous, looks past Wendy blankly, sees Mr Huggle, goes over to him. He looks at her in concern. Wendy stares after them, then looks at Grieg, who, turning, smiles at her. She glares at him, goes over to Veronica.

Veronica (*to an inaudible enquiry from Mr Huggle*) It doesn't matter.

Wendy Did he – do something?

Veronica glances at Wendy, tears in her eyes, shakes her head, looks away.

He said something, then?

Veronica shakes her head. Wendy turns, looks towards the door. It is open. Grieg has gone. She walks to the

*door purposefully, and out, closing it behind her. Cut
back to the party, Gwen at the hi-fi set, Stephen
standing beside her, watching, slight smile on his face,
and cut to his view of Leary talking savagely into
Amanda's face, Amanda smiling contemptuously,
McGonnigal just behind them, and cut back to:*

INT. THE STAIRS

*Wendy goes down them to the ground-floor hall. Turns
on the light, goes to the door that leads to the basement,
opens it, as from above thumps of dancing feet and loud
music come. Goes down to Grieg's door, her face set,
flings it open. Keep on her face, don't show Grieg.*

Wendy (*controlled, smiling with the effort*) You crashed
our party. (*Little pause.*) You helped yourself piggishly
to our drink, which you gulped down piggishly, you
insulted one of my friends, a girl who's incapable of
being unkind to anyone, even a pig like you, and then
you run off, like the cowardly pig you are. You'd bloody
well better go straight upstairs and apologise to my
friend before I get my husband and some of his friends
to throw you out, sitting tenant or no sitting tenant.

Cut to Grieg, facing her, watching her impassively.

Do – you – hear – me?

*Grieg, after a long pause, walks towards her. Wendy
steps aside to let him pass. He grabs her hand, jerks
her inside, slams the door. Wendy stumbles, nearly
falls. Steadies herself against the table, stares at him.*

Grieg (*after a long pause*) Enjoying your party?

*He comes over, stands close to her. Wendy stares at
him. He puts out his hands, one on each side of her
face. Wendy spits into his face. Grieg smiles.*

Wendy Let go of me!

Grieg stares into her face, his face very close. She stares back, increasingly as if mesmerised. Then he takes her hand, pulls her out of the basement door, tugs her up the stairs, very fast. She is trying to grab at something to pull herself back, he pulls her up the next flight, to the door of the party, puts his hand at the back of her neck.

Grieg Now who'll you send down for *your* apology?

Cut to:

INT. LIVING ROOM

Party in progress, dancing, etc. Stephen is hopping about with Gwen, Amanda is leaning forward, talking into Leary's face. Mr Huggle and Veronica are talking intensely. The door opens, Wendy comes in with a little stumble, straightens herself, whirls around, nobody notices. Grieg is standing at the door, staring at her. There is a long pause, then he smiles, leans forward, closes the door. Wendy remains looking at it. Suddenly there is a slapping sound behind, a little scream, Wendy turns around, as if dazed. Leary is holding his cheek, Amanda is walking away from him. A slight hush, then Leary strokes his cheek, laughter starts, slightly self-consciously, Leary walks after Amanda. Cut to Stephen, from Wendy's point of view. He looks towards her, makes a small amused face, then hops with Amanda out of the picture. Someone comes up beside Wendy, at first not seen properly. Wendy looks up at McGonnigal, his face, anxious, slightly pleading and cut to:

INT. BEDROOM

Wendy is lying on the bed, staring up at the ceiling in her pyjamas. Her arms are wrapped around her chest. Shouts from below, crashes, laughter, then the front door slamming. Pause. Then the sound of feet, slow, heavy, on the stairs. The door opens, slowly, Stephen comes in. He walks to the chair, sits down. Brushes hair away from his eyes, smiles at Wendy.

Stephen Well?

Wendy looks at him.

Make what you can of this. (*Speaks very carefully, smiling.*) They arrived together, they had their spicy little slap-up, they left together. He came back alone, she came back alone. He was ogling around for something, like possibly my wife, she stood watching him from a dark corner. He drank. She got his coat. They left together. (*Smiles.*) What do you make of this?

Wendy stares at him. His smile slightly unfocused.

Meanwhile back in the kitchen Aussie and Gwen were running amok all over my twelve-year-old PA, and your charity friend with the beard was cuddling a lady that definitely was not the bearer of his kiddies except possibly currently, actually and frankly. He fancies you, Leo Leary does. So observed the observer of all observed.

Makes a little laughing sound, stops, gets up, smiling vaguely.

Just a minute, darling.

Goes to the door, opens it, turns, smiles, close-up on his face, damp and his smile sickly.

Won't be a minute, darling.

*Cut to Wendy's face as sound of his feet running
down the stairs, then as the door is flung open below,
out on Wendy's face.*

INT. CHARITY OFFICE

*In on Veronica, sitting at the desk, going through a
ledger, her hand over her eyes. Cut to Gwen and Wendy,
seated at opposite ends of the desk, unwrapping packages.*

Gwen (*voice-over before she is seen*) Well, everyone
I saw was pissed to the newts, which is the only sign,
and there was that lovely Leary being slapped around.

*Wendy glances towards Veronica, who stands up
suddenly, and with jerky movements picks up her
handbag, goes out. Gwen raises her eyebrows, shrugs.*

One of her really bad days.

*Takes out of her paper a pair of baggy trousers, puts
them on the desk, as Wendy takes out of her paper
a pair of plus-fours, puts them on the desk.*

They were having a terrible time –

*Stops as the side door opens, Mr Huggle comes in.
Looks towards Veronica's desk.*

Mr Huggle Um, Veronica popped out, has she?

Gwen Yes.

Mr Huggle Well, perhaps I'll just, um.

Goes to the main door, and out. Closing it after him.

Gwen Oh Christ! What you could call a –

*Main door opens, Mr Huggle comes back in. He is
accompanied by a small man in a black suit.*

Mr Huggle (*going to the other door*) If Veronica – when she comes back, could you say the, um, accountant's dropped in?

He shuts the door. There is a pause. Gwen draws another package to her, shakes out another pair of voluminous and grubby trousers.

Gwen Now we're being rejected by one of those under-developed countries.

Wendy (*stands up abruptly*) Look, do you mind, I've got to get back, um, do you mind?

EXT. THE HOUSE

Wendy coming along the pavement, footsteps falter, then she goes quickly up the path, unlocks the door, goes in. Goes straight up the stairs to the living room.

INT. LIVING ROOM

It's in a filthy state; glasses, bottles, ashtrays everywhere. She looks around, trance-like, steps over bits and pieces, takes off her coat, puts it on a chair; it slips to the ground. She makes a weary gesture, puts it over the chair again, looks around her. Picks up a glass, shakes her head, puts it down again. Touches her forehead, then goes to the hi-fi, puts on some Mozart. Goes to the garden window, looks out. Shot of Grieg in the garden, sitting on a kitchen chair, reading a newspaper. Wendy licks her lips nervously, opens the window, steps away.

EXT. GARDEN

Grieg in the garden from behind, still reading the newspaper, strains of Mozart coming down. He lowers

*the newspaper, looks up. Shot of Wendy's face, jerking
away. He goes on staring. Pause. Wendy's face reappears,
she stares straight ahead, then looks down. Grieg stares
up, Wendy withdraws her head. Grieg gets up slowly,
stands in the centre of the garden, music still continuing.
Then shot from the window, the music very loud, looking
down at Grieg, looking up, then turning his head right.
Keep shot from the window, looking down as Wendy
comes into the garden, looks at him, walks towards him,
stops a few feet away. This, if possible, as the first
movement comes to an end.*

Wendy (*her voice heard faintly*) Pig!

*Grieg walks towards Wendy. She holds her ground
for a moment, then turns, walks quickly away. Grieg
follows. Wendy begins to run, Grieg's pace quickens,
the garden from above now seen as empty. There is a
sound from below, like a cry, then the slam of the
door, then cries from within, then hold shot of the
empty garden, music again in full flow, and fade out.
In on:*

INT. HALL

*Stephen comes into the hall, carrying his briefcase. He
looks tired. Goes into the kitchen. Comes out again.
Starts up the stairs.*

Stephen Darling!

*Gets to the living-room door, is about to open it, then
looks up the next flight, and cut to Wendy standing
halfway up the stairs, coming down, fully dressed in a
white frock, her hair done up behind her. She is
wearing Stephen's dark glasses.*

Hello.

Wendy (*tentatively*) Hello.

Stephen Still hungover?

Wendy walks down the stairs towards him, slowly and carefully. Stephen stands watching, smiling but slightly puzzled. When she is a stair above, thus making their heads on a level, he bends forward, kisses her on the forehead. Puts his hands on her cheeks. She winces, just slightly. He takes the glasses off, smiling. One of her eyes is bruised.

Christ!

Wendy (*bravely smiling*) I walked into the door. In the bedroom.

Stephen Poor darling. Will it be all right? It looks ghastly.

Wendy Yes.

Stephen kisses the air close to her eye. They gaze at each other for a moment, he puts the spectacles back on her nose, turns, stops.

Stephen What door in the bedroom?

Wendy The cupboard door. In the landing.

Stephen (*entering the living room, in its state of chaos*) God, what a tip!

Wendy (*follows, walking stiffly*) I'll do it tomorrow, I can't go anywhere looking like this anyway.

Stephen OK. (*Sinks down into a chair.*) God.

Shakes his head, then reaches out, turns on the hi-fi. Wendy stands beside him, then walks to chair opposite, sits in it, facing him.

Wendy How's Leary?

Stephen What? Oh, hungover and strangely absent when we needed him.

Smiles, touches his head, winces slightly, long pause, and on the two of them facing each other amidst the debris, fade.

INT. LIVING ROOM

The following morning. Wendy is in a sort of smock, a turban round her head, dark glasses on. She is plugging in the Hoover. She goes to the hi-fi, looks around her, looks towards the window. Licks her lips, looks quickly away. Picks up a few glasses with great efficiency, then puts them down again. Walks to the window as if in spite of herself, taking off her dark glasses as she does so and putting them in the smock pocket. Opens the window, looks out. Then withdraws her head, turns with a look that could be disappointment on her face, jumps. Cut to Grieg, standing inside the room.

Wendy (*very controlled, touching her glasses*) Please go.

Grieg walks towards her, then past her, to the window. Looks out.

Grieg Nice view.

Cut to the garden, stay on the garden, and Grieg looking down at it, as:

Wendy I don't care what you think of me – (*Still very controlled.*) Because frankly and honestly what someone like you thinks isn't very important anyway, and I'm perfectly prepared to concede –

Grieg steps away from window, out of camera which stays on the garden.

– that perhaps to some extent –

Little silence followed by squeals, sound of tussling, Wendy's squeals getting louder, glasses smashing, then sound of door shutting. Hold shot on garden, and:

INT. THE BASEMENT

Track over Wendy's clothes, scattered everywhere in the semi-darkness, then to her lying on the bed in the plastic overall, her hair loose. She is staring up blankly. The kitchen door opens, right. Grieg comes in, buttoning up his shirt. Picks up the secateurs, goes back towards the door.

Grieg The kettle's on, I'll have mine outside. *I've got* work to do. (*This with the very faintest touch of self-righteousness.*)

Wendy lies still for a moment, then fumbles in her overall pocket, produces the dark glasses, puts them on, stares up, and cut to:

INT. THE HALL

Grieg's basement-landing door, and the front door open simultaneously. Grieg and Stephen advance towards each other, Stephen does his skip and shuffle out of Grieg's way, nodding, smiling at him. Grieg nods impassively back, goes out. Stephen looks after him, then goes up the stairs.

INT. LIVING ROOM

Stephen opens the door, looks in. A shot of it in chaos. He closes the door, goes to the bedroom. Wendy is sitting before the mirror, dressed and with her hair pulled back, the dark glasses on. She looks at Stephen, at the door.

Wendy Hello.

Stephen How are you?

Wendy (*shrugs*) All right.

Stephen And the eye?

Wendy Blacker.

Stephen (*after a pause*) What have you been doing?

Wendy Having a bath.

Stephen You went to the office today, then?

Wendy No. (*Turns, lifts up the glasses to inspect her eye.*) You know I didn't. I was going to clear up the living room, remember.

Stephen Yes.

Wendy goes on inspecting her eye. Stephen laughs. Little pause.

Well . . .?

Wendy turns, looks at him impassively. Stephen shrugs.

It hasn't been done.

Wendy (*frowns*) No. We'll have to do it tonight. (*Shakes her head at herself in the mirror.*)

Stephen (*stares towards her*) We're in the studio tomorrow. So. (*Smiles slightly, a martyred smile.*) I'm getting stomach tension or something or other, inevitably.

Wendy Are you? (*Vaguely.*) Where?

Stephen In the stomach.

He looks at her reflection in the mirror.

287

INT. LIVING ROOM

The glasses gone. Order restored. But come in first on Wendy's overall, and the part of the Hoover from hands down to knee level. Then the Hoover stops, and cut to Wendy, in a chair, legs hanging over the side. She is watching Stephen doing the Hoovering. Still in the overall, Stephen crosses to the hi-fi; as he does so, sniffs.

Stephen Must say, a funny smell these things have got. (*Clutching at the overall.*) I don't know how you could bear to wear it.

Wendy It's only for when I've got something dirty to do.

Out, and in on:

INT. LIVING ROOM

In on Wendy. The hi-fi going. Bach. Then cut to Stephen in the armchair, sitting with his feet up, his collar undone. His face has a set, thoughtful expression; he is nodding his head very slightly to the music.

Stephen (*still jogging his head slightly*) You know, I've been thinking. The time's come to do something final about our friend downstairs.

Wendy Oh?

Stephen I don't know, I mean I met him in the hall this evening, and it suddenly got to me. Why *should* we put up with him? It's the way he somehow gets into everything.

Wendy I know.

Stephen And how do we know what he's up to, anyway? As far as we're concerned he could be up and down, in and out, all day long.

*Little pause, jounces his head in a lively fashion to
a lively piece of music.*

Know what I mean?

Wendy Yes, I do.

*Also jouncing her head slightly, both of them doing it.
Stephen extravagantly, Wendy demurely, as the record
ends.*

Stephen Isn't that smashing! (*Little pause.*) I don't know,
frankly and actually – (*Stops.*) God knows what Leary's
up to, he's off somewhere or other every ten-minute
break. Amanda just grins Cheshire – Something very
funny's going –

*Stops as music starts again. He sits listening to it,
looks at Wendy, frowns. She reaches up slowly, takes
off her dark glasses; there is a pause, her face very
serious, then it breaks into a sudden, frank, inviting
smile. Stay on this as she licks her lips, and cut to:*

INT. THE HALL

*Wendy goes down the hall, dressed to go out, very
determined, wearing the dark glasses. Hold on the door;
it opens, Wendy comes in. Back down the hall. Opens
the door to the basement. Goes down.*

INT. THE BASEMENT

*Wendy goes to the bed, sits down, takes the dark glasses
off, puts them down. Folds her hands into her lap, her
expression very patient. Fade out, then in on her sitting
there as sound of door from the garden opening, and
closing, footsteps. Wendy licks her lips, stares with her*

hands folded at the door, as it opens. Cut on her almost schoolgirl face, in on her face, hair hanging dishevelled, then she raises a mug to her mouth, sips from it. Lowers the mug, and cut to Grieg, standing in the kitchen door, also sipping a mug.

Wendy (*with casual malice*) Your days are numbered. My husband's decided to get rid of you.

Grieg pays no attention.

He'll knock you about and throw you into the street bodily. (*Little pause.*) He'll think of something. He's good with people. Jarring and oiling them. (*Pause.*) He's only started noticing you now that you're not around so much. What are you around so much for?

Grieg What's there to be around for?

Wendy (*after a moment, nods*) Thank you.

The telephone rings distantly. Wendy stares up at the ceiling.

That's probably him now.

Grieg It sounds like him.

They listen to the telephone. It rings a few more times, stops.

Wendy (*after a pause*) I'm going upstairs.

Standing up, we see her from the back; her dress is open, she is carrying a bundle of her underwear under her arm, stockings trailing down.

God, why are you so dirty?

Picks up one of the magazines from a pile, looks at it, shot of its cover, drops it back on the chair.

Such a pig.

Grieg (*slightly menacing*) Watch it.

Wendy stops, turns, looks at him. Come in on her face. Licks her lips. Upstairs, the telephone starts again. She stares at Grieg, who stares back at her. Then, in a whisper, excited and fearful:

Wendy Pig. Pig.

INT. LIVING ROOM

Stephen and Wendy as the night before, only come in on Wendy in dark glasses, from Stephen's point of view.

Stephen (*voice-over*) Do you still need those things?

Wendy nods.

I tried to get you this morning. Here and at the office. Nobody knew where you were.

Wendy I had an accident.

Stephen What? (*Cut to his face.*)

Wendy I tripped down the stairs.

Little pause, then looking at him very solemnly, lifts up her skirt, shows him a bruise on her thigh. Stephen stares at it.

So actually and everything I couldn't face the thought of all the grot of the office. I took the day off. (*Little pause.*) I was being naughty.

Stephen (*stares at her, licks his lips*) Um, Leary, um – (*Stops.*) Want some music?

Wendy shakes her head. Smiles at him. Gets to his feet, looks vaguely around.

Did we do the dishes?

*Wendy still smiling. Stephen staring at her as if
mesmerised.*

I'd better go over my shooting script, um . . .

Wendy (*tilts her head to one side, smiles lasciviously*)
Come over here. (*He goes over.*)

Reaches up, touches his nose, presses it.

You haven't told me yet who is doing what to whom.

*Draws his hand to her, and cut to Wendy and Stephen
on the living-room carpet. Clothes around them, his
folded into a neat pile, hers scattered indifferently. Cut
to their faces, Wendy is staring up, smiling. Bruise
showing. Stephen's is turned into the camera; it has a
slightly doped look, eyelids heavy. Then Wendy's face
moves off camera; stay on Stephen's as Bach begins.
His eyelids open.*

Stephen He's got something going all right. And it's not
with Amanda.

Eyelids begin to close again, and cut to:

INT.

*Come in on Wendy's face. She is seated on Grieg's bed,
hands folded in her lap. Suddenly she gets up, walks
across the room, opens the door, and out. As the kitchen
door opens, Grieg comes in, stands, as sound above of
front door closing. Grieg tilts his head to one side.*

INT.

*Before the charity office door. Wendy takes a breath,
adjusts her glasses, opens the door.*

INT. THE OFFICE

Wendy at the door, not seen, the office from her point of view. Veronica most prominent, staring towards her; a handkerchief to her mouth. Behind her, two men, tough and impassive, and the accountant from the earlier scene. Mr Huggle, plucking at his beard.

Gwen (*comes up beside her, from around the other corner*) Oh, I shouldn't bother, darling, we're closing up while Mr Huggle and his Veronica accompany these gentlemen to the station, to answer some questions about the books.

INT.

Stephen's figure, advancing up a long corridor with Amanda just behind him on one side, Leary, on the other, another girl behind him, PAs, ladies and gentlemen of the staff, clustered behind him. They advance into the camera, and as they pass, McGonnigal brings up the rear, carrying his briefcase. Cut to a shot of them from behind, McGonnigal making a little run to keep up. Stephen and McGonnigal are in ordinary clothes, also PAs, of course. But ladies and gentlemen are in evening clothes, as is Amanda. Watch the group from the back, they stop suddenly, then stand before a doorway, Stephen sitting on the desk, holding the telephone. Ringing sound, unanswered. Puts the telephone down, as McGonnigal's face appears at the door.

McGonnigal Um, Stephen . . .

Stephen looks at him blankly, then walks past him back into the corridor.

Could I just . . .

And cut to the procession, from long shot, walking down the corridor. It stops again.

Stephen Where's Leary?

Gazes at the throng, Leary not amongst them.

Amanda Darling, don't *you* know?

Stephen (*smiles at her, a feeble smile*) Look, I'll join you later, I've just remembered.

He goes off down one of the corridors, left. As he does so, Leary, unseen by him, wanders back to the group, out of one of the offices, as McGonnigal suddenly hurries after Stephen. Shot of Stephen walking down the corridor, McGonnigal hurrying after him, catching him in long shot. Then in on McGonnigal's face.

McGonnigal (*as if with an effort*) I want to know why you haven't been passing on my notes to the actors?

Stephen is staring at him blankly.

I must have made fifty notes, I've even tried to talk to Leary alone, but what with him nipping away all the time, and you getting between us, I haven't had a chance. In fact – (*working himself up*) I haven't had a chance since I arrived on the scene of my own play, which also doesn't have a chance, Stephen, and it doesn't have a chance because nobody, yourself included, and especially yourself, gives one goddamn about the style or the text, and now, with three hours before recording I can't get so much as a word with you.

He stares boldly and slightly fearfully up at him.

Stephen That's a very good point, Tim, don't you worry about it, leave it to me.

His gaze is abstracted. He puts a comforting hand on McGonnigal's shoulder, and hurries off down the next corridor.

INT.

The front doorstep. Stephen going furtively through the front door, then running on his toes up the stairs, flings open the bedroom door. The bedroom is littered with clothes, bed unmade. He stands staring, then goes downstairs to the living room, opens the door, goes in. Stares around, wanders across to the window, looks out. Grieg is in the garden, doing up his belt; he raises his eyes, looks towards the window, sees Stephen. They stare at each other, then Stephen turns away, goes downstairs. Opens the kitchen door. Plates, cups, etc. everywhere. He comes out, is about to go on down the hall, then stops. Turns around. Looks at the basement door. Walks apprehensively towards it. Down into the basement, stops before Grieg's door, then after a second, bends, looks through the keyhole. As seen through keyhole. Wendy, seen from in front, sitting on the bed, facing the door. She is tousled, dress partly opened, her legs spread carelessly. A mug of tea in her hand, her head over it. She raises her head, seems to be staring straight at him. Cut to:

INT. BASEMENT

Door, seen from Wendy's point of view. The doorknob turns, then slips back. Sound of feet running up the stairs, the front door slamming shut. Wendy continues to stare, then fiddles her hand across the bed, puts dark glasses on. Fade out. In on:

INT. BEDROOM

Darkness. The door opens, in. A small light goes on, illuminating Wendy's face, sleeping. Sound of footsteps moving towards her. Her eyes open blearily, cut to Stephen standing over her, his briefcase in his hand, then cut back to Wendy's face, her mouth spreading in a semi-conscious, sexual grin, and cut to Stephen's face, as he turns away, and cut to:

INT. LIVING ROOM

Wendy sitting in an armchair, looking towards the window, and cut to Stephen, standing at the window, looking down. He turns suddenly, his face twisted with pain, then walks quickly out of the room. Wendy gets up, goes over to the window, raises it, looks out.

EXT. GARDEN

Shot of Grieg, from her point of view, bending over a patch of bush, small shears in his hand. He looks up at her, looks down again. Puts the shears down. Then cut to Stephen, walking quickly across the garden, approaches Grieg, stands beside the shears. Cut back to Wendy, close-up, her lips open in excitement, then back to the garden from her point of view as Grieg, still bending, Stephen bending beside him, picks up the shears. Stephen staring down at the back of Grieg's neck as Grieg, still bending, holds out his hand. Cut back to Wendy's face, close-up; she closes her eyes in horror or in ecstasy, opens them, stares down. Grieg is snipping away with the shears. Stephen is walking away. Sounds of door slamming.

INT. LIVING ROOM

Stephen's footsteps. He comes into the room, brushes his hair away from his eyes, then goes across and sits down by the hi-fi set. Turns it on. Sits for a second, Wendy watching him from another chair. He sits, facing ahead, then begins to nod, almost imperceptibly, his head to the music. Wendy adjusts her dark glasses. Fade-out on this, and up on the two of them in the same position. Stephen staring at the television set, Wendy watching it indolently, the dark glasses pushed up to her forehead. On the screen: Leary's face, in his evening suit. Amanda in profile.

Leary (*speaking in faked-up Coward voice*) My dear lady, we ought to have exchanged teething rings in the registry office, or perhaps one of those ebony do-dahs in the shape of our respective throats, because that's what we spend our time sinking our respective bridge-work into.

As he concludes this, Stephen leans across, turns the set off. Sits staring ahead, then looks at Wendy, with her glasses up. She pokes them down with her finger, stares impassively back at him. Stephen gets up, walks across the room, to the door, goes out. Wendy watches. Gets up. The door opens again almost immediately, Stephen comes running across the room, his eyes and face mad, stands in front of Wendy, who remains sitting staring up at him. He begins to slap at her, crazy swattings. She makes a few weak defensive gestures, gets backed into a chair, her glasses knocked off. Stephen stands breathing heavily, making little crying noises.

Wendy Oh Stephen – (*Calmly and after a long pause.*) He does *much* worse.

INT. BEDROOM

Shot of bedroom, in disarray, clothes scattered everywhere.
From below sounds of Bach, very low. Camera tracks
around the room, takes in a heap of Wendy's knickers,
then pans out, and down the stairs, and in on:

INT. LIVING ROOM

The hi-fi on. Wendy and Mr Wycherley over by the
window. Stephen pouring a drink. Mrs Wycherley seated
in one of the Barcelona chairs.

Mr Wycherley Still cultivating *your* garden, I see.

Wendy Yes.

> *Mr Wycherley glances towards her. She remains*
> *staring down.*

Mr Wycherley I take it he's settled down, then. (*Drily.*)
For good. Eh, Stephen?

Stephen I don't know. Do *you* think he has, darling?

Wendy (*smiles*) It looks like it.

> *And cut to: Mrs Wycherley looking at Wendy and Mr*
> *Wycherley, their backs to her, still at the window, then*
> *at Stephen, who is now lolling in a chair, smoking a*
> *cheroot and playing with something out of sight.*

Mrs Wycherley I've been meaning to ask, what's the new
play like, is it as stylish as the last?

Stephen Not yet. But it will be.

> *He slips the glasses on over his nose. Mrs Wycherley*
> *again glances towards the window, where Mr*
> *Wycherley has just put his hand on Wendy's arm.*

Mrs Wycherley Just as long as you don't get yourself censored by that ghastly woman, the one that makes all the noise, you know what *my* feelings are about coloured and illegits, but she talks as –

Cutting to Mr Wycherley, his hand on Wendy's arm, Mrs Wycherley's voice over.

– if the whole country was an absolute marsh of vice and licence and what have you . . .

Cut back to Mrs Wycherley, staring towards Mr Wycherley.

Which I must say I take great personal exception to, *and* I like the right – (*turning to Stephen*) not to look at what's there to be seen, after all if people don't like it they can always switch off, can't they?

And cut back to: Mr Wycherley smiling at Wendy, who turns towards him. His hand still on her shoulder.

Mr Wycherley All right then?

Wendy (*vaguely*) Fine, thanks.

She moves away from him, he lets his arm drop. Cut to Stephen, who is watching Mr Wycherley with a little smile. Mr Wycherley looks towards him, meets his eyes. Stephen's smile remains, small but triumphant. Mr Wycherley turns back to the window, and Wendy crosses to Stephen, as:

Mrs Wycherley Which I must say, I quite frequently find myself having to do. Switch off, I mean.

Stephen smiling at Wendy. Wendy smiling back at him, nicely and yet almost impersonally, and from her to Mr Wycherley, turning away to stare coldly out of the window down on the garden, and finally to:

EXT. GARDEN

Grieg standing in the centre of the garden, his hands on his hips, staring up, seen from Mr Wycherley's point of view, and seeming to make, to the rising sound of Bach, a slow, obscene gesture.

MAN IN A SIDE-CAR

Introduction

I've forgotten every stage of writing *Man in a Side-Car* except its initiating image: the photograph in a newspaper of a young, pretty and already celebrated lady novelist, with a husband behind her elbow and a baby (or a cat) at her feet; that, and a subsequent report in probably the same newspaper that the marriage had broken up amicably. I suppose there were the routine drafts on drafts, but I don't recall even the usually memorable moment of completion. There was some fuss, though, when the play was sent out. Kenith Trodd, who had been involved in all my previous plays, first as script editor, then as producer, had left the BBC, probably in one of their periodic purges of talent, and no one there was sufficiently taken by *Man in a Side-Car* to offer it, except in a cursory way, to this or that director until Ann Scott, who had worked with Kenith Trodd and myself, rescued it from another producer's desk and brought it to the attention of James MacTaggart. To Ann Scott, then, my double thanks.

Because, in retrospect, the most important fact about *Man in a Side-Car* (for me, anyway) is that James MacTaggart directed it. We'd already worked together, some years before, on a small play of mine called *Pig in a Poke*, and got on sufficiently well to hope that we would again, some day. With *Man in a Side-Car* we went from getting on to friendship – we drank quite a few drinks together; had one or two small quarrels; and laughed a great deal – and professionally, had moved from clearly defined roles as author and director to rather more than trusting collaborators. So when I read through the play the other day to check it out for publication, I was still quite unable to separate the text from my (seven or so years later) vivid recollection of James's realisation of it. In fact, it now seems so inextricably his work as well as mine that in offering it up I feel that I am withholding rather more than simply his half. But then Gerald Savory or someone like him wiped the tape, of course. And now James is dead; and all I can do is dedicate the lesser half to his memory, in gratitude and continuing admiration.

First published in *The Rear Column and Other Plays*, Eyre Methuen, 1978.

Man in a Side-Car was first broadcast by BBC Television as 'Play for Today' on 27 May 1971. The cast was as follows:

Edith Gemma Jones
Gerald James Laurenson
Tommy David Collings
Mrs Merchant Sheila Beckett
David Geoffrey Matthews
Helen Yvonne Gilan
Dr Slocum Walter Horsburgh
Giles Jonathan Lawson
Waitress Tessa Lander
Men in Coffee Bar Roger Minnis, Steve King,
  Colin Richmond, Paul Barton
Girls in Coffee Bar Monica Wilding, Rosemary Turner
Three Men in Hospital Len Sanders, Bert Simms,
  Ernest Jennings
Two Nurses Constance Reason, Iris Fry
Ward Orderly Leonard Kingston

Director James MacTaggart
Producer Graeme McDonald
Script Editor Ann Scott
Designer Stuart Walker

Characters

Edith

Gerald

Tommy

Mrs Merchant

David

Helen

Dr Slocum

Giles

Waitress

Men in Coffee Bar

Girls in Coffee Bar

Three Men in Hospital

Two Nurses

Ward Orderly

INT. EDITH'S STUDY. DAY

It is a sparsely furnished room, with one picture, medieval and devotional, on the wall. There is a desk beside a window. The window looks out on to a path which is, in fact, a narrow drive. The drive curves round a bend and then on to a country road. The desk is an old-fashioned school desk, with a sunken inkwell and a ridge for a pen. Edith is writing into an exercise book at the desk. She uses a fountain pen that she dips into the inkwell. To her left is a pile of five exercise books, filled. Beside her, and behind her, past the window, is a bookshelf on which are arranged exercise books and novels. She is dressed in a long (as opposed to fashionably maxi) skirt, has hair swept down the side of her face, and in her cell-like room gives off a distinctly nun-like effect. She is in her early thirties. She is writing quickly and neatly onto the page, and at regular intervals is dipping her pen into the inkwell.

Edith (*voice-over, as she writes*) 'Mathilda began to discover that she had many things against Simon, and consequently and quite consciously began to develop a proportional esteem for herself. For example, Simon had begun to take instruction with a view to conversion. He approached his studies – for that was what he had made of the matter – with an academic devotion that was as inelegant as it was thorough, and spoke of the impending moment at church as if he were about to be awarded a prize for an achievement, an advanced degree for example. Mathilda, who had gone over to Rome at the age of

thirteen because she was in love with a girl, half Italian,
half Irish, wholly beautiful and almost twelve, at her
second boarding school, took her own Catholicism so
much for granted that she could afford to be witty at
its expense. Poor Simon was frequently shocked by her
little jokes, and the resulting strain between them – a
strain that confirmed Mathilda in her growing sense
of independence – led to some strange failures in bed.
These failures were, of course, entirely Simon's. Mathilda,
secretly enjoying them, marked them up as victories.
Simon might well entitle himself to an adjoining pew,
but his head would soon rest uneasily on the adjoining
pillow.'

> *Edith smiles as she writes the last few sentences.
> Cut to her face, then, as the smile stiffens, cut to the
> window beside her. Gerald, in goggles, a flowing scarf,
> gauntlets, and a very distinctive and expensive-looking
> leather coat with enormous buttons, is staring in at
> her. He turns, walks away. Edith turns slowly, as if
> sensing him there, a second after he has disappeared,
> frowns slightly, then goes back to her writing.*

'It turned out, in fact, that Simon, who in the early days
of their relationship, had so amused himself by making
fun of her own small aspirations, was unable to see the
comedy of his own larger ones. She came to the conclusion
and not at all reluctantly that her husband was a fraud.
She saw, with only enough pain to spicen the recognition
into anticipation, that there was little prospect of their
marriage lasting the course. She was too clever by half.
Indeed, she was too happy by –'

> *Her voice is interrupted by the explosive sound of the
> motorcycle starting. Edith's shoulders jump, her pen
> waits above the paper as the motorbike roars off.*

(*Her voice-over, writing.*) '– by more than half.'

EXT. PATH FROM THE COTTAGE. DAY

*Gerald on his motorcycle, which has an old-fashioned
side-car. It roars around the bend and out of sight, and
as it does so Mrs Merchant, wheeling a pram, comes into
shot. She is staring after the motorbike.*

INT. EDITH'S STUDY. DAY

Edith is now nearly at the bottom of the page. She writes:

Edith (*voice-over*) 'She knew the day would come when
she would say to her child-bridegroom – "If you were
half a man, you would go." And she equally knew that,
being half a man, he would. So many divisions could be
made to make a very simple sum.'

> *She turns the page; shot of the blank page, her pen
> hovers, then writes:*

'But Simon, if he was not capable of success, was finding
the consolations of malice. He –'

> *Edith smiles, screws the top back on her pen, puts it
> in the ledge, closes the inkwell, blots the page, closes
> the exercise book, then goes out of the study. Follow
> her as she enters:*

INT. GERALD'S STUDY. DAY

*Edith enters Gerald's study. There is a desk, a typewriter,
a camp bed, unmade, books, papers, etc., scattered
everywhere. There is an ashtray full of cigarette ends,
a pair of spectacles, a pipe half-smoked, an open box of
cheroots and, beside the typewriter, various sheets of
paper, some with fragments of typing on them. There is
a sheet in the typewriter. Edith makes a face, goes to the*

window, opens it, then goes out. Comes back in, looks down at the page, reads a few lines, goes out again, and follow her to the kitchen.

INT. KITCHEN. DAY

First come in on Mrs Merchant's face, smiling, then cut back to Edith, smiling, and she blocks the view for a second, then turns around, having lifted Giles out of his high chair, and is now cuddling him. Giles, who is about nine months old, not seen until that instant.

EXT. A RAILWAY STATION

The motorbike. Gerald appears with Tommy. Tommy is wearing a slightly ludicrous, very long, tatty overcoat. He is carrying an equally tatty overnight bag. They come to the motorbike; Gerald fishes into the side-car, hands Tommy a pair of goggles and crash helmet; they get in and on respectively.

EXT. COUNTRY ROADS

Gerald is driving as: credits.
   Follow them through country roads, and on them in different shots, some of Gerald in close-up. Some of Tommy, some from in front, some from behind, fading on the two of them in shot advancing as credits fade.

INT. KITCHEN. DAY

Edith is holding the bottle for Giles, while also drinking a cup of tea. Mrs Merchant is eating a proper lunch, as the noise of the motorbike outside. Edith glances up, then goes on feeding Giles. Sound of voices and Tommy's laughter outside the back door, then Gerald and Tommy enter, still in goggles and helmets.

Tommy Well, hello then.

He comes around, gives Edith a kiss, bends down, clucks at Giles. Gerald meanwhile is taking off his gear, smiling at Edith. Giles begins to cry.

Edith Your goggles.

Tommy Oh.

He takes his goggles off.

Gerald No, it's because you've taken the bottle away.

Edith glances at him, puts the bottle down on the table.

Tommy (*to Giles, who is still crying*) What is it, Giles, what's the matter, don't you recognise me then? You only saw me yesterday.

Edith Yes, but he cried then, too.

She picks Giles up, looks at Mrs Merchant, who gets up; they go out together.

Tommy It was wind yesterday.

Gerald Don't worry, I don't believe they *know*.

Tommy sits down, cutting himself some bread.

Tommy He never cries at me, normally. (*He shakes his head, worried.*)

Gerald For Christ's sake – he's not going to throw you out. Well?

Tommy What? Oh, well, like I said, they're interested, Gerald, certainly, the only thing that's holding them back, likely, is they're waiting to see the second act complete. (*He eats ravenously.*) That's all.

Gerald Did they have any constructive suggestions?

Edith comes back into the room.

Tommy I hope you don't mind, Edie – (*Holding up the bread.*)

Edith Please.

Neutrally, she begins to clear up.

(*To Gerald.*) Do you want anything?

Gerald Just some sense.

Tommy Well – well, no, well, he liked it, Gerrie. (*To Edith.*) That's Humphrey Jones, Edie, I worked with in Cardiff I mentioned to you who's got hold of that new theatre club in Chiswick, he's a smart bastard – no, all he said – (*back to Gerald*) was he liked its *tone* and that when we got it worked through to the curtain to let him be the first to refuse.

Gerald laughs.

You know what I mean, first *refusal* he wants, it's the next thing to an option. Edie, could I have one of those yoghurts if you've got one?

He turns around in a practised way, opening the fridge, takes out a yogurt.

Edith But he's not taking an option?

Tommy Well, I couldn't insist on it could I as – I'm a friend, see.

Edith (*ironically*) Well, that's all right then.

Gerald What does that mean?

Tommy is spooning down the yogurt at great speed.

Edith The director of a new theatre's likely to find himself with a lot of new friends as well. Or would he make it a principle to buy options on the work of strangers only?

Gerald Where's Giles?

Edith Having his nappy changed.

Gerald Mrs Merchant doing it?

Edith (*pretends to think*) Unless he's doing it himself.

Tommy But what really matters is that I could see he was excited by it, he wouldn't pretend over that, you know –

He is watching Gerald, who gets up, picks up the overnight bag, and goes out.

(*To Edith.*) He's not a complete bastard.

Edith Merely a clever one.

She looks at Tommy, who is smiling slightly shiftily. There is a pause.

Tommy Um, I was wondering, could you spare –?

Edith Please.

Tommy turns around, opens the fridge, takes out another yogurt.

What is it about?

Tommy What? Our play? Hasn't Gerrie told you?

Edith No. Nor have you.

Tommy Well, you never asked before. (*Laughs.*) I mean, I assumed . . .

He opens the yogurt, begins eating.

Edith Well?

Tommy Well. (*Laughs.*) It sounds very modish in outline, you know. (*Pause.*) Well . . . (*He laughs again.*)

Edith I like quite a few of the current modes.

Tommy Well, in fact it's about these four queers who ran a butcher's shop. Two of them draggy queens, see, and two of them butch –

Edith (*poker-faced*) Butch butchers.

Tommy (*laughs desperately*) That's one we did cut out, no, you see, it's the sort of sexual and emotional permutations and combinations – well, it's all in the dialogue and the tone, see, there's no plot as such, but if it's played in the right style it could be something special. (*Little pause.*) A cross between Racine and Orton. (*Little pause.*) Not just another commercial camp-up, Edie.

Edith Ah. An uncommercial camp-up?

Tommy Oh, Edie! (*Little pause.*) Why are you being so depressing then?

Edith Self-protection.

Tommy For Gerald you mean?

Edith Actually, I meant for myself.

Tommy I'm sure it'll come off.

Edith Yes. Almost at once. If it gets on.

Tommy Well, I'm very hopeful.

Edith (*stares at him unwinkingly*) Good.

Tommy (*finishes his yogurt*) I must say, it's nice to be back. I've missed you all.

Edith You've only been away for the night.

Tommy Yes, well, it feels like a couple of weeks.

Edith Perhaps that's because it was going to be. A couple of weeks. We all adjusted to that prospect.

Tommy Oh? You didn't expect me back today then?

Edith No. Not actually.

Tommy But Gerald phoned last night – he left a message with Stewart to come back as soon as they'd read it at the theatre.

Edith Ah. In that case it must have been an emergency.

She gets up.

Tommy Well, how's the novel going?

Edith I've done two days' work, since you last asked.

Tommy Oh, good.

As Edith goes out:

Humphrey Jones said he loved your last, to tell you especially.

Edith (*reappears, smiles*) Oh, good. (*She waits.*)

Tommy Yes, he loved it. (*Rather feebly.*)

Edith Good.

She goes out, and as she does so Tommy wheels round to the fridge.

INT. GERALD'S STUDY. DAY

He is sitting before the typewriter, spectacles on, staring down at the manuscript. The overnight bag is at his feet.

Edith stands at the door. Gerald, pointedly, doesn't look up.

Edith Can I speak?

Gerald (*still looking down*) You can.

Edith You summoned him back, then?

Gerald (*still looking down*) Yes.

Edith Why?

Gerald I was getting bored.

Edith We did agree that we might try two weeks without him.

Gerald Not quite. *You* said *you* could do without him. You asked me whether I could understand your feelings. I said I did. There was thus agreement about your feelings. None at all about policy.

Edith David and Helen are coming to dinner tonight. Or had you forgotten?

Gerald On the contrary. I specifically mentioned it to Tommy, by way of an inducement.

As Tommy appears behind Edith:

Edith was wondering whether you could really face David and Helen tonight. I've been reassuring her.

Tommy No, I'm looking forward to it, who are they exactly?

Gerald Her publishers. Manic depressers. But never mind – you'll have lots to eat. Edie'll make sure of that. And lots to drink. I'll make sure of that.

Tommy (*grins*) Ahh, just what I need.

Close-up of Tommy's face, beaming, seen from Edith's point of view, then she goes out.

INT. EDITH'S STUDY. DAY

Edith is at her desk, writing. See her from side, including a shot of the window.

EXT. GARDEN

Edith's point of view, from her study window: Mrs Merchant is sitting in a deckchair, reading.

INT. EDITH'S STUDY. DAY

Throughout this there's also the sound of a distant typewriter.

Edith (*writes, as voice-over*) 'He was turning into a way of life with a strong moral point of view. Mathilda would have found this boring if she hadn't known, indeed cherished the knowledge that this was merely a stage towards something even less consequential. During his time with her he had abandoned everything in turn. He had abandoned his art, for which he had no talent; and then his religion, for which he had had no feeling; and then his love-making, for which he had had no desire. Shortly he would abandon failure, for which he had no stoicism, in favour of a more sensational posture.'

> *There is the sound, dim, of Giles, crying. Edith frowns, makes to write another sentence, then turns to the window, raps on it, points.*

EXT. GARDEN

Mrs Merchant, Edith's point of view, gets up, goes off screen.

INT. EDITH'S STUDY. DAY

Edith turns back to her writing. Fade out. In on Edith writing again.

EXT. GARDEN

Mrs Merchant, Edith's point of view, playing with Giles, in his pram.

INT. EDITH'S STUDY. DAY

Edith (*voice-over*) 'Mathilda felt that although . . . (*the typewriter stops*) she had little time for Simon at the moment, she would manage to find some for his next phase. He promised, for a change, to be interesting. Also it would enable her to practise her newly acquired mercilessness, as well as to test her . . .'

All this over, as sudden shouts of laughter from Tommy and Gerald. She frowns, goes on writing, as the shouts continue . . .

INT. GERALD'S STUDY. DAY

Gerald and Tommy are crouched on the floor playing tiddlywinks with pennies and sixpences. Beside each is a pile of half-crowns. Tommy is playing. Come on them both from the door, then cut to Tommy's face. Frowning in concentration as he is about to wink a tiddly into the pot. He does so, and then another one, very practised, extracts two half-crowns from Gerald's pile, then moves back to do one a long way away, then shakes his head, moves forward to one closer in.

Gerald You're gutless, Tommy.

Tommy pays no attention as he takes aim, very serious.

For a quid?

Tommy (*looks up*) Let's see it.

Gerald reaches into his pocket, takes out a pound, puts it between Tommy and the cup.

And if I miss?

Gerald Oh, I never take anything from you, do I?

Tommy Done and done, boyo.

He crouches down, concentrating very hard. There is a sudden stillness, then he winks the tiddly in. He lets out a shout, reaches for the pound note. Gerald puts his foot down on the pound. See Gerald's face smiling from Tommy's point of view. Tommy crouching, Gerald standing above him.

Oh, come on, Gerrie, it's mine, I won it.

Gerald Not yet.

Gerald bends down, extracts the pound from under his shoe, holds it up, and as Tommy reaches for it, flicks it away from his fingers. He keeps this up for some time, Tommy clutching, Gerald whipping away, until Tommy suddenly closes on Gerald; they begin to wrestle, crashing about, clutching at each other, half laughing, half gasping, until they roll to the floor. Tommy has Gerald pinioned and is reaching for the pound, when:

Edith (*voice-over: focus on Tommy and the pound*) I hate to disturb you, but could you make less noise please.

There is silence, then Tommy gets up grinning sheepishly. He puts the pound note in his pocket. Gerald, still on the floor, turns his head, grinning, towards Edith.

Tommy Um. Oh, I'm sorry, Edie, it was my fault entirely, we had this idea about a wrestling scene, see, you know male wrestling is all the vogue now, on stage and screen, of course, we'll have it done in the nude, but we wanted to get . . . wanted to get . . .

He begins to laugh, helpless. Gerald still lies smiling, staring up at Edith.

(*Helplessly.*) Get – get – I'm sorry, Edie. Sorry.

Edith looks at them both, turns, goes out. On Tommy and Gerald. Tommy is still laughing, his laughter dying down. Gerald gets up, smiling. There is a pause, heavy, empty, then Gerald turns, goes to the desk, sits down. Tommy goes to the camp bed. Gerald sits staring at the typewriter.

Gerald (*after a pause*) What about a drink?

Tommy Oooh.

INT. SITTING ROOM. NIGHT

A table, laid for dinner. David, Helen, Tommy and Gerald sitting or standing, holding drinks. But come in first on Tommy's face, as he raises the glass to his lips. He is already slightly tight. Then take in David and Helen, sitting rather stiffly, and then Gerald, watching, smiling.

Tommy No, no look – (*Expansively.*) That the boys look like the girls and the girls look like the boys in Cannabis Street or Cannibal Street or wherever, that doesn't matter, see, that just gives us twice as many to fancy, doesn't it? Eh?

He laughs. Helen and David join in.

But you see unisex has been going on for years, yes it has, in the States they've had those creature-ladies and blue-ringed hair and goggles that are male martians, I'm sure of it, and in Russia, you know, more elemental, they've gone in a straight line with pills and operations, like that, to get the best of both worlds, childbearing muscle men – What about, no I'm serious, all of those shot-putters or putt-shotters and javelin throwers and mile runners the authorities caught shaving in the bogs, eh? Well, that's all right, who minds a bit of cheating in the name of sport, but look, reverse it for a moment, think of it this way, supposing yes supposing our test team, our fast bowlers, were really women, eh? Supposing these South African apartheid blokes were destroyed by an opening pair of fast bowlers from Yorkshire who had little ladies' problems and had to be rested for them, eh, well, wouldn't that be lovely, we destroy the white man at cricket with our ladies like we destroyed the black man with our ladies, eh? So what happens then to white supremacy – like male supremacy, down the flush bowl with it – (*Laughing.*)

Helen and David also laugh. Helen gets up.

Where are you going, Helen?

Helen I'm just going to see if Edith needs a hand.

Tommy Oh yes, oh, that's good, what about our World Cup side, eh, did it take a sex test, hormone count or whatever . . .

INT. KITCHEN. NIGHT

Edith is mixing something on the stove. Helen comes in.

Helen Can I do anything?

Edith (*suppressing slight irritation*) Oh, no thanks. I'm fine.

Helen I must say, we're enjoying Tommy. He's terribly funny.

Edith (*neutrally*) Ah – yes.

Helen He lives with you, does he?

Edith In a sense. He has done, off and on, since we were students. We take him so much for granted we scarcely know he's around.

Helen Gosh, I'd have thought that was quite difficult.

Edith Yes. It is.

Helen He's incredibly Welsh, isn't he?

Edith Sometimes. When he's had enough to drink.

Helen (*after a pause*) David's terribly excited about your new one. He says it's nearly finished.

Edith (*brightening*) Yes. Next month if I can keep it up – God willing, etc.

Helen I don't know how you manage.

Edith (*laughs*) By becoming extremely selfish. (*She takes a dish out of the stove.*)

INT. LIVING ROOM. DINNER TABLE. NIGHT

They are seated round the table, but come in first on Tommy's face; he is blinking slightly, and tighter. He raises the wine glass to his mouth as Gerald says:

Gerald Nappies.

David What?

Gerald Didn't we decide you'd call it nappies. You said, 'Let's be brutal, that's what it's all about.'

David (*doubtfully polite*) Nappies?

Tommy (*laughing*) Brutally would be crappy nappies.

Edith There isn't a title.

David I must say, I'm rather relieved.

Gerald But darling, didn't you – ah no, it was Giles that was all about nappies, brutally. I'm getting your children confused. (*To Helen.*) Do *you* have any children? I always forget.

Helen Yes, two actually.

Gerald Two *actually*! As opposed to metaphorically – like Edith's novels. Do you enjoy them?

Helen Yes, of course. They're brilliant. They're my favourites.

Gerald It's nice to hear someone being honest about their own offspring.

Helen and David laugh.

Helen I thought you were talking about Edith's novels.

Gerald Oh, do you think of them as your children, too?

Edith Helen was talking about her actual children, actually. As I think you've grasped.

There is a slight pause.

Gerald Well, I certainly have now, haven't I? What do you enjoy about them, Helen? All they do is eat, defecate and sleep. Extremely enjoyable for the baby, but slightly disgusting for the rest of us.

David On the contrary. Babies are –

Tommy Why does Giles get that rash on his bum?

Gerald It's their urine.

Gerald passes Tommy the wine. He fills his glass to the brim.

Acid in their urine.

Edith Could the rest of us have some, please.

Gerald looks at her, as if puzzled.

Gerald Oh the *wine* – I thought for a moment you meant –

Tommy erupts with laughter, as Gerald pours the wine around. After another pause, David says:

David Tell me – I've often wondered – how do people write plays together? Do you alternate scenes, or what?

Gerald Or what.

David What?

Gerald Yes.

David I'm sorry.

Gerald That's all right.

David laughs, clearly getting angry.

David I'm afraid I don't understand –

Tommy What?

David I said I didn't understand.

Gerald I'm sorry.

Tommy Why?

Gerald He didn't understand.

Tommy What?

Gerald How we write plays.

*Cut to Edith's face. She is watching Gerald and
Tommy through this, almost as if studying them.*

David (*controlling himself*) Anyway, what it amounts to
is that you've given up writing novels.

Helen Oh, did you . . .

She stops.

Gerald Writing novels? (*As if astonished.*) What novels?

David Oh come on, I read it.

Gerald Ah, my *novel.* I gave up writing that some
considerable time before it was published.

Edith It was a good novel.

Tommy (*emphatically*) It was a bloody good novel.

David Yes, I liked it.

Tommy (*vaguely, and with seemingly no sense of
context*) Christ.

INT. LIVING ROOM. NIGHT

*They are all sitting around having coffees and brandies,
but come in on Gerald, smiling, as Tommy says:*

Tommy (*voice-over*) No, well you see it was like this . . .
(*Falteringly.*) I was – she was a demi-vierge, can you
credit, of forty-three and a half, I think it was, and I was
a raw boy of thirty-one precisely, well I didn't know
what I was saying, excuse me a minute.

*The sound of Tommy's feet, stumbling. A door
slamming. Still on Gerald's face as we cut to a shot
of the group as a whole, evidently embarrassed, and
then cut to:*

Edith (*perfectly collected*) She could have stayed up. Got a Fellowship at Newnham. It never occurred to me she had a novel in her. Is it any good?

David Well, very accomplished and acceptably derivative.

Dreadful sounds off of Tommy being sick.

Edith Really? Derivative from?

Helen From you. I'd call it plagiarism.

More sounds from Tommy.

David Let's just call it flattery.

Gerald appears at the door.

Gerald Darling. (*Cheerfully.*) Where's the mop?

INT. BEDROOM. NIGHT

A double bed, with a bedside table on either side. On Gerald's a reading lamp, a bottle of sleeping pills, and a pile of paperback books, littered. On Edith's, a reading lamp, and a baby alarm. Also one book, Persuasion, with a book-marker in it. But none of this seen as yet. Come directly in on Edith's face, she is staring up at the ceiling. The sounds of Giles's breathing through the baby alarm are audible but not yet explained. There are sudden little cries, followed by the heavy breathing. Edith moves her arm, and turns down the baby alarm. As she does so, Gerald enters.

Gerald (*beginning to undress*) He's lying down. I thought he was heroic the way he came back in and told that story against himself, didn't you? Do you think he gave them pleasure?

Edith About as much as he gave me, I should think.

Cut to her face, as Gerald goes on undressing, off-screen.

When did you start getting him drunk? This afternoon? (*Little pause.*) You know, you do go very well together. You're so predictable, like a rather silly married couple that everyone else has outgrown. How do you see yourself? As a *succès manqué*? Does he represent your last hold on your old self, attractive, dominating, etc., and so forth?

Gerald climbs into bed, lies down beside her.

The glamour is entirely in the vocabulary. A failure. An unhappy husband. A desperate man. Try – flop. Flop's the right word for you. No Graham Greene connotations, no dimmed brightness, no forlorn flickers of promise. Flop. You're a flop and Tommy's a miserable, despairing parasite. What the Americans call a bum.

INT. HALL OUTSIDE THE BEDROOM. NIGHT

Tommy is standing outside the door, listening. He is in a state close to collapse, exhausted.

Edith (*voice-over*) What was interesting *and* poignant, about his performance tonight, was its desperation. Didn't you feel it? (*Sharply.*) Don't do that!

Gerald (*voice-over*) Why not? We always used to celebrate the guests' departure with a spasm of analysis and a bout of love.

Edith (*voice-over*) What I'm celebrating tonight has nothing to do with you. In fact, that *is* what I'm celebrating. I witnessed Tommy's desperation and your malice this evening without even embarrassment. He was sad and you were trivial, and really I quite enjoyed it.

Like recognising a perfect definition. Your behaviour was definitive. I said don't!

Tommy puts his hand to his forehead.

INT. BEDROOM. NIGHT

Gerald is leaning over Edith, grinning, Edith is staring up. The sound of Giles's breathing is audible.

Edith Would you please turn out the light? Because if you're going to go on grinning anally down at me, I'd rather not see you.

Gerald maintains his position.

You don't really think they're going to do your play, do you? Surely you know Tommy better than that. I do, anyway. He never showed it to them.

Gerald goes on grinning down at her.

What you've written is a flop. A flop's flop. And Tommy knows it.

Gerald Do *you* know what I've got against you? Your chin. You've got the chin of a boxer. The tension of not punching it is driving me mad. I'd like to have you in the ring, belting away at your chin. Your novels stink. They make you lots of money and you sell the film rights, but they stink.

He rolls over, turns out the light. There is a pause.

Edith (*in the darkness*) Yes, but Tommy still didn't show your play to anyone. Not even a Welshman. He'll be leaving in the mornmg.

Gerald Oh no he won't.

Edith Do you want a bet?

INT. GERALD'S STUDY. NIGHT

Tommy is sitting on the camp bed. He begins to take off his shoes and socks. He looks forlorn, beaten. His hand moves, and he picks up a piece of bread, puts it into his mouth, chews on it desperately, and on his face:

INT. KITCHEN. DAY

Come in on Tommy's face, munching, as if carried over from the last scene.

Edith (*voice-over*) You're a pig.

Tommy looks startled, then cut to Edith looking down at Giles, to whom she is giving a bottle.

Tommy And he'll grow up to be a big strong pig, like me, see.

Edith looks at him coolly, goes on feeding Giles.

(*Clears his throat apprehensively.*) Um, while we're on the subject of pigs, Edie, in relation to myself see, I – well, I've been awake all night, worrying and guilty – I thought – (*attempts a charming smile*) I'd outgrown that kind of thing, it must have been the train journey and being tired with it, you know.

Edith From here to Waterloo is thirty-five minutes.

Tommy (*laughs*) Yes, that's true, well you know British Rail. (*Laughs.*) Anyway, I thought I had an apology to make.

Pause, he looks at Edith, who addresses herself to Giles.

I did like your friends, very charming I thought they were. (*Pause.*) I hope I'm forgiven then.

Edith looks at him, makes as if to speak as:

Mrs Merchant (*comes through the door*) Good morning.

Edith Good morning. He's just finished.

Lifts Giles out of the chair, hands him to Mrs Merchant.

Mrs Merchant (*taking him*) And how's my ba-ba today?

As she carries him out, Edith suppresses a grimace of irritation.

Tommy It's funny the way she talks to him like a sheep, eh? (*Laughs.*)

Edith You know I'm going to ask you to leave, don't you?

Tommy stares at her, licks his lips.

It's time, Tommy. You've been with us since we started living together – and that was a year before we got married. Four years, interrupted by short breaks of three months or so, and your six months' spell in Cardiff. Now I want you to go, and not to come back.

Tommy (*staring at her helplessly*) But – Edie – because, you mean because of last night? I'll never – never – I promise –

Edith You see, you talk to me as if I were your older sister, or mother, someone you make promises to, that you're slightly frightened of, that will look after you and make everything all right again. (*She shakes her head.*) I don't feel protectively towards you. Not any more.

After a pause Tommy nods his head.

Tommy (*with dignity*) Could I stay then until we've completed the play? It'll only be to impose on you another week or so?

Edith Why? You know the play's no good. You didn't take it to anyone in London.

Tommy Do you think I'd lie about a thing like that?

Edith Yes. (*Smiles.*) Don't look so incredulous. You lie a great deal. About things like that, and more important things.

She gets up, comes over, stands behind him, touches his shoulder.

Just go, Tommy. Like a good boy. (*Both tenderly and ironically said.*)

Tommy (*turns, clutches at her hand*) But what will I do – what?

The door opens. Edith moves away from Tommy as Gerald comes in.

Gerald Good morning.

INT. EDITH'S STUDY. DAY

Edith is watching Mrs Merchant and Giles.

EXT. GARDEN

Mrs Merchant is wheeling Giles in the pram down the path.

INT. EDITH'S STUDY. DAY

Edith turns, sits down at her desk, opens the exercise book, unscrews the top of her pen, dips it in the ink, makes as if to write. Her pen hovering over the page, as she reads the previous sentence:

Edith '. . . could not deny that the excitement the process of cleaning up gave her . . . (*Begins to write.*) . . . was oddly pleasant, and although cerebral in its planning was becoming – was becoming – was becoming – (*Lifting the pen up, she gazes down at the paper.*) cerebral in its planning – was becoming – (*She dips her pen into the ink, it hovers over the page*) – was becoming –

INT. GERALD'S STUDY. DAY

Tommy is sitting on the bed, hands clasped between his legs. Gerald is sitting at the desk chair, doodling.

Gerald Why?

Tommy Because she told me to.

Gerald I haven't. (*Little pause.*) What will you do? Go home to Llanelli?

Tommy No, I'll go to London.

Gerald You've been to London.

Tommy I can always wash dishes for a bit.

Gerald No you can't. Not any more.

Tommy (*after a pause*) No.

Gerald Where will you live?

Tommy Well, I can – perhaps I can go and stay with someone for a time, until I've settled down.

Gerald No you can't. They won't have you. Not any more.

Tommy No.

Gerald It's all ended, all that, Tommy. They're all married, to one sex or the other, they've got houses or flats, children or positions, one or two are even dead. They'd like to see you now for ten minutes in a pub, from an accidental meeting, and even so they won't ask you your address or give you theirs. There's nothing for you in London.

Tommy (*after a pause*) And do you know, I can't do it any more, I can't, Gerrie. I'll tell you something: it frightens me, London. Not just people who don't want to hear my voice when I telephone them, or the pubs nobody goes to any more, no, it's the whole place, the whole feel of the place and all eleven million of them, however many it is, it makes me feel too little.

Gerald That's because you're too old. So what will you do, Tommy?

Tommy I don't know. I don't know. Of course Edie's right. I can't go on like this, living off you.

Gerald Why not?

Tommy Because – (*thinks*) she won't let me. (*Laughs.*)

Gerald Well, there's always this, isn't there? (*He holds up the manuscript.*) Perhaps this will save you, if Humphrey Jones is to be trusted.

Tommy But there's still the second act –

Gerald Is Humphrey Jones to be trusted?

Little pause.

Tommy?

Tommy (*looks at Gerald*) No.

Gerald You didn't take it to him then?

Tommy No, Edie's wrong about that, I took it to him, and I walked about for two hours while he read it, it was very kind of him, you know, on the spot he read it, and then I went back and he told me he thought it wasn't very interesting, straightforwardly and honestly, like a good friend should. So he's a good friend, you see. I've got a friend in Humphrey Jones. He'll always turn me down on the spot.

Gerald But it doesn't matter what Humphrey Jones thinks, does it? *You've* still got confidence, haven't you? *You* still like it, don't you?

Tommy (*after a pause*) No. I think it stinks, you know.

Gerald So what will you do, Tommy?

Hold on his face, staring at Tommy.

INT. EDITH'S STUDY. DAY

Come in on her pen nib, poised above the page. Then it stabs down, begins to write.

Edith (*voice-over*) 'Positively sexual in its execution. (*Repeats.*) And although cerebral in its planning was becoming positively sexual in its execution. She had felt the same sensation when completing her General Paper for her Oxford Scholarship. She was in control, the prize was hers. In the very exactness with which she organised and made lucid her originality there was a respect for convention that could have been interpreted as contempt. So poor Simon's career as her husband was about to be brought to a neat finish, with, of course, a respect for the conventions that marked her contempt for him. Under these circumstances it would have been delightful to make love to him for a last time. She would see if it could be arranged. The method of dispatch was so orderly, surely a bravura flourish could be permitted. She –'

She is interrupted by the roar of a motorcycle from outside. She turns to the window, looks out.

EXT. GARDEN

Edith's point of view from window: Gerald, in his gauntlets, helmet and goggles, is starting the motorbike, while Tommy in his ludicrous overcoat, is getting into the side-car. The motorcycle roars off, up the path.

INT. EDITH'S STUDY. DAY

Edith smiles contemptuously, returns to her exercise book, dips in her pen.

Edith (*voice-over continued*) '– now saw her mercilessness as a quality of mind –'

INT. WIMPY BAR IN A SMALL TOWN. DAY

Gerald and Tommy are seated at a table.

Gerald Has it occurred to you that if she hadn't met us when she did, she'd never have written a word? Not a word. Except possibly for a few academic reviews in academic journals. She didn't aspire to creation. She had a first from Oxford and a great gift for thinking dully about dull books. She only took up novels because I was finishing mine and you were in the middle of thinking about beginning yours. If I'd been a weightlifter, she'd have gone in for that.

Tommy In the end, she'd have lifted heavier weights.

A Waitress puts a coffee in front of Gerald, a Wimpy, a piece of cake and a coffee in front of Tommy.

337

Gerald It took me two years to write my novel, Tommy. Do you remember?

Tommy, who is raising the hamburger to his mouth, nods.

It was gestured at, at the bottom of long reviews on other novels.

Tommy I remember.

Gerald And in three years, she's written four novels –

Tommy (*his mouth full*) Five almost.

Gerald And she gets whole reviews to herself, with a photograph inset that was taken when she was twelve. She gets interviewed on average once every three months, with sometimes a reference to myself in the text, or a picture of me striking a husband's pose to the left of her elbow, or with an ear and half an eye showing behind Giles's face. But that's not it, no, that's not it. What it is, is that she sits there in her chaste little cell over her bloody exercise books imitating a schoolgirl imitating a nun, and she still doesn't know how to write a novel. She has a special little gland that other people haven't got, that functions away glandularly, and it makes her richer and richer and more and more famous, and that's not it, either, no, that's not it, it's not even the sum of the injustices of her victories and successes, it is simply that she's killing me. Killing me, yes, that's it.

Tommy Killing you?

Gerald Oh, I don't mean that she's ending our marriage. She's doing that. You today, me tomorrow. Your departure is the means to my end. I mean, she's making me dead.

Tommy You hate her then?

Gerald I'm in love with her. You know, the way one might be with a schoolgirl or a nun. Aren't you?

Tommy What? In love –?

Gerald Oh come on, Tommy. You've *always* been in love with her. I've only just started.

Tommy shakes his head.

Why, you've slept with her, haven't you?

As Tommy stares at him, transfixed:

That year when we were living together. All three of us. Didn't you sleep with her?

Tommy Look, Gerald, I don't know what you're talking about.

Gerald Didn't you fancy her, then?

Tommy (*laughs*) Well of course, that's a different question, isn't it?

Gerald No it isn't. Everyone was sleeping with everyone. I took it for granted you did with her.

Tommy Why didn't you ask me before, then, if you've thought that?

Gerald I wanted to preserve the proprieties. It doesn't matter any more. So you can tell me. (*Smiling.*) How often did you sleep with my wife?

Tommy (*laughs*) Well you know, I can't remember. You know, Gerrie –?

Gerald You do remember, Tommy. Was it once –

Holds up a finger.

Twice –

Holds up two fingers. Tommy holds up two fingers.
Gerald continues to hold up two fingers also. They sit
staring at each other, holding up two fingers. Then
Gerald smiles.

Did you enjoy it?

Tommy (*shrugs*) Well, no. (*Lowering his fingers.*) It
wasn't very successful, it was you she wanted, see.

Gerald I'm sorry to hear that.

Gerald begins to laugh. Tommy also laughs. Gerald
draws Tommy's cake to himself, and while he is
talking, covers it with various condiments, pepper,
salt, mustard, tomato sauce, etc.

Sometimes when you're walking along a street you see a
schoolgirl with her satchel, her legs they go down, very
vulnerable, almost pitiful, into their socks and shoes. Do
you know what I mean?

Tommy is staring in horror at the cake.

And one in a hundred has a face, exquisite, sealed off,
and you put out of your mind what you know goes
through theirs, and you feel it inside you, caught between
cherishing and despoiling. (*Little pause.*) The desire to
rape nuns is, of course, conventional fantasy. I won't
bore you with it. Here – you've had my cake. Now eat
yours.

Gerald pushes the cake at Tommy.

Tommy Like hell I will, boyo.

Gerald It's the price you have to pay, Tommy. If you're
to inherit my mantle.

Tommy shakes his head, laughing uncertainly, and
then stares down at the cake, back at Gerald, and on
his face.

INT. EDITH'S STUDY. DAY

Register the sound of her laughing quietly, over the last shot of Gerald. Edith writing.

EXT. GARDEN

Mrs Merchant and Giles approach up the path.

INT. EDITH'S STUDY. DAY

Edith writing.

Edith (*voice-over*) 'And so he departed, for the last time, from their bedroom, with his tail between and not metaphorically, his legs. With his clothes bundled in his arms and his face bulging with unconsummated aggression, he was not a particularly dignified spectacle. But he had pathos, of a kind that Mathilda knew –'

She turns, looks out of the window.

EXT. GARDEN

Edith's point of view, Giles and Mrs Merchant now in the very middle of the path.

INT. EDITH'S STUDY. DAY

Edith (*voice-over*) '– in the solitary (*writing quickly*) but by no means lonely years to come. She – she –'

Edith stops, smiles at the page, then screws the top on to her pen, closes the inkwell, blots the page, closes the exercise book, stands up, stares, smiling, out of the window.

341

EXT. GARDEN. DAY

From Edith's point of view. Mrs Merchant lifts Giles out of the pram.

EXT. COUNTRY ROAD. DAY

The motorcycle is roaring at great speed along the road. Cut from Gerald's face, impassive behind goggles, etc., to Tommy's eyes staring in fright. Tommy attempts to attract Gerald's attention, the motorcycle roars on, past the camera, see it from behind, suddenly slowing and then stopping. Tommy scrambles out of the side-car and runs, clutching his stomach, to the bushes.

EXT. GARDEN. DAY

Edith is pushing Giles in the pram slowly up the path, towards Mrs Merchant.

EXT. ROAD. DAY

The motorbike roaring along the road. Cut from Gerald's face to Tommy's, crumpled in misery.

EXT. GARDEN. DAY

Edith, Mrs Merchant, Giles, in the middle of the path as before. Sound over of the motorbike, which, as they look up, is roaring towards them, and cut to their reactions, then to Tommy's face, stiff with horror. Then Gerald's, indecipherable behind the goggles, etc.

INT. LIVING ROOM. DAY

Come in directly on Gerald's face, now without goggles, helmet, etc. He is sitting impassively. Then take in Tommy, sitting on the sofa, clearly shaken. The door opens, Mrs Merchant comes out, walks past Gerald, stiff-faced. Gerald follows her with his eyes, then looks towards the door, as Edith comes out, closing it behind her. Baby noise off from Giles.

Edith You nearly killed us all. Do you realise that?

Gerald It *was* a close thing, wasn't it? Old Tommy would have thrown up his gâteau vinaigrette if he hadn't already thrown it up.

Edith Are you being defiant, or are you actually a little mad?

Gerald A little mad actually. (*He gets up and goes to the door.*) You've got a lunatic on your hands. I give you warning. (*He smiles, goes out.*)

Tommy (*to Edith, who is staring after Gerald*) Edie . . . um, you know, he's, well –

Edith turns, looks at him.

It's – it's – look, Edie, he isn't well, there's something wrong with him, I don't mean he tried to run you over or anything like that, see, but he might do something desperate, if you ask me.

Edith And if I ask you, what would you suggest?

Tommy You shouldn't be alone together, not just now, Edith.

Edith Tommy, I asked you to go. Are you going to, please?

Tommy He hates you, you know.

Edith Of course he does. Why should he make an exception of me? He almost certainly hates you too.

Edith goes out. Tommy stands for a moment, on his face an expression of rage.

INT. GERALD'S STUDY. DAY

Gerald is lying on the camp bed, smoking a cheroot. Tommy comes in.

Tommy I'll stay if you tell me to . . .

Gerald (*looks at him*) *Tell* you to?

Tommy Yes.

Gerald Well, I won't. I'd prefer you gone. I need you somewhere else, Tommy.

Tommy, after a moment, goes to his suitcase under the camp bed, drags it out, begins to shut it.

Could I have my shirts back, please?

Tommy I've soiled them.

Gerald The soil may belong to you, the shirts belong to me.

Tommy takes out the shirts, puts them on the bed, closes the suitcase.

How romantic, to travel light. You don't mind if I don't take you to the station after all?

Tommy (*looks at him, after a pause*) Will there be a train?

Gerald At the station? Well, if you don't find one there, you won't find one anywhere.

344

Tommy (*suddenly firm*) Could I have my coat, please?

Gerald It's behind you.

Tommy The one I inherited.

Gerald Inherited?

Tommy The one I ate that cake for.

Gerald Oh, you misunderstood me. I was speaking poetically.

Tommy (*desperately*) What is it you want me to do, then? What?

Gerald Go.

Tommy turns, goes out of the door.

INT. EDITH'S STUDY. DAY

Edith is standing at the window looking out, and from her point of view, through the window, sees Tommy plodding up the path.

EXT. GARDEN. DAY

From Edith's point of view, Tommy plodding up the path. He is carrying his suitcase, and wearing his ludicrous overcoat.

INT. EDITH'S STUDY. DAY

For a moment Edith looks uncertain, as if perhaps on the verge of calling out to Tommy.

EXT. GARDEN. DAY

There is the roar of the motorbike and Gerald comes into view, stops beside Tommy, talks to him. Tommy gets into the side-car.

INT. EDITH'S STUDY. DAY

Edith turns away to her desk. She sits down at it, stares ahead for a moment, unscrews the top of her fountain pen, opens the exercise book, then sits staring at the page. On her face.

INT. BEDROOM. NIGHT

Edith is lying in bed reading Persuasion. *Beside her the baby alarm is on. The sound of Giles's breathing. Hold on this, then the roar of the motorbike, and immediately, from the baby alarm, Giles's cry. Edith starts, sits still, then makes as if to get up. The crying stops. She gets back into bed, sits tensely. A few muffling noises from the box, then silence. Sound of a door opening and closing, footsteps. Gerald comes in, closes the door behind him. On his face is an expression so impassive that it is sinister. He begins to get undressed.*

Edith I think you'd better sleep in the study. As it's free now.

Gerald No, I'll sleep with you tonight. It'll be the last time.

Edith Yes.

There is a silence as Gerald goes on undressing. Keep on Edith's face, watching him. It is very composed, but a hint of excitement.

Gerald By the way, Tommy informs me you've slept with him.

Edith Really?

Gerald You did then?

Edith Tommy is a liar. I've never gone in for adultery.

Gerald I wasn't asking after your religious habits. I was indirectly asking whether you and Tommy had ever copulated with each other.

Edith Are you hoping he did? Do you think that jealousy is less demeaning than envy?

As Gerald gets into bed:

I'd be grateful if you'd wash. You're dirty.

Gerald lies staring up at the ceiling. Edith picks up Persuasion.

Gerald There is, I suppose, the faint possibility that Giles isn't mine?

Edith Would it make any difference if he weren't?

Gerald (*reaches past her, turns off baby alarm.*) I'd like to think he'd disgust me just as much if I were sure he were.

Edith You are literally hateful. Full of hate. *Did* you try to harm him this afternoon?

Gerald suddenly rolls over, looks down at her, then takes the book from her hand, and drops it over the edge of the bed. Edith laughs. Gerald puts a hand on her breast.

(*Ironically.*) Oh dear.

Gerald slaps her.

You don't have to do that. I'm yours.

Gerald stares at her blankly, and Edith smiles. He begins to make love to her. As he does so, Edith's hand comes out, turns on the baby alarm. Her hand withdraws but stay on the baby alarm. A few small cries come from it, and cries from Edith, then on a full cry from Edith, cut to: Edith's face, she is flushed and smiling. A small, triumphant smile. Then take in Gerald beside her. He is lying, staring up. She turns towards him.

Oh dear. (*Pause.*) I'm sorry.

Gerald goes on staring up. Then suddenly he begins to cry. Edith stares at him, her smile becoming suddenly uncertain.

Gerrie – (*Whispered.*) Gerrie –

And aghast she puts her hand to his head, stares into his face. He is still crying.

Gerrie –

He stares at her pathetically. He rolls away, gets out of bed, picks up his clothes, goes to the door, turns, stares at her. On his face, an expression of dreadful malevolence. He goes out. Edith stares after him, makes as if to follow him, then lies back; hold on her face, suggesting time passing. Her expression tense. Then the roar of the motorbike, the sound fading away. A pause.

(*Her voice slightly shaky.*) That's that, then. (*Little pause.*) Consummatum est. (*She laughs, still shakily.*)

INT. GERALD'S STUDY. DAY

Hold on the room, in its slovenliness. Then Edith comes on camera. Purposefully, almost violently, she rips the covers off the camp bed. Then a series of shots, montage, of her cleaning out and cleaning up the room, with a kind of fanatical intensity, culminating with two last shots, sustained longer than the others, of her wrapping up Gerald's manuscripts in brown paper, tying them into a parcel, then putting the hood over the typewriter. Move back to the door, where Edith stands when she has finished. Take in the room, bare and as if purged. She turns, goes out.

INT. BATHROOM SINK. DAY

On Edith's hands, as they are briskly washing themselves, Edith's face in the mirror as she combs her hair.

INT. EDITH'S STUDY. DAY

She goes to the window, stands for a second, then turns to her desk, picks up the exercise books to the left, the ones filled, holds them almost devotionally, smiles. She puts them down, sits down, takes out her pen, opens the inkwell then turns the exercise book open. The page is blank. She frowns, turns back a page. Also blank. She picks the exercise book up, riffles through it, blank. In horror she picks up the filled exercise books, riffles through them. On the last page of the last exercise book, scrawled in large letters: 'Go back to page one.'

INT. KITCHEN. DAY

Edith is sitting at the table, staring ahead. Her face is over-composed, as if against panic. She gets up, goes to the phone, opens the address book beside it, begins to dial. Then cut to shots of her finger on different telephone

numbers, dialling with the other finger, to suggest
numerous phone calls being made, then cut to Edith
sitting at the table again. There is the sound of a motor
car outside, a honk. She gets up, picks up a coat and
handbag, already arranged on a chair, goes to the back
door, opens it. And finds herself facing Mrs Merchant,
Giles in her arms. Edith blinks in a shock of recognition.

Edith Um, um – I've got to go to London on – um,
something urgent. Could you do Giles until, I, um – if
I'm late? It's terribly urgent.

Mrs Merchant Of course, it's nothing serious, is it?

Edith Yes. (*Makes to go.*)

Mrs Merchant I'll tell Mr Dunlop you've gone.

Edith Oh, he won't be – Yes, if he comes, tell him he
must wait for me. He must. All right?

She looks at Giles, kisses him as if remembering, goes
out.

EXT. GARDEN. DAY

Shot of Edith, from Mrs Merchant's point of view,
getting into a taxi.

INT. DAVID'S OFFICE. DAY

Come in on Edith's face, seen from David's point of
view. She looks exhausted.

Edith Credit where it's due. It's effectively humiliating.
I spent the morning on the telephone to people I haven't
seen for months, for years. Asking them if they'd seen
my husband. They hadn't, of course. But they found the

question interesting. One or two hinted that I'd dropped them with my success. I longed to say that I'd been merciful. If I'd dropped them when I'd been a failure they'd have had to attribute some fault to themselves. This way I gave them the opportunity to blame me. The afternoon I spent in familiar half-forgotten pubs, not knowing whose eyes to dodge and whose to catch. None of them looked as if they could have belonged to my past, but they might all have belonged to *his*. I don't know. I can't remember. How could I? (*Little pause.*) I should have thought. I should have *thought*. But it was the one unthinkable thing. (*Little pause.*) But he thought of it. Why didn't I? I should have slept with them under my pillow, had them chained to my wrist, hidden them under the floorboards, until he'd gone. (*Little pause.*) But I've worked out this much. He wouldn't have put the black ones there if he'd decided to – (*with an effort*) destroy the other ones. He'd have left torn pages, or embers, or nothing. He *must* be going to use them – as hostages, so to speak. (*She smiles.*) What shall I do? (*Lips tremble.*) David?

She attempts a smile. On her face.

EXT. DRIVE. DAY

Taxi coming towards the drive. But carry on shot of Edith's face from previous scene, and then cut to:

INT. KITCHEN WINDOW. DAY

Mrs Merchant's face staring out, desperately worried.

EXT. GARDEN

Mrs Merchant's point of view. A taxi draws up, beside a car. Edith gets out, paying the taxi driver hastily, looks at the car, begins to run towards the house. Mrs Merchant hurries to the door, opens it, and see her face worried, from Edith's point of view.

Mrs Merchant I don't know what's wrong, Dr Slocum's with him now.

Edith runs past her.

INT. GILES'S ROOM. DAY

Terrible cries coming from Giles. Dr Slocum is straightening up from the cot, stethoscope dangling from his ears. He turns, stares at Edith, his face severe. Edith stares back at him, panic-stricken. Mrs Merchant comes in behind her.

Edith Oh God, what's the matter?

Dr Slocum I've not the slightest idea. His lungs are in excellent shape, at least.

Edith (*confused, shouting*) What?

She goes to the cot, looks down at Giles. She picks him up. Giles begins to calm down.

Dr Slocum But whatever it was, I can't believe it was worth calling me out for. We've got the summer flu epidemic on our hands, you know.

Edith Called – who called?

She looks accusingly at Mrs Merchant.

Mrs Merchant (*indignantly*) I didn't –

Dr Slocum The call was from your husband. (*Packing his bag.*) He said your child needed attention.

As he straightens, on his face, cut to:

INT. BEDROOM. NIGHT

Edith is in bed, reading. The book held up to her face. She lowers the book. She is crying, silently. She wipes her eyes with the sheets, lies still for a moment. Then turns out the light. There is a pause. The light comes on again. She lies staring ahead, as if trying to remember something, then suddenly turns her head to the baby alarm, which is silent. She stares at it in panic, then grabs it, turns up the sound. Still nothing. She makes to get out of bed, suddenly remembers the on-off switch. Fumblingly she checks it, turns it to 'on'. The sound of Giles breathing. She turns the light on. Picks up the book, resolutely, begins to read.

Edith The sod! The hateful sod!

Fade into a shot of Edith asleep, the light on, the book open beside her. It is still night. There is, over, the distant noise of the motorcycle, very muted, being driven at the lowest possible throttle. Her eyes flicker open. She stares ahead, then sits up as the noise goes on, slightly louder. The noise stops. Cut to her face, listening, waiting. Sounds of a key in the lock, a door opening, closing quietly, footsteps, other doors opening and closing. Then silence. Edith gets up, goes to the bedroom door, opens it. Follow her through to:

INT. VARIOUS ROOMS. NIGHT

Gerald's study. On to her own study, the door is open. She goes to it.

353

INT. EDITH'S STUDY. NIGHT

What appears to be Gerald's back – it is, in fact, Tommy, in Gerald's coat. His head is bent low as he fumbles inside Edith's desk. Cut to her face, resolute as she walks quickly and softly over, puts her hand on his arm. Tommy jumps, looks up. Edith stares into his face, see it full in camera, from her point of view, then back to Edith.

Edith What do you want?

Tommy Oh, I'm sorry Edie. (*Nervously.*) I – I – was just – well, see, the thing is Gerald asked me to get something for him.

Edith He's got them all. There aren't any more.

Tommy What? Sleeping pills? He says he hasn't, Edith, no, look. (*He holds a bottle out in the palm of his hand.*) He said you kept an extra bottle in your desk –

Edith You came here for that?

Tommy (*shrugs*) Well, he asked me to come and get them, Edie. He said he needed them.

Edith (*after a pause*) What are you doing in his coat?

Tommy Well, he gave it to me in the end, you see. I won it in one of our bets. It was a cake I had to eat, he –

Edith Where is he, Tommy? Where is he?

Tommy Well, I promised him I wouldn't say. He said you'd ask, he made me promise, Edie.

Edith He's got my exercise books, you know. My novel. I want them back.

Tommy Of course you do. Of course.

Edith He's not in London then?

Tommy No.

Edith Has it occurred to you that he's ill?

Tommy looks at her as if wavering. Edith goes to him, clutches his arm.

Tommy, take me to him. (*Little pause.*) Please.

Tommy looks at her. She is pleading, but there is something deliberately sexual in her appeal.

Please? (*Wonderingly.*) Don't tell me anything. Just take me to him. You didn't promise him you wouldn't do that, did you?

Tommy No. (*Little pause.*) Do you mean now?

Edith (*gently*) Please, Tommy.

Tommy (*after a pause*) But what about Giles – you couldn't leave him all by himself then, could you?

Edith, as if realising, shakes her head.

Edith I'd – I'd – (*Stops.*) Well then, ask him to give me a ring, will you please?

Tommy Yes. Yes, I'll do that.

He hesitates, then takes Edith in his arms, kisses her gently on the mouth, then stands hesitant.

I'll tell him to give you a ring then.

He goes out. Keep on the door, sound of doors opening, then Edith goes to the hall, and through to:

INT. KITCHEN. NIGHT

Edith goes to the window, looks out.

355

EXT. GARDEN. NIGHT

There is a figure on the seat of the motorcycle, in crash helmet and goggles, indistinct. She stares towards it, through the window, assuming that it is Tommy. The figure raises an arm, in salute, then Tommy appears, in goggles and helmet, climbs into the side-car. All this from Edith's point of view.

INT. KITCHEN. NIGHT

Edith stares at the motorbike, then, realising, runs to the kitchen door.

EXT. GARDEN. NIGHT

Edith opens kitchen door as Gerald, on the seat, kicks the motorbike into life; it cruises up the drive. Cut to Edith's face, and from that cut to:

INT. EDITH'S STUDY. MORNING

Edith is sitting at the desk. She stares blankly ahead, then takes a fresh exercise book, opens it. She picks up her fountain pen, lifts the lid of the inkwell. Dips the pen in. Her pen hovers. She writes:

Edith (*voice-over*) 'Mathilda felt that – Mathilda felt that she – Mathilda felt – Mathilda – Mathilda –'

Having stopped writing, she turns her head, looks out of the window, and, from her point of view, cut to:

EXT. GARDEN. DAY

Shot of Mrs Merchant, with Giles in the pram, just leaving the house.

INT. EDITH'S STUDY. DAY

Edith suddenly screws the top back on her pen, snaps the inkwell shut, very quickly hurries out of the room.

EXT. GARDEN. DAY

Shot of Mrs Merchant and Giles as if through the study window, as Edith runs up to her, takes over the pram, begins to push it. Mrs Merchant walks beside her, as, over, the sound of the telephone ringing. Edith stops. Turns around, runs back to the house, all this seen as through the study window, then cut to:

INT. KITCHEN. DAY

Edith hurrying to the telephone, picks it up a fraction after it stops ringing. The dialling tone is audible. She stands holding it, then puts it down. She stands looking at it, then goes back to the open kitchen door.

DAY

From Edith's point of view at the kitchen door, Mrs Merchant and Giles, waiting.

Edith (*shouting*) I shan't be coming. You go on.

Mrs Merchant turns, goes down the path. Edith watches, then turns, goes back in, shuts the door.

INT. KITCHEN. DAY

Edith goes to the stove, puts on the kettle, and cut to Edith sitting at the table, drinking a cup of tea. The telephone rings. She leaps up, goes over to it, picks it up.

Edith Hello. Hello.

There is a click of the receiver being replaced at the other end. She puts the telephone down, goes back to the table. Sits. The telephone rings again. She leaps up, it stops ringing. She stares at it. She sits down, almost gingerly. It rings. She gets up. It stops ringing. She remains poised between sitting and standing, staring at the telephone, and cut to:

INT. GILES'S BEDROOM. DAY

Come in on Giles, nappy off, then come in on Mrs Merchant, dropping the dirty nappy into a bucket. She smiles down at Giles and cut to Edith at the door; she comes in, stares down at Giles.

Edith Hello, darling.

Mrs Merchant I was just going to do his rash.

Edith Were you? I'll do it.

As Mrs Merchant opens the jar of ointment, Edith dips her finger into it, takes some ointment out on the end of her finger, when the telephone rings. Mrs Merchant turns towards the door, as if to answer the telephone.

I'll get it.

She pushes past Mrs Merchant, handing her Giles, and leaves the room. Mrs Merchant looks at Giles, then puts her finger into the jar, as the telephone stops ringing. There is a short pause. Edith reappears. Mrs Merchant, not seeing her, is about to apply the cream.

(With a tight smile.) I said I'd do it.

She is still holding her fingers ahead of her. On them, baby cream. Mrs Merchant steps aside, offended.

*Edith advances towards Giles, as the telephone rings.
Edith stiffens, then making an immense effort, goes
on dabbing the cream. The telephone goes on ringing.
She goes on dabbing the cream, finishes, wipes her
fingers. The telephone is still ringing. She turns to Mrs
Merchant.*

Would you do his nappy, please?

She walks out of the room, and cut to:

INT. KITCHEN. DAY

*Edith walks steadily towards the telephone, picks it up.
She waits a second, as if expecting a click. There is a
pause.*

Edith Hello. (*There is a silence.*) Hello. Giles?

Gerald Gerald.

Edith (*smiles very slightly*) Gerald. Yes.

Gerald You asked me to give you a ring.

Edith Yes. (*Ironically*) Thank you.

Gerald I've given you several. I shan't be giving you any
more.

*Click, as he hangs up. Edith stands there, holding the
receiver, then bangs it down, then picks it up and
bangs it down several times, in a fury. Stops, begins to
walk away. The telephone rings. Edith turns, stares at
it, then picks it up.*

Edith? Gerald here. Hello again! Look, old girl – it
occurred to me you might want something. Is there
anything?

Edith (*controlling herself*) You know what I want.
(*There is a silence.*) Don't you?

359

Gerald (*after a pause*) Me?

Edith I want my novel back. (*Long pause.*) Are you there?

Gerald Yes – yes, I'm here. Is there anything else you want?

Edith I'd like to talk to you. Properly.

Gerald Would you like to see my room? Where I'm living, and how I've settled down?

Edith Yes. (*Quickly.*) Where is it?

Gerald Oh, better to pick you up, I think. If you don't mind riding in the old side-car, that is?

Edith No. That'll be all right.

Gerald Say in an hour.

Edith Yes. Yes. In an hour.

Gerald In an hour.

> *Click as he puts the telephone down. Edith replaces the telephone, turns, sees Mrs Merchant standing before her, holding Giles. Looks at her, looks at Giles, then, as if realising.*

Edith Oh. Mrs Merchant. Um, would you mind terribly holding the, um . . .

> *Cut to:*

INT. KITCHEN. DAY

Mrs Merchant, her face staring out of the window.

EXT. GARDEN. DAY

*From Mrs Merchant's point of view. At kitchen window
see Edith walking down the path to the motorbike.
There is a man sitting on it in Gerald's coat, goggles, etc.
Edith says something to him, cut to:*

Tommy All I know, Edie, is he told me to bring you.
Isn't that all right?

*Edith, after a pause, gets into the side-car, it roars off.
And cut back to:*

INT. KITCHEN. DAY

Mrs Merchant at the window, turning away. And cut to:

EXT. HOTEL. DAY

*The motorbike pulling up before a large shabby house
converted into a shabby private hotel. Tommy gets off.
Edith gets out, Tommy takes Edith's arm, they walk up
the steps to the front door, and cut to:*

INT. HOTEL. DAY

*They go up grubby stairs, passing a lounge-type room,
from which comes the noise of a television set. Then up
more stairs past various doors with numbers half-erased.
They reach the last two doors, next to each other.*

Tommy This is his, Edie.

Edith I think I'd better do this alone, if you don't mind.

Tommy Of course, Edie.

*He turns, to go to the other room, stops as Edith
makes to knock.*

Look, I'll be in here if you need me. See.

*Edith looks at him, then turns to Gerald's door,
knocks. There is no reply. Edith knocks again, then
turns the handle. The door opens. She goes in. The
light is on. The bed is unmade. There are clothes
spilled everywhere, and a general sense of muddle and
squalor. Propped against the mirror there is a note, on
which is written: 'This is my room.' Edith reads the
note, turns, looks around. Makes as if to go out, then
turns, goes to the chest of drawers, cupboard, bed,
each one in turn, hunts rapidly through them, then
stops, stares around, and cut to: Tommy's room. It is
in the same condition as Gerald's. Tommy is sitting in
an armchair. Come in on his face, looking towards the
door, then cut to:*

Edith (*at the door*) He's not there. (*Little pause.*) Of
course.

Tommy Oh.

He gets to his feet, as if about to go and look.

Edith He's not there. He never intended to be. Where is
he?

Tommy I don't know. (*Little pause.*) Edie, I don't know.
Look, he said I was to pick you up and take you to his
room, seeing as you wanted to see it, that was all, Edie.

Edith (*advances towards him*) You're lying. You're lying.
(*Stands in front of him.*) All the money you've borrowed
and never mentioned again – all the food you've guzzled –
the drink you've got drunk on to give yourself the
courage to bore and insult my friends – who do you
think buys him those shirts you make dirty, his coat –

that coat – *I* gave it to him, my books gave it to him, to you – you owe me, you owe me. (*Punching at his chest.*) Now you tell me, tell me, tell me!

Her voice is rising hysterically, and cut to the hall, before the front door. Tommy holds the door open for Edith. She steps out, he follows, his hand on her arm. He closes the door, and from the doorstep, their point of view, cut to:

EXT. HOTEL. DAY

Gerald in Tommy's coat, on the motorcycle, driving away. Tommy and Edith stand staring after him, and cut to:

EXT. DRIVE. DAY

Come in on Mrs Merchant, medium shot, coming up the drive. Her walk – seen from in front – is jerky, odd. Hold, then cut to:

INT. TAXI. DAY

Edith is sitting forward, staring towards Mrs Merchant, who is walking towards them; she taps on the glass, stops the taxi. She opens the window and leans out of it. Close-up of Mrs Merchant's face, seen from Edith's point of view. Tears are streaming down her cheeks. She makes to open her mouth, closes it, clearly very distraught. But there is something sinister in the effect. Edith gets out, starts after her, clutches her arm. Mrs Merchant turns, says something, Edith says something then turns, runs towards the house. Tommy has got out of the taxi, and is following slowly. He stops, turns back to the taxi.

INT. KITCHEN. DAY

Edith flings open the door, shot from inside the kitchen, then a brisk montage as she runs through the house, comes to Giles's room, goes in. Giles is asleep. Edith turns, comes out, walks back to the kitchen. Tommy is standing just inside the door.

Edith He's here somewhere.

Tommy Is he?

Edith He must have been. He's just sacked Mrs Merchant.

She goes to the door, looks out.

EXT. GARDEN. DAY

From Edith's point of view at kitchen door, sees taxi still there. There is a short, intense silence, then Gerald's motorbike starts up (not seen) and roars around the house into sight, up the drive, past the taxi and away. There is a pause.

INT. KITCHEN. DAY

Edith turns, looks at Tommy.

Tommy (*licks his lips*) I haven't got any money, Edith.

Edith What?

Tommy For the taxi. To get me back to Guildford, see.

Edith starts to laugh, stops, opens her handbag, fumbles in it. Then looks at Tommy.

Edith You've got to make him come here and talk to me.

She takes a five-pound note out of her wallet, hands it to him.

Will you?

Tommy looks at the money, then at Edith.

Tommy This is a fiver, did you know, Edie?

Edith (*after a slight pause*) I haven't got anything smaller. That's all I have.

Tommy puts his hand into his pocket.

Tommy Oh, look, I've got a pound. I won't need this after all.

He hands it back to Edith.

Thanks.

Edith Please, Tommy. (*Cut to her face.*) Please.

INT. EDITH'S BEDROOM. NIGHT

Edith is asleep, Persuasion *lying open beside her. The lamp is on the floor, lampshade tilted, to soften the light. The baby alarm is on. Gentle sounds of Giles breathing. Keep on Edith's face. She sits up suddenly, stares around. Gets up, walks to the door. There should be something almost somnambulistic in her movements.*

INT. LIVING ROOM. NIGHT

She goes down the hall, opens the door to the living room. Stands blinking. Then cut to Gerald sitting in a chair, in Tommy's coat, facing her. Cut back to Edith.

Gerald (*smiling, voice gentle*) I've come, you see.

Edith Yes. (*Quietly.*) Just a minute. I'm not properly awake. I've got to be awake to say the right words, haven't I?

She smiles, goes out.

INT. BATHROOM. NIGHT

Cut to Edith washing her face under the cold tap.

INT. LIVING ROOM. NIGHT

Then cut to Edith, drops of water still on her face, coming back to the sitting room. It is empty. She stares around as Gerald comes out of Giles's room, closing the door quietly.

Gerald It's all right, I haven't gone. (*He sits down.*)

Edith You've grown so expert in your games. (*Smiling, gentle.*) They're very literary. Literal, in fact. That's why I have to get the right words.

> *She is walking slowly towards him, then crouches down at his feet, takes his hand.*

There. I've got you.

> *Gerald puts his hand on hers.*

Gerald I didn't realise you wanted me.

Edith Please, Gerrie, could I have it back? Please. (*She smiles up at him.*)

Gerald (*carefully*) Would you say you wanted it more than anything?

Edith Is that what you've been proving to me? I knew it already. I've known it since I started writing – since about the third paragraph of my first novel. It's the only thing nobody would ever have to prove to me. I'm not ashamed, either. I'm not ashamed.

Gerald And what would become of me, if I gave it back? How would I sustain your interest? You've tried to catch my every move, these last few days.

Edith You could come here again, if you wanted. For as long as you wanted. And Tommy too.

Gerald Would you love us?

Edith (*after a pause*) I would do my best.

Gerald I could make love to you?

Edith (*with a slight, malicious smile*) You could do your best.

Gerald Ah! (*He smiles. Touches the side of her cheek.*) And if it's too late? If I haven't got the exercise books any more?

Edith (*thinks, then very carefully*) I think I'd like to see you die.

Gerald (*nods*) Then it's too late for me. I haven't got them any more.

Edith stares up at him, frozen. Then slowly gets up, walks to a chair opposite, sits down, looks at Gerald. She tries to smile.

Edith What did you do with them?

Gerald (*shakes his head*) It doesn't matter any more. Not to me. (*He puts his hand into his pocket.*) Did you find the right words, do you think?

Edith's mouth is trembling, but her voice is controlled, as if with a tremendous effort.

Edith I shall start again. And once I've started, what you've done won't mean anything.

Gerald is holding sleeping pills – not of course registered by Edith – in his cupped hand. He begins to pop them into his mouth, as if they were Smarties.

Gerald You'll be able to say of me – (*popping them into his mouth nonchalantly*) that I was literal to the end.

Edith Perhaps doing it again is only right. It'll be different, there will be things to add, but – above all – you won't be here. What you've done *will* mean something. But to me. Not to you. You're so much waste, got rid of. And there's nothing more you can do to hurt me, you see.

Gerald I know. That's the appalling thing about you.

Edith (*smiles*) Would you go now, please. (*Getting up.*)

Gerald Oh. Aren't you going to stay? I thought you wanted to see me – um, die. (*Modestly.*)

> *Edith stares at him, aghast. Gerald throws the last few sleeping pills into his mouth, swallows them down with a gulp. Then shows her the bottle.*

Isn't that what you wanted?

Edith (*after a pause*) How many have you taken?

Gerald Twenty-two.

Edith You're a child. A nasty child.

> *Long pause, she stares at him. Gerald is staring up at her.*

Gerald And my games are so literal. But the words *were* yours. Weren't they the right ones, after all?

Edith (*after a pause*) Do you want me to telephone for a doctor, then? If you do, say so.

Gerald Oh, that's *your* business.

Edith I'll do what *you* tell me to do.

Gerald Then – do whatever you think is best. You have your church, your art, and your education. If the maxims you derive from each should conflict, you will have to choose.

Edith (*after a pause*) How do you feel?

Gerald A trifle nervous. But physically tip-top. The system needs about twenty minutes to absorb them. After that it's downhill all the way. But I believe the decline can be arrested until I go into a coma.

Edith In other words, you can reach the telephone unaided.

She turns, goes out. Cut to Gerald's face; he smiles, uncertainly. There is a pause. Edith returns, walks past him, into Giles's room. There is the sound of a protest from Giles, sleepy. She comes out, carrying him. Walks past Gerald, and out of the room. Cut to Gerald's face. He sits resolutely. Crosses his hands in his lap. Licks his lip. His face twitches slightly. He raises a hand, scratches at his cheek as if he had an itch there. Then lowers his hand, raises it, scratches again, blinks.

INT. BEDROOM. NIGHT

Edith is sitting up in bed, staring ahead. Giles is lying beside her, asleep. She picks her watch up from the table, looks at it, puts it down. She turns, looks down at Giles, and cut to his face asleep. Edith's hand, shaking, goes to his hair, touches it and cut from this to:

INT. LIVING ROOM. NIGHT

Gerald's face, eyes closed, mouth open in a yawn. His hand is resting against his cheek. His eyes blink open. He stares blearily around, heaves himself up, gropes forward, stands swaying, and cut to:

INT. BEDROOM. NIGHT

Edith is sitting up, staring ahead with great intensity. She closes her eyes, opens them. Suddenly there is a crash, eerily distanced. Her head jerks in alarm as the room fills with heavy breathing. She looks towards the baby alarm. The breathing is coming from it. She jerks her head away, stares ahead. Then reaches out a hand trembling slightly, to the alarm, turns it off. Then she sits with her head sunk on her chest, eyes closed. Fade out on this, and fade up on Edith lying, her face sideways on the pillow, her thumb in her mouth, staring into Giles's face, also sideways on the pillow, thumb in his mouth, asleep. She straightens slowly, turns to the baby alarm, still sucking on her thumb. She reaches out a hand. Turns on the knob. The breathing is now stertorous, rasping. She turns the knob off quickly, blinks and, as if coming to herself, swings her legs out of bed. She hurries out of the bedroom and cut to:

INT. HALL. NIGHT

Edith is in the hall, and from her point of view, cut to the door to Gerald's study. It opens. Edith is staring at it, making incomprehensible noises of fear. Tommy is standing there, in Gerald's coat, goggles pushed up on his forehead, helmet and gauntlets under his arm.

Tommy I'm cold. (*Slightly whining.*) He told me to wait outside, with the bike, where is he then?

Edith's lips move for a second. She gives a ghastly grin.

Edith Asleep.

Cut to:

INT. GILES'S BEDROOM. NIGHT

Come straight in on Gerald, lying on the floor, snoring heavily. The baby alarm microphone close to his face. Then cut to Tommy's face, shocked and bewildered, staring at Gerald.

Tommy Ohh – Ohh – look now – look – Edie we've got to – look. (*Little pause.*) What are we going to do, then? What are we going to do?

Cut to Edith's face. She is staring at Tommy. Cut to:

EXT. DRIVE. DAWN

In on Gerald's face, in close-up, in goggles and crash helmet. Then draw back, to see him in the side-car, with his head back and his mouth open, breathing deeply. Then his face is drawn slowly out of camera and cut to Tommy and Gerald, on the motorcycle and side-car respectively, pulling quietly down the drive, from Edith's point of view watching from the window, then cut to her face at the window, staring out.

EXT. FIELD. DAY

A path across a field. The motorbike travelling slowly and eerily across it, and from a distance, see the motorcycle stopping. Tommy pulls Gerald out of the side-car, lowers him to the ground, then Tommy walks away, running, walking, running, and cut to:

EXT. MRS MERCHANT'S HOUSE. DAY

The gate to the front door, Mrs Merchant standing before it, arms akimbo. Edith, with the pram.

Mrs Merchant I've never been spoken to like that before. Never in my life.

Edith He'll never speak to you like that again. I promise. (*Little pause.*) He left me – just after he – he'd spoken to you. He said he wouldn't come back. (*Little pause.*) We've always had such a good relationship, Mrs Merchant. (*Little pause.*) Please. We need you, Giles and I. We do need you.

INT. KITCHEN. DAY

Come in on Tommy's hand, raising a cup to his lips, then to his face. He looks desperately tired. Edith sits opposite, watching him.

Tommy Could it be murder, Edie?

Edith It was suicide.

Tommy But legally? I mean, if the police –?

Edith He wanted to kill himself. He wanted to do it in the way that would hurt me most. He was determined to be hateful to the end. (*Little pause.*) He had the right to kill himself. I had the right to defend myself from the consequences of his doing it here.

Tommy You said yourself he was ill. He needed help –

Edith looks at him very coldly.

Edith Well, you didn't give it to him, did you?

Tommy No. I gave it to you instead.

Edith Why?

Tommy You know why, now. Don't you?

Edith Are you in love with me?

Tommy I've always been, Edie. Always. (*Little pause.*) And did Gerrie ask you about it? About whether we'd ever slept together?

Edith (*after a pause*) No. Anyway, it was a long time ago.

Tommy Still, he asked *me*. I was just wondering –

Edith What did you tell him? (*Little pause.*) *Did* you tell him?

Tommy Certainly not. No. I told him it was ridiculous.

Edith And so it was. It always is. Quite ridiculous. Everything is ridiculous. Gerald's death.

The telephone rings. Edith and Tommy stare at each other. She gets up, lifts the telephone from the receiver, staring at Tommy, then turns away, puts it to her ear.

Hello. (*Little pause.*) Yes, it is. (*Brightly smiling.*)

INT. HOSPITAL WARD. DAY

Edith and Tommy walking along it, past various beds, to a bed near the end, screened off. There is a Nurse with them. The Nurse pulls back the screen and cut from Tommy's face and Edith's face to a man, sitting up, grinning, his arm in a sling, having his pyjamas changed, and cut to Tommy and Edith walking on to the next bed, screened. The Nurse opens the screen for them, and cut to Gerald's face on the pillow, eyes open, breath very faint, then Edith is sitting in a chair beside him, Tommy standing beside her. He looks down at Gerald's face, he

makes a sound, turns his face away, clutches at Edith's
hand, and on the tableau:

INT. KITCHEN. DAY

Tommy and Edith sitting at the table, a cup being raised
to Tommy's lips.

Edith (*almost desultory*) That's your fifth cup. You'll be
ill.

Tommy (*after a pause*) Four, I've only had four cups.

Edith That's still too many.

> *Little silence, as Mrs Merchant comes into the kitchen,*
> *walking on tiptoe. She stops by Edith, looks down at*
> *her compassionately.*

(*Wanly smiling.*) I'll be all right. Really. Tommy's going
to look after me, for a little.

> *Mrs Merchant gingerly touches Edith's arm, she goes*
> *out. There is a silence.*

You had two cups in that ghastly room, and two in the
hospital canteen. It's your fifth.

Tommy (*thinks, nods*) Fifth. (*Little silence.*) I won't have
any more.

Edith What are you going to do now? Are you going to
stay here?

> *After a pause, Tommy nods.*

I won't want you here.

Tommy I know.

Edith But you'll stay anyway?

374

Tommy Yes, I will, Edie. I don't mind being inferior, see. I don't mind.

Edith looks at him, with a weary smile.

Edith I shall despise you.

Tommy Sometimes. Other times you won't notice me, even. And I'll be nice to Giles. (*Little pause.*) I have no shame.

Edith No. That's your strength, isn't it?

Tommy Of course people will despise you for living with me.

Edith I'm quite strong too.

She gets up, goes out of the kitchen.

INT. EDITH'S STUDY. DAY

She enters, turns on the light, goes to the window, looks out. Suddenly she crosses herself, closing her eyes and lowering her head. She smiles ironically, turns to the desk. On the desk are the exercise books, neatly piled, and as the camera comes in on them sounds of great chords of religious music, organ, which go on as Edith approaches the desk slowly, as if in a trance, picks them up as if holding something sacred, turns around, her eyes aglow. The music still going on, solemn and magnificent, and:

Tommy (*at the door*) So he put them back, then?

The music stops. There is a silence.

Edith You see. You see. I was bound to get them back. I'm a novelist. (*In a whisper.*) That's all I am. That's all I want to be. I shall go on writing novels until I die.

If God is good to me, I shall die as I finish a sentence. His Will Be Done.

> *Cut to Tommy's face, staring at her; stay on his face as organ music, over, starts again, gently, mixing into Edith at her desk.*

EXT. GARDEN. DAY

The organ music going on, as through the window to her side we see Mrs Merchant in a deckchair, holding Giles in her arms, in an accidentally religious posture, and kneeling beside her, Tommy, beside whom is a small jug of soapy water. He has his hands to his face, as if in prayer, blowing a mighty bubble. This shot freezes into a still, as the organ music continues, and:

Titles superimposed. Fade out.

PLAINTIFFS AND DEFENDANTS

To Alan
for Ben, Simon, Peter and Charles

Plaintiffs and Defendants was first presented by BBC Television on 14 October 1975. The cast was as follows:

Peter Alan Bates
Hilary Rosemary McHale
Charles Dinsdale Landen
Jeremy Daniel St George
Joanna Georgina Hale
Sallust Simon Cadell
Josh Benjamin Whitrow
Mrs Sawsbury Rosemary Martin
Mr Rose Victor Langley
Man 1 David Rose
Doctor Tom Kempinski

Director Michael Lindsay-Hogg
Designer Richard Henry
Producer Kenith Trodd

Characters

Peter

Hilary

Charles

Jeremy

Joanna

Sallust

Josh

Mrs Sawsbury

Mr Rose

Man 1

Doctor

INT. JOANNA'S BEDSITTER

Peter is lying in bed, staring blankly into camera.

Joanna (*voice-over*) . . . the thing about Josh, you see – well, he didn't discover about himself until he was nearly thirty, it must have been awful for him.

Peter (*politely*) Must have been.

Joanna (*voice-over*) He's still the only person in the world I can talk to. Except you. I can talk to you, right?

Peter Right.

Joanna You and Josh. You're incredibly different, though. He's a great talker and you're a great listener.

Cut to Joanna, sitting in the corner of the bed, one shoulder hunched, smoking.

(*After a pause.*) I'm being boring, aren't I, sorry.

Sounds of Peter moving.

Is it time, then?

Peter (*beginning to get dressed*) Well – nearly, I'm afraid, Jo.

Joanna (*sits watching him*) It's funny how I always want to say something and then stop myself, all except this time. I'm sorry.

Peter (*dressing*) Say what?

Joanna Something to stop you going.

Peter What have you said?

Joanna Nothing.

Peter Oh, I see.

Joanna Do you want to go, is that it?

Peter Of course not.

Joanna We've never spent a night together. Never.

Peter No. I'm very bad-tempered in the morning.

Joanna Are you?

Peter Yes.

Joanna I can't imagine you bad-tempered. Or anything but polite. No other moods except polite and randy. You are still randy for me, aren't you?

Peter laughs, slightly embarrassed. Joanna laughs.

You're the only man I've ever wanted, in this way. Ever.

Peter What are you going to do this evening?

Joanna Oh, see Josh, I don't know. Do something to keep my mind off.

Peter But that cover you're designing –

Joanna I'll start on that after midnight. I like to work after midnight.

Peter (*straightening from doing up his shoes*) You don't think that being freelance cuts you off a bit? I know working in an office has its hazards, but –

Joanna I wouldn't get much of a lunchtime, though, would I? And I need long lunch hours, right? (*Smiling.*) When you have them?

Peter smiles.

I like them better even than evenings like this. The afternoons afterwards are like dreams, but the nights go on a bit. Go on then, make a run for it before I begin –

Peter comes over, bends to kiss her. Joanna's arms go around his neck, clasp him. Cut to Peter's face, in Joanna's clasp, slightly desperate.

No claims, right?

Peter I'll see you soon.

Joanna (*letting him go*) Do you know when exactly?

Peter Not exactly.

Joanna But soon?

Peter Of course. It's going to be a hell of a week or two –

Joanna smiles, pained. Nods. Peter raises his hand in salute, goes to the door, opens it. All this from Joanna's point of view. Peter closes the door. When it's almost closed, see Joanna from his point of view. She is sitting hunched, lighting another cigarette. She turns her face, looks towards him. The door obliterates her as it closes, and on the closed door, titles begin.

EXT. TURKISH BATHS

Titles continue. Peter enters.

INT. TURKISH BATHS

Titles. Peter washing himself vigorously.

EXT. TURKISH BATHS

Peter emerging, and:

INT. PETER'S HOUSE. HALL.

He enters, puts down briefcase, touches his hair, glances at watch. Then goes down hall, opens door to kitchen. Cut to:

INT. KITCHEN

Hilary, in her late thirties, is bent over a pile of papers marking them. Her briefcase is on the kitchen table. She looks up, smiles.

Hilary Hello.

Peter Hi. (*Smiles back.*)

Hilary Won't be a minute. (*Goes on marking.*)

> *Peter picks up a mug from a kitchen shelf, sits down at the table with it, pours himself some coffee.*

You eaten?

Peter Yes, I had a bite.

Hilary Good. (*Scribbles something on the bottom of the essay.*) You know that staff meeting last week – where I made a few brief points about marking adults as if they were children, and the resistance from almost everyone?

Peter But you carried the meeting.

Hilary Until this evening. When a deputation of students demanded to know why we'd stopped grading their essays – they said it wasn't fair, as it meant they didn't know where they stood.

Peter God!

Hilary Well, this one knows where *she* stands all right. (*Pushing the essay away.*) C-question-mark-plus.

Peter She'll want to know more about that question mark.

Hilary How did the case go?

Peter (*thinks*) Oh, we lost. And the lecture?

Hilary All right after ten minutes. I slid from *Little Dorrit* to *Bleak House* and got pretty knowing about the law. You look very dapper.

Peter Do I?

Hilary Oh, of course, the party – how was it?

Peter I didn't go.

Hilary Why not?

Peter Didn't feel in the mood.

Hilary has got up, comes around behind him, puts her hands on his shoulder, kisses him.

Hilary Your hair's wet.

Peter Is it? (*Feels it.*) I had a shower.

Hilary A *shower*, where?

Peter I had a game of squash with Sallust. My pupil. It seemed a better idea than the party.

Hilary And who won?

Peter He did. Quite convincingly, actually.

Hilary Darling, do you think you *ought* to play with him? He must be much younger than you and in top-notch condition –?

Peter Oh, I gave him a run, you know. (*Yawns.*)

Hilary How's he getting on?

Peter Oh, all right – gets on my tits now and then – passes me notes on points that help the judges while away another fifteen minutes of my life – ambitious little sod – he's all right.

Door opens. Jeremy enters, he is about sixteen.

Hello.

Jeremy Hi. Is there an apple?

Hilary In the bowl on top of the fridge.

Jeremy goes over, takes an apple.

Peter Did you go to the flicks?

Jeremy What?

Peter Cinema? (*Little pause.*) Moving pictures. Movies. You said at breakfast you were going to the movies.

Jeremy Oh. Yeah. (*Bites into his apple.*)

Peter What did you see?

Jeremy Oh, that famous Renoir thing.

Hilary *La Grande Illusion*?

Jeremy thinks, shakes his head.

Peter *La Règle du Jeu*?

Jeremy Yeah.

Peter I wish I'd known it was on, I could have just done with that this evening. That marvellous little Jewish count – the rabbit shoot – every time I think of his face it makes me want to cry.

Jeremy What, the rabbit's?

Hilary Didn't you like it, darling?

Jeremy Yeah, I did. Quite.

Peter Oh come on, Jeremy!

Hilary Darling, if he didn't like it, he didn't like it. They've got to discover their own classics –

Peter Well, what are they?

Hilary Darling, what's your idea of a classic?

Jeremy Classic? (*Thinks.*) I never think about whether it's a *classic* or not. Just about whether I liked it.

Peter And you didn't like *Règle du Jeu*?

Jeremy (*who has been moving towards the door*) I said I quite liked it.

Hilary That's true, darling. He did say he quite liked it.

Jeremy goes out.

Peter (*after a pause*) He didn't like it.

Hilary Perhaps he tried, though.

Peter Is that what the question mark's for? In C-question-mark-plus.

Hilary You didn't give him much chance.

Peter A chance? With Renoir? He claims to be what they call a film buff, which I thought might mean that he could end up editing or directing or even reviewing the bloody things but he talks as if he already distributes them.

Cut to:

INT. BEDROOM

Hilary in bed, reading, spectacles on, seen from Peter's point of view, as he hangs his trousers on the chair. She looks up.

Hilary I don't remember getting you yellow knickers.

Peter No, I picked up a fresh pair, for the game, I'd forgotten. (*Coughs.*)

Hilary That cough. You've got to stop.

Goes back to her book. Peter climbs into bed, lies staring ahead, and cut to a blown-up picture of a Junior Colts cricket eleven, seen from Peter's point of view. First, the picture as a whole, then various faces, ending with possibly the young Peter's. Cut back to his face, smiling slightly, then frowns as a very light snoring noise impinges. He turns, looks down at Hilary, who has fallen asleep. Peter gently takes the book from her hands, puts it on her side of the bed, then the spectacles, lays them on top of the book, looks down at her face, cut to Hilary's face, in sleep. Peter kisses her forehead, and cut to:

INT. PETER'S ROOM IN CHAMBERS

Sallust sitting in a corner. Peter gesturing a woman in her middle thirties into a seat. With her, Rose, a middle-aged solicitor, who also sits down.

Mrs Sawsbury (*after a pause*) I didn't realise there'd be two of you –

Peter Mr Sallust is my pupil. It's customary for him to sit in, I hope you don't mind. He'll be helping me with your case. Mr Rose, I've had a look at the statement Mrs Sawsbury gave you – there are just a few things I'd like to clear up. Did you explain to Mrs Sawsbury?

Rose She knows you're to be her counsel.

Peter Good. Mrs Sawsbury, I'll have to ask you some fairly brutal questions, but they're questions the other side are bound to put to you, so we must be quite clear on your responses, all right?

Mrs Sawsbury Yes.

Peter Now – (*Looking at the statement.*) Now your present income comes entirely from the alimony settled on you by your husband, that's right, isn't it?

Rose Yes.

Mrs Sawsbury No, I've got a job now.

Peter (*glances at Rose very briefly, then away again*) What job?

Mrs Sawsbury Usherette, in a cinema.

Peter West End cinema?

Mrs Sawsbury Yes.

Peter And what does that bring you?

Mrs Sawsbury Twenty pounds a week.

Rose You didn't mention this to me, Mrs Sawsbury.

Mrs Sawsbury I only started last week. But I've been looking for work for a long time – we can't live on the alimony, not these days.

Peter No, of course not. And you haven't asked for more from your ex-husband?

Mrs Sawsbury No, I never wanted his money anyway, I'd rather do without his help. (*Looks at Rose.*) I thought it would make a difference if I could bring them up without his help.

Peter What hours do you work?

Mrs Sawsbury Three afternoons and three evenings.

Peter Sounds rather nice. And who looks after the children?

Mrs Sawsbury I've got them into one of the council nursery schools.

Peter But your oldest child – the boy, Kevin – is old enough to go to school, isn't he?

Mrs Sawsbury I've got the choice until next year. They can stay at the nursery until half past five.

Peter Oh yes. Very practical. (*Little pause.*) And in the evening? On the three evenings –?

Mrs Sawsbury I have a friend who looks after them.

Peter Gives them their tea and puts them to bed?

Mrs Sawsbury And stays in with them.

Peter You don't pay your friend?

Mrs Sawsbury No, I don't.

Peter A real friend, then. (*Smiles, little pause.*) Now what do *you* estimate your husband's income at?

Mrs Sawsbury Well, it varies – I know it's got more since he left – but it goes from year to year.

Rose In his statement he puts it between four and five thousand a year. Three and a half would be more accurate.

Mrs Sawsbury Anyway, I don't see what that's got to do with it, besides, he's got another child now. That's what's so unfair.

Peter It's part of their case that he can give your children certain advantages, you see.

Mrs Sawsbury He can't give them my love.

Peter What about your ex-husband's new wife?

Mrs Sawsbury They don't *know* her – except as somebody who stuffs them with chocolates and takes them to the pictures. And their coloured TV, of course, but they're not advantages, are they?

Peter (*smiles*) Only if you like Westerns.

Mrs Sawsbury Lucille hates them.

Peter But you'd agree that they get on reasonably well with her? Your children do –

Mrs Sawsbury They don't mind going.

Peter Do they look forward to it?

Mrs Sawsbury Only for the treats. But they wouldn't miss them if they weren't promised by their father.

Peter looks quickly at Rose, who acknowledges the look, then down at the statement.

Peter Mrs Sawsbury, I said some of my questions would be brutal. Well, here's one. Are you ready?

Mrs Sawsbury nods.

Are you living with anyone?

Mrs Sawsbury It's my flat, I've the lease.

Peter Well then, is anybody living with you?

Mrs Sawsbury No.

Peter It's very important, Mrs Sawsbury. The other side claims that there is a man – they have evidence –

Mrs Sawsbury No.

Peter The friend who looks after the children. Is it a man or a woman?

393

Mrs Sawsbury (*after a pause*) A man.

Peter And does he ever spend the night in your flat?

The telephone rings.

Sorry. (*Picks it up quickly.*) Hello. (*Little pause.*) Look, I'm sorry, but I can't talk, I'm in the middle of a conference. (*Little pause.*) I can't say at the moment. Sorry. Goodbye. (*Puts the telephone down.*) Sorry. (*Looks momentarily distracted.*) Um, yes – does he, Mrs Sawsbury?

Mrs Sawsbury Well only sometimes, when he's late back.

Peter And does he spend those nights in your bed? I'm sorry, Mrs Sawsbury.

Mrs Sawsbury (*after a pause*) Yes.

Peter And do you have any plans to marry?

Mrs Sawsbury He's a Catholic, and so's his wife. (*Pause.*) Well, why not, we're both lonely, his wife hates him, she doesn't mind, his daughter's grown-up, *she's* married now, nobody cares – and *he's* got somebody in *his* bed, hasn't he, and if he can do it, why shouldn't I?

Peter I'm not judging you, Mrs Sawsbury, but I must know, for your sake, what we're to expect in court.

Mrs Sawsbury Well, what *am* I to expect? I mean, he can't just come after two years without doing anything except send his cheques in, and take my children away because he's got more money than me because he can work and I can't and because he's married again. He can't do that – that's not justice, is it?

Peter Why do *you* think he wants them back?

Mrs Sawsbury To spite me.

Peter He says he loves them.

Mrs Sawsbury Then why did he leave them in the first place? If you love people you stay for them, don't you? I didn't take them away from him, he took himself away because he said he couldn't stand it any more, and now he's trying to take them away. Everything's always come so easily to him, but they're not going to. I won't let them. (*Pause.*) I won't, you know.

Cut to:

INT. PETER'S ROOM IN CHAMBERS

Mrs Sawsbury and Rose gone. Peter sitting back, smoking, Sallust watching him.

Peter Well, Tommy, what do you think?

Sallust She's very unengaging.

Peter Well, not to her elderly Catholic lover. Nor, perhaps, to her children. So possibly not to the judge – at least, if he's elderly, Catholic and childish. Some of them are.

Sallust I hope she doesn't get on to her ex-husband when she gives evidence. It'll seem as if she's only hanging on to them to spite him.

Peter He's a swine. No, he probably isn't.

The telephone rings. He hesitates, fractionally, picks it up.

Yes. Oh, well put her through, please, I'm free now. (*Listens.*) Yes, yes, that'll be all right. Goodbye. (*Puts the telephone down.*)

INT. JOANNA'S BED-SITTER

Peter and Joanna are standing in the middle of the room.

Joanna I've got a lot of ham and assorted crudities.

Peter I'm not hungry, thanks.

Joanna There's some Scotch.

Peter God no. I've got some briefs to look at this afternoon. Well, how are you, then? Been, um, doing anything interesting?

Joanna Oh, a few covers from those people where we met.

Peter Good.

Joanna A few ups and downs with Josh, right?

Peter Josh?

Joanna That friend of mine I told you about. His affair with that actor came to a sticky end, I'm sure I told you. (*Pause.*) Anyway, he's been in one of his depressions, losing hair and fattening, so I've been on call as his favourite mother. It's too ridiculous.

Peter Poor Jo. (*Little pause.*) Poor Josh, come to think of it.

Joanna laughs, and cut to Peter suppressing wince.

Joanna Sorry about phoning. But your coming around at lunchtime was such a habit and then you stopped – I worried whether you were all right, right?

Peter No, I'm sorry I had to be so circumspect, there was somebody with me. (*Pause.*) Sorry, by the way, I haven't been able to get around, it's been very difficult, what with one case and another . . . haven't had a moment . . . How'd you get hold of my work number, by the way?

Joanna I looked it up.

Peter That was very clever of you.

Joanna (*laughs*) Matter of fact, I did manage to get a glimpse of you.

Peter Where?

Joanna On the Tube, actually. I was in the next carriage and saw you through the windows, it was weird.

Peter Weird, really? What was I doing?

Joanna Well, do you really want to know? (*Laughs.*) Well, you were smoking and you had some work in your lap, and you were looking at a girl who was sitting a bit down from you. She was very young and she was reading an enormous book. I made one of those calculations only unlib spinsters are supposed to make, you know, that she could just about have been your daughter.

Peter (*lighting a cigarette*) How long did you watch me for?

Joanna Oh, a few stops. Any of your cases been interesting?

Peter Only if you're interested in mess. And defeat.

Joanna Well, one side usually wins, you told me, right?

Peter At the moment, I appear to be representing the other side. Why didn't you join me at one of the stops?

Joanna I wasn't sure you wanted to see me. To tell you the truth, I was following you.

Peter (*after a pause*) Really? How far?

Joanna Well, to your front door. And then Jeremy came up on his moped – it was Jeremy, right? He went in.

Peter On a moped and through the front door, yes, that was probably my son.

    Joanna laughs. There is a pause.

Joanna I shouldn't have told you, right? I swore to God I wouldn't.

Peter It doesn't matter.

Joanna It matters to me, as I'm trying to cut down on humiliations.

Peter That's because you know you're – (*hesitates*) worth more than a lunchtime doss-down with a married man.

Joanna That's all it's been, then?

Peter Well, it's not been much else for you, I shouldn't think. Jo, I'm sorry, it was all my fault, I know that.

Joanna (*smiles in pain*) Well, I thought *you'd* give me my cards with some style. I mean, be original . . .

Peter I'm sorry.

Joanna For the past two weeks, since you stopped coming, I've been waiting by the phone. I didn't dare go out, even if it meant missing a chance of a commission. I even thought you might be ill. (*Laughs.*) I worried for you, or an accident or – (*Shrugs.*) Is it because of following you?

Peter You did know I was married, I told you at once. I have a life – (*Pause.*) Also I meant it when I said you were worth more – I mean – (*Smiles.*) There are lots of males between homos like Josh and husbands like me, it's sad that you should waste yourself –

Joanna Couldn't you say outright that you've stopped fancying me and I've become a nuisance?

Peter I've stopped fancying you and you've become a nuisance.

There is a pause, Joanna shocked.

Is that really any better? It's certainly not true. I still fancy . . .

Joanna (*cutting in*) Yes, well, you can go now, if you want.

Peter makes to say something, checks himself, goes to the door.

Peter I'm sorry about the clichés. My manners have been appalling, right the way through.

Joanna stares blankly, smoking. Hold on her, then cut to:
Peter beginning to close the door behind him.
Joanna lets out a wail, which turns into a scream. She gets up, races crazily around the room, wailing, knocking over work table etc.
Cut to Peter's face, appalled, caught at the door and on this cut to:

EXT. LONDON SUBURBAN GARDEN

Point of view from upstairs window. Alison, very pregnant, Hilary and five children ranging from three to twelve. Their cries muffled. Cut to:
Charles's face, staring out of the window.

Peter (*voice-over*) If I hadn't gone back I'd have spent the next three months waiting to hear of her suicide – or worse.

Charles (*waving, smiling down*) Would she really go that far?

INT. STUDY

Cut to Peter on a polystyrene bag, in an ascetic male preserve: do-it-yourself bookcases, school textbooks, unmarked and marked school essays on the desk. Around the walls there are pictures of school groups. One of these is the same as the one in Peter's and Hilary's bedroom.

Peter The point is, one doesn't know. At least, I don't. But once I *had* gone back in, it was bound to move in a fairly predictable sequence, a slap on the chops to stop her hysterics, a cup of tea to soothe her, a cuddle to stop her trembling, a fuck to – (*Gestures.*)

Charles (*sits in the opposite polystyrene*) Do you think that's ended it?

Peter I don't know. There's no way of glossing a fuck, is there? I tried to make it forlorn and farewell.

Charles Couldn't you have said something?

Peter What? If I said anything ambiguous, she would have ignored the other and real meaning. If anything explicit –

Charles You'd have been picking up the furniture again. I thought you'd decided to give up that sort of thing anyway.

Peter This sort of thing I never tried to take up.

Charles Well, casual affairs.

Peter Yes. Although there's nothing casual about this one now. Yes, I had given it up. But there was a party and I – I had some fantasy that I might be lucky with some pertly careless little creature – dreams, dreams. Because there was old reality standing by herself in a corner and myself gravitating ineluctably towards her as usual. I can't explain it. (*Little pause.*) She's ghastly! Look, old cheese, you did mutter something about a –

Charles gets up, goes to Scotch, syphon and two glasses on the desk.

Charles But in bed, surely?

Peter Yes, but so ravenous. Making love to somebody you can't stand but who's infatuated with you makes you believe you have a soul. Otherwise why do you feel so rotten? And afterwards the mandatory post-coital cigarette, she smokes with a shoulder hunched – (*Imitates Joanna smoking.*) And if I attempt a joke, her *laugh* – (*Imitates Joanna laughing.*)

Charles laughs. Peter laughs slightly, offers Charles a cigarette. Charles with a slight smile shakes his head.

And then the endless squalid complications of turning up at home smelling just right – not freshly showered but not, of course – oh God! (*Sits depressed for a moment.*) You've given up smoking.

Charles Apparently I'm lucky in my metabolism. I scarcely suffered. I had to take over the soccer one afternoon, and I couldn't keep up with the under-fourteens. And I suppose I believe schoolteachers ought to set an example – and as a father, come to that.

Peter I set just the right example for Jeremy. He models himself on everything I'm not. My vices have moulded an ascetic. Have you given up alcohol too?

Charles Well – yes, really.

Peter Christ, Charlie!

Charles You don't think –

Going to the window, looking down. Cut to:

EXT.

From Charles's point of view. Alison and Hilary talking, children playing.

Charles (*voice-over*) You don't think you should tell Hilary?

Peter (*voice-over*) Good God, why?

Cut to:

INT. STUDY

Charles Well, if this girl's as unstable as you say, she might – you know. And it would be better if it came from you first.

Peter I'd rather take the risk. She's finding her new lectureship exhausting enough – I don't want to create any unnecessary – (*Gestures.*)

Charles Yes, but if the girl does – it would be much worse. Besides, she'd understand, surely?

Peter Understand what? That I'd been unfaithful to her for ten years, on and off. You don't think she'd settle for one infidelity, do you – we'd be working back through our married life together – (*Shudders.*) The habits of confession and recrimination root very quickly, you know. I hear enough of them at work, I don't want to go through them at home. (*Gets up, goes to the window, looks out.*) When's it due?

Charles Next week some time.

Peter Alison looks amazingly sprightly.

Charles Oh, she scarcely notices any more. Except when she's not.

Peter Will this be your last?

Charles Only if it's a boy. She'll go on until she produces one –

EXT. GARDEN

From Peter's point of view. Alison, Hilary and the children. Joined by a nubile girl of about fifteen.

Peter (*voice-over*) How old *is* Caroline?

Charles (*voice-over*) Fifteen.

Peter (*voice-over, keeping Caroline in perspective as she bends over one of the other children*) Mm.

Charles (*voice-over*) Something I better warn you about, Pete.

INT. STUDY

Peter turns, faces Charles.

Charles We've gone vegetarian, I'm afraid.

  Cut to:

INT. PETER'S AND HILARY'S KITCHEN

Peter is washing up a few dishes. He is in his pyjamas. Jeremy enters, goes to fridge, takes out a bottle of milk, pours some into a glass.

Peter Is that all you want?

Jeremy Yeah.

Peter Have a good day?

Jeremy It was all right.

Peter Get a lot done?

Jeremy Mmm?

Peter Work. You were going to spend the day on your work, weren't you? Your A-levels?

Jeremy I've just come in.

Peter I know you've just come in. But before you went out –

Jeremy I did some.

Peter (*after a pause*) Good.

Jeremy (*goes towards the kitchen door, stops*) The telephone kept going.

Peter Oh. Who was it?

Jeremy I don't know. When I answered they hung up. From a call box.

Peter Probably for you then?

Jeremy No.

Peter How do you know?

Jeremy Because they wouldn't have hung up when I answered.

Peter But the call boxes these days – (*Turning away.*) The vandals have scarcely left one intact. (*Turns back.*) Tell me –

Jeremy is exiting from the kitchen. Peter turns back to the sink. Above, the sound of the telephone ringing. Cut to:

INT. BEDROOM

Hilary is lying in bed, spectacles on, reading. One hand extended casually over the telephone. Sound of a cough, door opening, closing.

Hilary God, that cough of yours.

Peter Wasn't that the phone?

Hilary Yes.

> *The telephone rings. Hilary picks it up, gaze still on the book, waits.*

348 0720. Hello. (*Puts the telephone down.*)

Peter Who is it?

Hilary Don't know. The pips are doing their endless pipping –

Peter Probably somebody for Jeremy.

Hilary Shouldn't think so.

Peter Why not? (*Getting undressed.*)

Hilary He's very considerate.

Peter (*looks at her in astonishment*) Even if he were, he'd hardly be phoning us up, as he's already in the house. One of his friends –

Hilary Not at this hour.

> *Peter gets into bed, lies back, looks across at the Junior Colts picture.*

I wish Jeremy had come today. Caroline's really very nice –

Peter A little young, surely.

Hilary What did you and Charlie talk about upstairs, or were you just hiding?

Peter Oh, about all the things he's given up. Which is really the last twenty years, when you think about it. What did you and Alison talk about?

Hilary Her womb. She was admiring it for its fertility – rather as one admires Dickens for his.

Peter (*laughs*) Macrobiotic. Onion and parsnip stew, Russian salad, fruit salad, no alcohol, Christ! (*Coughs slightly.*)

Hilary It's economics, of course. They can't have children *and* all the other vices. They do look extremely healthy on it, though. (*Pause.*) Well, they're our best friends. You and Charlie had a grubby public school dorm affair when you were passing through adolescence together, and you did your National Service at the same barracks. So now they're our best friends at thirty-eight.

Peter I neither had a dorm affair nor did my National Service with Alison.

Hilary And I suppose they'll be best friends to the end, won't they? They'll go on and on, Sunday lunches and monthly dinners until something happens to change them, a death possibly. (*Shudders.*) Why did I say that? (*Laughs.*) Anyway, I suppose we love them, don't we?

Peter I don't know. Old friends are like old habits. Once you've got them it's too late to wonder whether you actually want them. (*Coughs.*)

Hilary If Charles can do something about his smoking, can't you?

Peter Mmm.

Hilary (*turns her head, looks at him*) Don't you care that I care?

> *Peter turns his head, looks at her, puts his hand out, touches her on the cheek, then suddenly leans over, kisses her.*

Please make an effort.

> *Peter kisses her more passionately, then more passionately again. She pushes him away.*

That's not the issue. Besides, I've got a hard day tomorrow. I'm giving a lunchtime lecture as well as the evening seminars. And a Board of Studies meeting –

> *Peter looks at her, falls back on the pillow.*

Oh, don't take offence. (*Pause.*) All right, do.

> *Turns out her light, turns her back on Peter. Peter, his light still on, lies staring across the room, and cut to the photograph of the Junior Colts. See it in close-up, then moving from face to face, pausing on a face that could be Peter's.*

(*Voice-over.*) Look, it's not bloody fair, I must get some sleep if I'm to cope tomorrow!

> *Peter blinks, turns. Hilary is sitting up in bed, glaring at him.*

Please turn out your light!

> *Leans across him, turns it out. There is a silence.*
> *A very slight cough from Peter.*

Give us a cuddle then.

Another silence, then the sound of Peter getting out of bed.

(*After a pause.*) Pete?

The sound of the door closing.

(*To herself.*) Silly bugger!

INT. KITCHEN

Peter is sitting at the table, smoking.

Hilary (*at the door*) Do you prefer this to sleeping with me?

Peter It's more stimulating.

Hilary stares at him, then goes out, closing the door, emphatically. Peter sits for a moment, then stubs out his cigarette, gets up, hesitates, goes out.

INT. BEDROOM

Hilary is in bed, her light on. Peter gets in beside her, puts his light off.

Hilary Well, what *is* the matter with you?

Peter Nothing.

Hilary Then that's all right then, isn't it?

Turns her light off. There is a pause. Hilary turns her light on, looks down at Peter, lying with his hands folded under his head.

You're being exceptionally childish.

Peter What?

Hilary turns her light off.

Peter (*turns his light on*) What do you mean – childish?

Hilary turns away from him.

Peter Christ!

Turns his light off. There is a pause. Hilary turns her light on. Looks at Peter again, gets out of bed. Peter sits up, stares after her, as Hilary goes out of room.

Oh Christ!

Gets out of bed, follows Hilary out, slamming the door behind him.

INT. KITCHEN

Hilary and Peter sitting opposite each other, smoking.

Hilary (*talking in a whisper*) . . . no use your blaming me, I'm upset by it too but I can't help it. But you know I'm not off you, and you know I love you, it's just that – it's a strain, at the moment, I keep revolving the next day's lectures or what's worse, last week's, I really wonder whether I should have undertaken them, I don't seem to have the stomach for addressing large groups on – and I keep wondering whether I'm boring them or stupefying them and what the difference is. (*Pause.*) Am I in danger then?

Peter (*also whispering*) What? What of?

Hilary Of your looking elsewhere. I don't think I could bear that.

Peter Don't be silly.

Hilary I do worry about it, you know. And the unfairness of it.

Peter It's not at all unfair. I *was* being childish –

Hilary No, I meant the unfairness to me. Or us. Women.
How when I'm in my forties, which is tomorrow almost,
you'll still be very attractive –

Peter So will you.

Hilary And then when I'm in my fifties – or when you're
in your sixties even, going by current trends – I'll just be
a woman in my sixties as far as you're concerned –

Peter You don't believe that.

Hilary I'm talking about my worries, not my beliefs. I can
perfectly well imagine myself struggling not to check
your pockets or your underwear drawer before doing
both probably – it's very humiliating. (*Pause.*) You know
damn well I'm not frigid –

Peter (*emotionally*) Darling! (*Takes her hand.*) Look, let
me tell you –

Door opens. Jeremy enters. There is a pause.

Jeremy Anyone want a cup of tea?

Hilary Darling, shouldn't you be in bed?

Jeremy I've got a free class tomorrow. (*Putting the kettle
on.*) Don't have to be in until ten.

*He sits down. Hilary and Peter exchange glances.
There is a silence.*

Hilary What have you been doing?

Jeremy Oh, nothing really.

Hold on the three of them for a moment.

Peter (*after a long pause*) So much for Pascal.

Jeremy What?

Peter Wasn't it Pascal who said that all human evil came from our not being able to sit alone in a room, doing nothing?

Hilary (*brightly*) If we *could* all do that, there wouldn't be any humans left to do it.

Cut to:

INT. BEDROOM

Lights out.

Hilary (*voice-over*) I know he does.

Peter So do I. In that it would be most unnatural if he didn't. But that would only account for the odd half-hour of his day, surely. What does he do for the rest of the time?

Hilary Recuperates.

Peter laughs, so does Hilary and cut to:

INT. PETER'S ROOM IN CHAMBERS

Rose, Mrs Sawsbury, Sallust and Peter. Peter clearing his throat, waits.

Mrs Sawsbury But it was only the once. It only happened the once. He doesn't drink heavily as a rule, but he was feeling very low, his daughter's husband had been very rude to him, and he went to the pub. He's not a drinking man. I don't know where they got hold of this – this sort of lie.

Peter The trouble is, it's not exactly a lie. He did hit them, unfortunately.

Mrs Sawsbury Only the boy.

Peter And pushed the girl.

Mrs Sawsbury He didn't hurt them.

Peter Probably not – as they made so much noise. They wouldn't if they had been really frightened.

Mrs Sawsbury He's very fond of them, and they know it. He was ashamed afterwards, he cried.

There is a pause. The telephone rings on the desk.

Peter Excuse me. Who? Look, I can't take any calls, I'm – what? Who? I haven't got an appointment – (*Listens.*) Well, he can try then. (*Puts the telephone down, slightly abstracted.*) Sorry. (*There is a pause.*)

Mrs Sawsbury It's not fair if something like that counts against us. Will it?

Peter (*pulling himself together*) One can never be quite sure what does count. We'll do our best to make the judge understand.

INT. CHAMBERS

Peter and Sallust.

Peter They've got a private detective, of course.

Sallust Shouldn't we get one?

Peter It's too late. They'll be living their lives as if we already have.

Sallust Of all the times to get drunk and clout the kids! Do you think we've got a chance?

Peter Of what?

Sallust Of winning.

Peter Oh yes. So has opposing counsel. I shouldn't think anybody else has, though.

The telephone rings.

(*Answering it.*) Still there? (*Looks at his watch.*) All right. (*Puts the telephone down.*) Don't feel up to anybody else's misery just at the moment.

Door opens.

Mr James, isn't it?

Josh Yes.

Josh enters. He is in his mid-thirties, with a strained, unhappy-looking face.

Peter This is my pupil, Mr Sallust. You haven't come to us through a solicitor, have you, Mr James?

Josh No.

Peter I should warn you that really you should see a solicitor.

Josh It's a private matter, you see. (*Pause.*) About a friend of mine. Miss, um, Pelley.

Peter (*puzzled for a second, then controlling himself*) Oh. Then perhaps, Tommy –?

Sallust Of course.

He goes out. There is a pause.

Josh I don't know if she's mentioned me to you – Josh.

Peter Yes, I believe she did, once or twice. (*Lights a cigarette.*)

Josh I'm sorry to come in on you like this – I didn't know what else to do.

Peter waits.

I'm frightened.

Peter What of?

Josh Her. *For* her, that is. You see, I went around last night, she wasn't normal. Well – even for her. She was talking rather wildly –

Peter What about?

Josh You. She hasn't stopped that, but there's a kind of despair, you know, beyond her usual – desperation – (*Looks at Peter.*) You see, you're the third man in a row to go wrong on her.

Peter I see. (*His hand is trembling slightly.*) I was under the impression that you and she –

Josh Oh no. I'm homosexual. I slept with her once or twice, when she needed comforting. I expect she makes more out of it to other people – at the moment I'm no use to her. I would be if I could.

Peter I don't know what I can do.

Josh If you could just bring yourself to talk to her – she wouldn't let me in this morning, but I could hear her through the door, whimpering – I know how awful this must be for you, I'm sorry to ask.

Peter sits smoking, trying to control himself.

I expect all you wanted was a quick lay. It's not fair, is it?

Peter (*smiles shakily*) Thank you.

Cut to:

INT. JOANNA'S BEDSITTER

Joanna is in bed, in pyjamas. Peter is sitting in the chair beside the bed.

Peter But surely you must see a doctor.

Joanna (*smiling bravely*) No, it's only flu, I tell you. (*Laughs.*) You would come around suddenly after all this time and catch me in this state. (*Lights a cigarette.*)

Peter Should you?

Joanna Won't hurt me. (*Affectionately.*) Anyway, the number *you* smoke –

Peter Yes.

Joanna I couldn't actually make out from our last time whether you were going to come back.

Peter Well, now you know. (*Smiling.*)

Joanna Yes. I feel better – you've got a medicinal smile.

Peter That must mean it's hard to swallow.

Joanna What? (*Laughs.*)

Peter Can I make you some tea – or –?

Joanna (*shakes her head*) You've been very busy then?

Peter Yes.

Joanna I haven't followed you again.

Peter What about phoning?

Joanna (*looks at him*) Mm?

Peter Have you tried phoning me?

Joanna I won't do it again. I just wanted to hear your voice . . .

Peter Instead you heard my wife's and my son's.

*Joanna lies down, turns her face away, begins to cry.
Peter looks at her with a kind of desperate irritation,
then moves over to the bed, takes the cigarette away
from her fingers, puts it into the ashtray.*

Joanna (*puts one hand into his lap*) You want to go,
don't you?

Peter No – it's just that I've got to be back in chambers –

Joanna You can go now, if you like.

Peter No, no, I can stay on a bit.

Joanna (*cries out*) I love you.

Peter closes his eyes in horror.

I won't do anything to make you unhappy, I swear. If
I can just see you –

*Peter fumbles with his free hand for a cigarette.
Cut to:*

INT. HILARY'S AND PETER'S BEDROOM

*Hilary is lying in bed, staring up at the ceiling. Her face
is tight with anger. There is the sound of coughing, Peter
enters, naked. He is carrying his clothes. He dumps
shoes on the floor, goes to a drawer, chucks pants and
socks onto the chair.*

Hilary How's Jeremy?

Peter He's in his room.

Hilary But how is he?

Peter I don't know. He's in his room and I'm here.

Hilary I thought you might have looked in on him, to say goodnight.

Peter I said it from my usual place, a tentative foot or two on the other side of his door.

Hilary Yes, but I thought you might have looked in on him tonight.

Peter Really? Why?

Hilary To apologise.

Peter For what?

Hilary For being so offensive.

Peter Offensive? I thought we were having a high-powered discussion as to the relative merits of Laurel and Hardy –

Hilary *You* were having the discussion.

Peter I allowed him to display the full range of his critical vocabulary. I counted five 'whats', and seven 'yeahs', and six 'all rights'.

Hilary We know you did. You counted them out loud, if you remember. He merely said that he *quite enjoyed* Laurel and Hardy.

Peter No, he didn't. He said they were all right. And that's all he said.

Hilary Why should he say more – especially under an assault like that.

Peter I've heard you talk about students in your seminars with *their* 'all rights', and 'quite liked its' –

Hilary Jeremy is not a student in my seminar. He's our sixteen-year-old son. Whose behaviour, I might say, was remarkably adult under the circumstances.

417

Peter And who provides the circumstances? Not every youth these days is lucky enough to have a father who conforms to the propaganda, crop-headed, authoritarian, grammatical –

Hilary His sole offence this evening was to be younger and nicer than you.

Peter That makes two offences, both serious. (*Gets into bed, coughs slightly.*) Anyway, *he* didn't seem to mind.

Hilary If you really think that, then you're being stupid.

She switches off her light. Peter lies staring angrily ahead. Cut to Junior Colts picture.

You've been ghastly all evening. The one evening I have off during the week and when Jeremy's home – all of us having a proper family dinner together, which I spent the afternoon thinking about and getting ready – and you come home scarcely able to look at anyone, you drank too much before the meal, and then ruined the meal with your egoistical . . . It was unforgivable.

Peter You think that unforgivable? You should come to court one day and find out the sort of thing *my* sort of people don't forgive each other.

Hilary Would you like Jeremy – and myself – to be that sort of people?

Peter At least I'd know where I was. A son who scarcely addresses a remark to me, a wife who moralises and blackmails.

Hilary hits him. They sit glaring at each other, then Hilary collapses back on the bed. Peter remains sitting upright, staring at the Junior Colts picture. Cut to it, then back to Peter, as sound of muffled sobs over. He sits staring impassively, then turns, looks down at Hilary. Hilary is lying, her shoulders shaking. Peter looks down at her, his expression quite detached, but sad. He leans over, then puts his arms around her, lifts her up against himself.

I'm sorry. I didn't mean that.

Hilary struggles against him, almost frantically. He clutches her to him.

(*Soothingly.*) Don't, don't, don't, don't.

Hilary subsides. Occasional deep sobs.

You know I love you. (*Strokes her hair. Coughs very slightly.*) You know that.

Hilary And who else do you love?

Peter Jeremy.

Hilary And no one else? No girl or woman that –

Peter No one else. Nothing else either. Perhaps that's my trouble.

Hilary You used to love your work.

Peter It's not very lovable at the moment.

Peter strokes her hair, then kisses her on the mouth. Kisses her again, more passionately. Begins to caress her. Hilary at first resists, then acquiesces, then begins to respond with passion. Cut to Peter lying back, coughing.

Hilary (*leaning over him, concerned*) That was a race against time. Or death, it felt like. You certainly don't love yourself, do you?

The telephone rings. Hilary and Peter look at each other.

Hilary 348 0720. (*Listens.*) Pips.

Looks at Peter, puts the telephone down thoughtfully.

Peter (*urgently*) Take if off the hook.

He reaches across. The telephone rings. Hilary picks it up.

Hilary 348 0720. (*Waits. Pause.*) Which hospital? (*Little pause.*) Yes, we'll take the call. Here – *you'd* better –

She hands the telephone to Peter.

It's a hospital – they've reversed charges.

Peter (*clutching the telephone, waits, then*) Hello – I can't hear – which hospital? (*Listens.*) Who?

Hilary watching intently.

Yes, it is. (*Pause.*) Charlie, hello! What – oh Charlie, wonderful – it's Charlie – a son!

Hilary (*smiling*) Thank God!

Cut to:

INT. JOANNA'S BEDSITTER

Joanna, fully dressed, is sitting on a corner of the bed, smoking. Peter is standing.

Joanna I thought this was one of your late nights. When you're not expected home –

Peter Yes, it is.

Joanna And so you've just looked in to say you could only look in, right?

Peter Well, to see how you were. I've got a long-standing engagement with my pupil.

Joanna What's the point of your coming around then?

Peter I thought you liked me to.

Joanna Not like this. There's no point to it.

Peter What will you do this evening?

Joanna Don't worry.

Peter Well, you'll be all right?

Joanna Yes, thanks.

Peter OK. Well – see you next week perhaps. Right?

Goes to door, opens it; as he closes it, cut to shot of Joanna, from his point of view sitting as if indifferent on the bed. The door closes on her and cut to:

INT. HALL

Peter, on the other side of Joanna's door, apprehensively listening. Then turns, walks away, swinging squash bag and briefcase, with an air of release.

INT. SQUASH COURT

Peter and Sallust playing. Peter, running rather flounder-ingly, his face working, breathing hard, loses the point and rests collapsed against a corner, coughing.

INT. CHANGING ROOM

Sallust under a shower, Peter sitting on a bench, shaking. Towel around his middle. He has a cigarette, unlit, in his mouth. Sallust emerges.

Peter Was that a cold shower?

Sallust Mmm.

Peter Christ!

Sallust Well, I go on sweating for hours if I have a hot one. And as I'm taking my girlfriend to the opera –

Peter Didn't know you liked opera? (*Little pause.*) Didn't know you had a girlfriend, either. Well, I must have assumed you had –

Sallust I won't have her for long if I have to keep taking her to the opera. How do you feel?

> *Peter grunts.*

You used to be pretty good once, usedn't you? (*Towelling himself vigorously.*) Very nice touch –

Peter Not really. It's always been cricket for me. Sometimes I still remember a particular shot – I'd never done it before, it was in an under-fifteen match – it was a late cut. I didn't even know I was going to do it – or was doing it – (*gets up, demonstrates*) until I'd completed it – like this – and the ball was at the boundary. The one moment in my life when I felt a touch of sublimity. (*Laughs.*) I try and recall it occasionally, before I go to sleep. (*Begins to dry himself.*)

Sallust You know, it just struck me the other day that I was twenty-eight and already too old to be any of the things I still dream I might be – a professional tennis player – or –

> *He stands, with a wondering look. Peter turns, looks, smiles.*

Peter Eh? What?

Sallust (*vaguely*) Actually, a – um –

> *He collapses to the floor. Peter runs to him, lifts up his head.*

Peter Tommy, Tommy . . . God . . . Tommy.

Two men, carrying squash bags, appear at the end of the dressing room, come towards Peter, one of them smoking. Then hurry forward, bend over to look at Sallust.

First Man Can you do that? Your mouth, kiss him? That business?

Peter looks at him, then bends over, begins a clumsy kiss of life on Sallust.

I'll go and get . . .

He hurries off.

Peter, with Second Man crouching beside him, goes on kissing, draws his mouth away.

Peter I can feel him, he's beginning –

Peter puts his mouth back over Sallust's, and on his life-kissing, Second Man beside him, a cigarette between his fingers. Cut to First Man, standing, scratching meaninglessly at his cheek. Second Man standing beside him, smoking another cigarette. A Third Man, possibly a doctor, kneels by Sallust, and now wearily straightening. Peter observed in the distance, almost obscurely, sitting on the bench, staring blankly ahead and smoking. Various other figures around, including a porter. The Doctor gets up, goes over to Peter, sits down beside him.

Doctor OK?

Peter I felt his breath coming. Out of his mouth.

Doctor It was probably your own breath coming back at you, I'm afraid.

Peter He just keeled over.

He gets up, walks mechanically over to Sallust's body.

Doctor They'll be here in a minute. You look as if you could do with –

Peter bends down, picks up Sallust's towel, puts it carefully over Sallust's genitals.

I'm sorry.

Peter (*Meaninglessly*) He was my pupil, you see.

Stay on group as long as possible, then cut to:

INT. COLLEGE LECTURE ROOM

Hilary's face, seen through the glass-and-wire panels of the door. She is talking, spectacles on, from notes. As she talks, she lifts her head, as if from instinct, looks towards the door, and:

From Hilary's point of view, see Peter on the other side of the glass.

INT. CHARLES'S STUDY

They are sitting on the polystyrene sacks, as before. But first, Charles's voice-over, as image maintained from previous scene.

Charles One of our boys did that – he was fifteen.

Cut to him, pouring a healthy dose of Scotch into two glasses.

Perfectly fit. Suddenly collapsed on the football pitch. In the midst, so to speak.

Peter (*taking a glass*) Thanks.

He is by the window, offers Charles a cigarette.
Charles takes it.

What is it?

Turns, looks out of the window. Cut to:

EXT. GARDEN

From Peter's point of view. Caroline appears, walking
slowly. Hilary and Caroline at further end, bent over
pram.

Peter (*voice-over*) Halfway upon this way of life I'm lost
upon –

Charles (*voice-over*) Having had twenty years –

Jeremy appears, walks after Caroline, catches up with
her. Says something. Caroline shrugs.

Having had twenty years, twenty years of *entre deux*
guerres, no, that's something else –

Cut back to:

INT. CHARLES'S STUDY

Peter's face, turning impassively away from the window.

Charles (*smoking*) The worst is to come, I suppose. The
death of friends, all the deaths in waiting, including our
own. But it's the death of children that haunts me.
Sometimes in the night –

Peter Don't!

Charles (*grunts*) What was he like?

Peter Just a pupil. Callower than some, in fact I took
less notice of him than most of my recent ones until our

game – we talked for the first time, you know, the way people do after squash – I patronised him a bit, ignored him quite often, and tried to conceal my irritation when he passed me damned stupid notes in the middle of a plea. He was all right. (*Little pause.*) I don't know.

Charles Everything else all right?

Peter Mmm?

Charles That girl?

Peter Oh God, I don't know. I'm keeping it at bay, for the moment.

Charles What?

Peter Whatever conclusion there's to be. (*Notices Charles's cigarette.*) Thought you'd given up?

Charles Started again in the hospital waiting room. (*Inhales deeply, coughs.*)

Peter (*coughs*) Still, that's something to celebrate.

INT. THE COURT

Judge enters, everybody rises, then sits, and as Counsel for Mrs Sawsbury rises, the camera cuts from face to face, on Mrs Sawsbury sitting behind Peter, with Rose, to Mr Sawsbury, to the Judge, then back to Mrs Sawsbury, tautly apprehensive, then to Peter turning, smiling encouragingly. Mrs Sawsbury smiles tightly back.
  Credits.

TWO SUNDAYS

To Alan
for Ben, Simon, Peter and Charles

Two Sundays was first presented by BBC Television on 21 October 1975. The cast was as follows:

Charles Alan Bates
Peter Dinsdale Landen
Alison Rosemary Martin
Hilary Georgina Hale
Boy Steven Gover
Bowler Andrew Burleigh
Housemaster Benjamin Whitrow
Schoolmaster 1 Victor Langley
Schoolmaster 2 Simon Cadell
Children Paul Stencil, Benjamin Bolger, Daniel Bolger,
  Amelia Bolger

Director Michael Lindsay-Hogg
Designer Richard Henry
Producer Kenith Trodd

Characters

Charles

Peter

Alison

Hilary

Boy

Bowler

Housemaster

Schoolmaster 1

Schoolmaster 2

Children

INT. MORNING

Bowler, waking in the morning. Blinks, looks about him, makes a move to get out of bed. Cut to:

INT. PETER'S BEDROOM

Peter getting out of bed, looks and clearly feels dreadful.

Peter Oh Christ!

Hilary (*off*) Mmm?

Peter It's eight-thirty.

Hilary (*off*) Wha –?

Peter Eight-thirty. (*Little pause.*) Eight-thirty. (*Little pause.*)

Hilary (*off*) Mmmmm.

Peter Shan't tell you the time again.

Hilary (*off*) Won't have to. I know. It's eight-thirty.

Peter But it won't be the next time you ask.

Hilary Good.

Peter (*glares at her*) We've got a long bloody drive.

Hilary I've got a long bloody drive. (*Off.*) You've got your usual bloody hangover.

Peter turns, goes out in his underwear and cut to:

EXT. PLAYING FIELDS

Charles, running across school playing fields, in long shot. The sound of bells ringing, several boys walking, sitting. He comes closer and closer, his head swaying, eyes slightly glassy, breathing heavily until he's full in camera and then gone on past it. Hold on the school playing fields, and cut to:

EXT. SCHOOL YARD

Different school, although this is not explicit. Several boys again, this time wearing school suits, in some cases gowns, white shirts. Come in on a Boy in a gown, sitting, reading.

Boy *'Je suis le roi d'un pays pluvieux.'*

> *Sound of bells. He looks up, then around, as if looking for someone. Then bends over his book. See him from a sudden point of view that turns out to be Bowler's. Boy is smiling, as cut to:*

EXT.

Bowler, from Boy's point of view, advancing towards him in grey flannels, white shirt, carrying cricket boots. Gets to him.

Boy Good morning then.

Bowler Hello.

Boy Unusual togs for a Sunday morning.

Bowler They've put me down for a nine net.

Boy I expect you'll enjoy that.

Bowler It's for the Junior Colts.

Boy Gratters. (*Ironically.*) And luck.

Bowler We're fagging Refec at break.

Boy To hell with all that.

Bowler We'd better go.

Boy gets up, they move towards a building, slowly, and cut to:

INT. PETER'S AND HILARY'S KITCHEN

Hilary, dressed, is drinking a cup of coffee, reading a paper. Peter is leaning against the fridge door, dressed, drinking coffee, smoking. He coughs slightly. Hilary glances at him.

Peter Where's Jeremy?

Hilary In the toilet.

Peter The toilet!

Hilary That's the word they use.

Peter Who?

Hilary Everyone in the Juniors, from the Headmistress down. They always say it.

Peter Always? (*Going to the fridge.*) Lively conversationalists then.

He opens the fridge door, takes out a bottle of wine.

Hilary What's that?

Peter Bottle of wine, isn't it?

Hilary For breakfast?

Peter For lunch. Last time they were on some herbal rubbish, I'm not risking that again. If he doesn't hurry, we won't make it for lunch. How can an illiterate spend so long on the lavatory?

Hilary (*calling*) Darling! Darling!

And cut to:

INT. CHARLES'S STUDY

Charles, still in his running shorts, etc., sweat dripping off him, is standing at his desk, one plimsolled foot on a chair, turning over the pages of a manuscript.

Alison (*off*) Are you in there?

Charles Yes, darling.

Listens, hand on a page. Alison's footsteps off. Charles closes the manuscript, puts it unhurriedly away, as:

Alison (*at door, she is very pregnant*) They've started breakfast.

Charles I'll just have a shower.

Alison Couldn't you after?

Charles Oh, I pong fearfully.

Alison Well, we've got a lot to do, I haven't started the casserole . . . and I would like to tidy up . . .

Charles (*following her out*) Don't worry, darling, We'll cope.

Cut to:

INT. SCHOOL CORRIDOR

Boy and Bowler, walking down a passage. They stop.

Bowler I thought we weren't allowed in Music until after prep.

Boy No, it's all right on a Sunday.

Bowler You sure?

Boy So I'll see you there after your nets. There's something I particularly want you to hear . . .

Schoolmaster (*off*) Hey, you two, aren't you fagging Refec?

> *Cut to Master, at end of passage, not seen clearly, just a shape.*

Boy (*off*) Sir.

Bowler (*off*) Sir.

Schoolmaster Come on then.

> *Seem to be coming in on him, instead come in on:*

INT. CHARLES'S AND ALISON'S KITCHEN

Three boys, aged eight, six, four, around the table. A girl, aged two, in a high chair. All eating.

Charles Well, we've got a jolly nice day in store for you chaps, haven't we, Mummy?

Alison A jolly nice day.

Charles (*sits down*). We must all be particularly nice to Jeremy, until he's used to us. He'll be the odd one out.

One of the Boys (*off*) Don't like Jeremy.

Charles (*cheerfully*) You've forgotten him, it's been such a long time.

Voice But I remember I don't like him.

Other Voice Nor do I.

Charles Then let's begin by pretending to like him, and if we practise hard, we'll end up by doing it.

INT. PETER AND HILARY IN A CAR

Peter is slumped down, smoking. Hilary is driving. Jeremy is in the back, strapped in.

Peter How did this come about, anyway?

Hilary It was a conspiracy. The wife of your oldest friend invited the wife of his oldest friend and her husband, the oldest friend, to lunch. We wanted to ruin your Sunday.

Peter You didn't have to accept.

Hilary I had no choice. That's not true, I had a choice of any one of the next eight Sundays.

Peter Then why didn't you choose the eighth?

Hilary To avoid having this conversation then. (*Pause.*) It'll give Jeremy someone to play with, won't it, darling?

Jeremy (*off, after a pause*) I hate them.

Peter Then you, at least, shouldn't be too bored.

   Cut to:

INT. CHARLES'S STUDY

Charles is putting the manuscript into a large brown envelope. Sound of car drawing up, opening and closing

*of doors, voices in greeting. He goes to the window,
opens it, and as if from his point of view cut to:*

EXT.

*From point of view of music-room window, looking
down over school yard. The yard is full of boys going off
in different directions, walking together, separately, some
standing in groups. Bowler comes into picture, now
dressed as Boy, only without the gown. He looks up, and
cut to:*

*Alison, Hilary, Jeremy, with other children, in the
garden, and Peter, from his point of view looking up,
seeing Charles, who is smiling down. Cut to Peter's face,
smiling slightly, and looking up, and cut up to:*

INT. MUSIC-ROOM WINDOW

*Boy at it, indistinct, looking down, seen from school
yard, Bowler's point of view. And cut to:*

INT. CHARLES'S STUDY

*Peter in it, lighting a cigarette, sighing. Suddenly looks
towards the door, as it begins to open. And cut to:*

INT.

*Music-room door opens. Bowler enters. He is dressed as
in previous scene. He looks towards gramophone, cut to
Boy, just putting record on. He turns.*

Boy It's to be Berg.

Bowler Oh.

Boy bends over gramophone. Bowler sits down, adopts a listening posture. Boy fiddles with the gramophone, then as scraping noise of needle on the pre-music grooves, walks to sit down, and cut to:

INT. CHARLES'S STUDY

Charles enters, carrying a quarter of a bottle of Scotch and two glasses, one of which has a long drink in it.

Charles Sorry. I got it in specially and then forgot where I put it.

Peter Very sweet of you.

Charles puts the full glass down on the desk, opens the bottle, makes as if to pour, stops.

Charles You'd better look after yourself –

Peter Thanks. (*Little pause.*) What are you drinking?

Charles (*little laugh*) Ribena, actually. I seem to have acquired an addiction to it – because of the children – well –

Lifts his glass. Peter has poured, lifts his glass, coughs slightly.

Charles Well – (*As if trying to think of something to say.*) Oh, there's something I wanted you to hear. It might amuse you – one of my sixth-formers did it.

He goes over, turns on a tape recorder, sits down. Peter makes an expression of bored irritation when Charles's back is turned, sinks down, sips, smokes. Charles sits down, as tape whirrs. There is a long silence. There is a ping, followed by two more pings. Silence. Peter makes an expression. Sudden crashing of chords, and cut to:

INT. MUSIC ROOM

The climax of the Berg record. The two boys sitting. The record stops. Boy gets up, goes over, takes the record off, keeps his back to Bowler. Bends over to put the record back in its sleeve.

Bowler (*after a pause, clears his throat*) It's jolly bloody good.

Boy (*looks at him*) Yes?

Bowler Well, I liked it.

Boy But did it make you laugh?

Bowler Laugh.

Boy It's very and fantastically witty.

Bowler *You* didn't laugh.

Boy Oh, I know all the jokes.

Bowler Then what did you put it on for?

Boy Your entertainment, of course. And I wanted to concentrate on the grief, for once.

He puts on another record, walks back, scratching pre-music begins, and cut to:

INT. CHARLES'S STUDY

Peter sitting back, cigarette drooping from his lips, eyes half closed as if in boredom, occasionally wincing. See his face from Charles's point of view, then his eyes taking Charles in. Charles from Peter's point of view, staring at him, looking away.
Through this, over, on the tape, lavatory flushing, dogs barking, bird calls, savagely discordant violins. Then

silence. Tape whirring. A sudden girl's scream, terrible, from the tape. Silence.

Peter raises his eyebrows interrogatively.

Charles I'm not quite sure whether this is part of it. The silence I mean. (*In a low voice.*) It goes on for twenty minutes.

Peter Oh. (*Short pause.*) May we not acknowledge it? Rather than listen to it. Or whatever it is one does to silence.

Charles (*after another short pause*) Yes, yes, perhaps one had better – I just wanted you to get a sense of its effect. (*Gets up, goes over, bends for a moment.*) Once or twice I've fancied I heard something *behind* the silence. But it's never the same, so I suppose it must be imagination. (*Turns it off.*) Perhaps that's what he intends. Well –

He looks at Peter eagerly.

Peter A sixth-former, did you say?

Charles Yes, but quite young. Just sixteen. A precocious lad. I have hopes he'll pull off an Oxford place, at the very least. He's utterly individual. I think I told you last time we had quite a business coming to a policy on hair styles?

Peter (*clearly not remembering*) Oh yes.

Charles And finally decided on a completely liberal view. Well, you can imagine what we got – hair to the shoulders, Afro-styles, the lot. (*Laughs.*) Except from young Tedhurst. Young Tedhurst went bald.

Peter Really? Disease or design?

Charles Oh, design, I'm sure. And now this, for his Creative Arts Project. Most boys wrote stories, or painted, or built things, you know – but young Tedhurst – (*Gestures to the tape-machine.*)

Peter What will you say to him?

Charles The truth of course. That I think it very, very interesting.

Peter Well, that should do the trick.

Charles How do you mean?

Peter That a bald, sixteen-year-old futuristic musician is entitled to exactly the same attention as any other boy.

Charles (*puzzled*) Well, of course he *is*.

Peter Yes. (*Pause.*) Anyway, you're obviously still enjoying school, then.

Charles Oh, yes. Last year they tried to promote me into more admin and less teaching, but I wasn't having it. Those that can't aren't going to have *that* taken away from them. (*Smiles.*) By the way, did I mention to you, I've taken over the Junior Colts, soccer *and* cricket.

Peter Really?

Charles I thought that would surprise you.

Peter For the exercise?

Charles Partly. Of course I have to take further exercise to keep up with them. A run every morning before breakfast.

Peter Christ!

Charles I'm up to four miles.

Peter Christ!

Charles I really feel quite marvellous for it. (*Little pause.*) Well, how about you?

Peter Oh, I'm not fit enough to take exercise.

Charles But you're all right?

Peter Yes. Oh yes thanks. Well, you know – (*Grunts vaguely.*)

Charles And publishing? Anything changed? Last time you sounded a bit depressed –

Peter Then nothing can have changed. I'm still editing the waste-products of immigrant intellectuals. We've just started a new paperback series. 'Mind-Formers of Our Time.' Monographs on people like Marcuse, generally by people on whom we can do monographs in a few years' time.

Charles But you *were* very excited over a novel you'd received – a quite unexpected first novel, I think it was.

Peter Was I? Oh yes – that got a few nice reviews. Nothing special happened – I suppose one or two people might have bought it.

Charles But you're still doing novels, aren't you?

Peter Now and then. We have to keep up a list, for appearances' sakes. But of course with rising costs and declining literacy – (*Gestures.*)

Charles Still, it's good that you are, for whatever reason. (*Pause.*) What about your own – you had one on the way, didn't you?

Peter No. Rather yes, but no. Not any longer.

Charles Don't say you've given it up?

Peter I've already done my bit as publisher to add to the world's stock of unread books. I have no right to add to it as an author. (*Pause.*) Besides, it wasn't any good.

Charles How do you know?

Peter I assessed it in my second capacity, I decided it was probably worth more than a straight rejection, but that I wouldn't have recommended it for publication. In fact, I'd probably have taken the author out to lunch and gently discouraged him. Which is precisely what I did do. A bloody good lunch, too – oysters, Guinness and strawberries. Thus proving that I may be a poor novelist, but I'm a decent enough editor.

Charles Still, it must have been, well, painful for you.

Peter It was a relief, actually. I haven't the stamina to drink, smoke *and* write, in the evenings.

Charles Well, perhaps it would be worth giving up, for something really important.

Peter That's what I did.

Charles Under the circumstances – (*Hesitates.*)

Peter What?

Charles Oh just something rather ironic. But it can wait. (*Pause.*) Well, the thing is –

He stops, looks towards the door. Peter also looks towards the door, which is opening. Cut to:

INT. MUSIC ROOM

A Schoolmaster, in a gown, standing at the door. Boy and Bowler on their feet as Mozart comes to an end on the gramophone.

Schoolmaster Mysteriously Mozart from the other side of the door. While from the other side of the window something fashionably atonal. Berg?

Boy Sir.

Schoolmaster When it shouldn't really be either, as you're both down to fag for seniors at Refec. Didn't you hear the Refec bells between the Berg and the Mozart?

Boy Sir, we were just going, sir.

Schoolmaster (*looks at them thoughtfully*) Good. By the way, isn't there some pettifogging regulation about the Music Room. *Is* one allowed to use it before six o'clock prep?

> *Boy and Bowler look at each other, seen from Schoolmaster's point of view.*

Boy We thought on Sunday, sir . . .

> *Boy looks towards him, and as if we're going to see Schoolmaster from his point of view. Cut to:*

INT. CHARLES'S STUDY

Alison, the pregnant lady from the garden, at the door.

Alison What are you two chaps up to? Lunch is ready – at least, the children have all washed their hands, and Hilary's arranging them around the table –

> *Peter is getting up.*

– on which I'm just about to plonk the casserole, so if you're going to get up some of our brew, darling, you'd better nip about it sharpish.

Charles Do you like home-made beer? I've been following that chap in the *Guardian,* sometimes it turns out all right.

Alison It's actually jolly delicious.

> *Alison holds the door open as first Peter then Charles pass; see them from her point of view, and then her eye going to the ashtray containing Peter's stubs, and his glass and the Scotch, as over:*

Peter As a matter of fact, I did bring along a small contribution –

Alison makes a sardonic expression, closes the door, and cut to:

INT. SCHOOL REFECTORY

Sound of voices. Come in on knives and forks plying between plates and mouths, then cut to: Boy's face, standing behind larger boys, who are eating. Then see him from the perspective of Bowler, also standing behind older boys, at a different table. There are other younger boys (clearly acting as fags) behind different tables. Boy smiles to Bowler, then in response to an order from one of the older boys, moves to fetch a jug of water. Bowler receives an order at the same time, comes back with bread, puts it down on the table, and cut to:

INT. CHARLES'S KITCHEN

An enormous table, around which the four boys from the garden are seated. Charles, behind the table, is on his feet and plonking bread down on the children's plates; Peter is moving around the other side, pouring out orange squash. Alison is at the head of the table, serving casserole into bowls. Beside her, in a high chair, is Nindy, the little girl. Hilary is seated, serving vegetables into the bowls. On the table several bottles of home-made beer and two bottles of white wine. All this taken in fleetingly, then cut to Peter's face, sardonic, and then to Charles, intently the father. Charles suddenly looks towards Peter, who smiles more intimately than in the study. Charles smiles back, while over:

Alison Does Jeremy eat aubergines?

Hilary He's worth trying. Doesn't Nindy manage her fork well?

EXT. SCHOOL YARD

Lots of boys milling about, talking, then come in on Boy's face, as he and Bowler slightly cut off from the others by a notice board.

Boy Gratters.

Bowler Oh, shut up!

Boy I was only saying 'gratters', isn't that what chaps say to chaps when chaps get selected for the Junior Dolts.

Bowler Anyway, I'm only down because Duff is infirm.

Boy Duff is infirm? But only mentally surely, not physically.

Bowler I mean, *in* infirm, you know jolly well. I didn't select myself, you know, I was selected, you know. Surely you can understand that.

Boy What?

Bowler That it's not my fault.

Boy What's not your fault?

Bowler If I happen to get selected because I was bowling off-spins in the nets, I didn't know I could bowl off-spin even, so it's not my fault, is it?

Boy But it's your fault when you smirk about it.

Bowler I'm not smirking! (*Turning around on him.*)

Boy No, it's quite true, you're not. Coming for a walk?

Bowler No.

Boy Why not?

Bowler Because I can't.

Boy Why can't you?

Bowler Because I'm meant to be playing, that's why.

Boy But your match isn't until Thursday, it said on Notice.

Bowler It's squash, this afternoon.

Boy Oh, squash!

Bowler It's the House Shield semi-finals.

Boy Gratters!

> *Cut to:*

EXT. CHARLES'S GARDEN

Charles and the four boys are playing soccer on the lawn. See them from Peter's point of view. Then take in Peter watching them. He is sitting in a deckchair at the end of the garden with a bottle of wine at his side, a cigarette in one hand, a glass in the other. He looks up suddenly, and to his right, at the approach of Hilary, not yet seen, and cut to:

INT. SPECTATORS' BALCONY, SQUASH COURTS

Come in on Housemaster's face, looking down, as off, in the court, Bowler's voice:

Bowler (*off*) Oh, jolly good serve.

> *Sound of rallies punctuates the conversation.*

Housemaster Some verse?

Cut to Boy with an exercise book open on his knees, a pencil in his hand.

Boy Sir.

Housemaster Why here?

Boy Well, supporting House too, sir. It's the House Shield semi-finals.

Housemaster Ah, well that's very keen of you. Let's hear a mite of applause then.

Boy He hasn't done anything to applaud yet, sir, he's behind love-four.

Bowler (*off*) Jolly good serve.

Boy Five-love.

Housemaster Then you must applaud his opponent. That's the done thing, isn't it?

Boy Sir.

Housemaster Then kindly do it.

Bowler (*off*) Jolly good serve!

Boy applauds, and on him clapping and looking first down, into the court, then up again, as if at Housemaster, seen as if from his point of view, but cutting to:

EXT. GARDEN

Hilary's face, from Peter's point of view, their voices carefully lowered, as over the sound of Charles, shouting encouragement.

Hilary You might show willing.

Peter But I'm not.

Hilary It's a little embarrassing for Jeremy, though, *his* father not playing.

Peter It would be more embarrassing for him if I did. He hates football too.

Hilary But at least he's joining in.

Charles (*off*) Oh, hard cheese, Jeremy.

Peter Poor little sod had no option.

Hilary Well, I must say, you present a very pretty spectacle –

Alison (*off, advancing*) I say, would you mind looking?

Peter What?

Hilary (*looking down*) Oh well done, Nindy.

Peter looks down, on his face a sudden grimace.

(*Under her breath.*) Say something! (*Aloud.*) Marvellous, darling!

Peter Yes, brilliant.

Cut to the Little Girl, holding chamber pot for inspection.

Alison (*behind*) Isn't she a clever girl! (*Claps.*)

Hilary also claps. Peter also claps.

Daddy, Daddy, Nindy's done a lovely little jobs for Pete, right into her potty!

Charles bounds up, sweat running down his face, breathing deeply.

Charles What a clever girlie. (*Claps, and sinks exhausted to the porch.*)

Peter (*sotto voce, to Hilary*) What do they do when she does a lovely big jobs?

Hilary lets out a laugh, suppresses it, turns, moves off after Alison, who is leading Nindy, carrying the pot, away. From the garden, noises of game continue. Charles sits recuperating, seen from Peter's point of view, then cut to:

You seem a bit done in for a chap who's up to four miles and the Junior Colts.

Charles (*over, panting*) It's the heat.

Cut as if back to Charles, and instead to:

INT. SCHOOL SHOWERS

Bowler is sitting beneath the clothes peg on a bench opposite the showers. He is stripped down to his shorts, and is taking off his socks. He sniffs at them in fascinated disgust, drops them to the floor, looks up, as:

Boy (*voice-over, off*) Hard luck.

Cut to him as he enters, stands uncertainly.

Bowler I pong.

Boy comes over, sits down on the bench beside him.

Bowler I don't know how you can sit there.

Boy Why not?

Bowler Because I pong.

Boy That's because you've been running about, losing.

Bowler gets up, takes off his shorts, goes to the shower.

Bowler I wouldn't have, if you hadn't been there.

Boy Run about?

Bowler Lost! You put me off.

Boy But it doesn't matter, you losing. Master told me so.

Bowler looks at him, goes under the shower and cut to:

INT. CHARLES'S BATHROOM

Charles drying his face. He finishes, stares ahead, makes a face as if reaching a decision. Puts the towel back, and cut to:

INT. CHARLES'S STUDY

Peter is staring blankly ahead, hand around a glass; cigarette in his other hand. Suddenly sighs, as if with boredom. Coughs slightly.

INT. SHOWERS

Boy is still sitting, staring down. Cut to Bowler sitting opposite him, towel around his waist, putting on socks. As he does so, glances furtively at Boy. Glances away. Draw the camera back, to take in the two of them. Then cut to:

INT. CHARLES'S STUDY

Charles, full face. He is closing the door, looks at Peter. Take in the two of them, Peter making a small effort at a greeting. Charles turns away. Camera on him. His face, for a second, desperate. Turns around, looks at Peter.

Charles Sorry.

Peter What? What for?

Charles All this. Family casseroles, soccer on the lawn, home-made beer. You must hate it.

Peter Of course, I don't.

Charles (*smiles*) It's the only way Alison knows of doing things.

Peter It's a splendid way. Besides, don't forget I didn't drink the beer or play soccer and the casserole was delicious. And so was the home-made bread.

Charles The beer's really not at all bad.

Peter Look, why don't we meet in town for lunch sometime?

Charles We always decide to do that.

Peter Nothing could be easier to arrange.

Charles Fine.

There is a pause.

Peter I'll give you a ring early in the week, just as soon as I've checked on my office diary –

Charles Right. (*Little pause.*) One gets such odd fragments of information, doesn't one? From each other. But usually not the sequels.

Peter Yes. It's very . . . tantalising.

Charles I mean. I take it everything's all right, to do with that girl –

Peter Girl?

Charles The one you were having an affair with.

Peter Oh. Oh yes. (*Little pause.*) Which one was that?

Charles The Australian.

Peter Ah, yes. Long gone. All the way back to Australia, thank God! That was a long time ago.

Charles You were worried that Hilary might find out, you thought she'd make trouble.

Peter Hilary?

Charles No, the Australian.

Peter That's right. Yes, yes, she did go through a period of Antipodean bluster. I think she just wanted to liven me up a bit. She found me boring, when it came to it. She had some idea that adultery should be, well, more spectacular, especially in the literary world. At least a few *éclaircissements*.

Charles Anyway, Hilary never did find out?

Peter Christ, no. She wouldn't really have done anything underhand – she was all right. She was quite nice actually. Her book's done quite well, too, considering it came at the tail end of all that business. Have you read it?

Charles shakes his head.

In the Afterword, which she had stuck in afterwards, so to speak, there's an account of an affair she had with a married chap who used to bring a spare pair of knickers to her flat in his briefcase. That was me. Hilary thought it was funny.

Charles That it was you?

Peter No, no – just the description. She read it out to me, bits of it, of course she hadn't the least idea –

Charles Good God, what did you do?

455

Peter I laughed too. It struck me as really quite exceptional, to lie in bed listening to one's wife innocently reading out an account of one's adultery . . .

Charles Yes, I can see . . . (*Laughs.*) Anyway, that's all over.

Peter Mmm. Yes.

There is a pause.

Charles I remember your saying that if you got out of *that* one intact you'd make sure there'd never be another.

Peter Did I say that?

Charles Don't you remember?

Peter Well, there have been so many since . . .

Charles You mean now?

Peter Not really, no. Well, one of the editor's secretaries – she's worse than me. She keeps a supply of VD pills in her bag, makes me take them . . . Extremely organised. Oddly enough, I hear she's not a very good secretary.

Charles Where do you do it?

Peter Mmm? (*Slightly shocked.*)

Charles No, I was just curious. Sorry.

Peter No, it's all right. In my office, at lunchtime, or after hours – when she's not going on somewhere more interesting and I don't have to get home for anything.

Charles But isn't that risky?

Peter Not really. I lock the door and leave the key in –

Charles Surely people suspect.

Peter I imagine there are the usual jokes. But as long as they don't reach Hilary – (*Pause.*) The most depressing

456

thing, you know, *the* most depressing thing, is that I used to feel a certain amount of post-coital tristesse. Well, guilt. But these days I can scarcely be bothered to feel shifty when I get home. Extra-marital sex is as overrated as pre-marital sex. And marital sex, come to think of it.

Charles Then why do you have it?

Peter (*sighs*) I don't know. Well, the first time is still quite fun, it's having to go on and on.

Charles Why do you?

Peter From politeness. I mean, one can't just have it off, tip one's hat . . .

Charles But you still love Hilary, don't you?

Peter What?

Charles Hilary.

Peter What?

Charles (*after a long pause*) Love Hilary.

Peter Christ! (*Pause.*) Of course I do. (*Pause.*) There's not a day at the office, when the telephone rings, not a day when at least once – (*pause*) I don't have a spasm of terror, and think: 'Not this time, please let nothing have happened to her this time. Or Jeremy.' You know. I'm frightened for them. I want to die before they do so at least I shan't spend my last years – first me, and then Hilary, and then after a long intermission, Jeremy. That seems only fair except that I know that life doesn't work on fair principles, which are anyway formulated by types like me in Greenwich . . . Who knows? Who knows what . . . I'm frightened for them. (*Pause.*) I know she is for me. (*Pause.*) Christ, that's a marriage, isn't it? (*Pause.*) Bloody hell, of course I love . . . (*There is a pause.*) What do you mean?

Charles gets up, walks restlessly around the room. Peter watches him, then loses interest, concentrates on his drink.

Charles There's something . . . (*Stops.*)

Peter (*not paying attention*) Mmm?

Charles The irony is . . .

He looks at Peter, then turns, opens the drawer of his desk, takes out a bulky and large brown envelope.

Look.

Charles hesitates, then, making up his mind, carries it over to Peter, hands it to him. Cut as if to Peter's face, but instead to:

INT. SHOWERS

In on Bowler's face. He is now dressed and holding a sheet of paper. Boy is standing, turned away from him.

Bowler About me?

Boy That's right. Didn't you recognise yourself? I thought you would as it's so complimentary.

Bowler Well, I can't . . . I've only read it once. (*Little pause, looks down, tries to read it again.*) It's difficult, with you sitting there – Well, you, I mean, you just stick it in my hand –

Boy I'm putting you off again, am I? You can't win at games when I'm watching, you can't read when I'm watching –

Bowler Why don't you stop watching then?

Boy You like being watched.

458

Bowler Rubbish, what bloody rubbish! It's a lousy poem, it's just bloody rubbish!

Boy (*trying to control a shaking voice*) I'm glad I showed it to you. I was sure I'd get an intelligent assessment.

Bowler They're right about you, what they say, you're just a pseudo, really, loping about listening to music and scribbling poems and not doing anything at all.

Boy (*his voice now shaking*) The irony is that I thought you might have a touch of intelligence. The irony is that you're an extremely stupid sort of little person. The irony is I've been wasting my time on you.

Bowler (*shouting*) Then why don't you leave me alone?

Boy (*shouting*) Yes, why don't I?

They stare at each other. Over the end of this scene:

Charles (*shouting*) That's enough, boys. Either play sportingly, or don't play at all. Don't forget, it's only a game.

Cut to:

INT. CHARLES'S STUDY

In on Peter looking down at the envelope in his lap. He picks it up surreptitiously, as if weighing it, also tests its bulk with his thumbs. A general sense of his being aghast. Then looks towards Charles, and from his point of view.

Charles (*leaning out of the window*) Ali darling, do you want me to come down . . .?

Alison, off, in the garden, voice not audible.

Jolly good, thanks, darling.

Straightens from the window, closes it, pauses, staring out, then turns. Looks towards Peter.

I was going through one of those passages that one goes through, you know, feeling a bit desperate, not sure I could go on – (*Gestures.*) Then one day, just after I'd got back from my run I just – sat myself down and began it. I didn't intend it to come out as a full-length novel, I had no idea.

Peter Well, these things happen.

Charles Even now I can scarcely believe I've finished it. Or whether what I've finished is something *there*, you know, created. Or therapy. (*Little pause.*) I expect you'll be able to tell me, no punches pulled. (*Smiles.*)

Peter smiles.

What I do know is that it in a sense saved my life.

Peter Well, that's certainly to its credit. Has anyone else read it?

Charles No.

Peter What does Alison feel about it?

Charles Actually, she hasn't read it either. In fact, I'd better warn you – um, she doesn't even know I've written it. Oh, she knows I've been working on something, of course, but I've rather let her go on thinking that it's the Molière translations, you know, the ones I started just after we came down. (*Pause.*) Actually, I'd rather she didn't know, well, at least just yet. You'll be able to help me there, too. You see, it's about us?

Peter Us?

Charles Well, our marriage. (*Stares at him.*) It's *not*, of course, but there are certain – well, I wouldn't want

460

Alison to think it *was* about us, is perhaps the best way of putting it. There are inevitable similarities – especially between myself and the central chap. There's a chap who's a little like you in it too, only superficially. For one thing, he commits suicide.

Peter Well, there at least he's a little unlike me. If only superficially.

Charles No, no. I meant the other chap.

Peter Oh, the chap a little like you?

Charles Mmm.

Peter Can you tell me why, or would that ruin the suspense?

Charles No, no. As he commits suicide on the first page. And the last.

Peter He does it twice?

Charles No, it's the same suicide. The structure is complex. Circular. But I hope organic. (*Pause.*) He commits suicide because he's unhappy really, that's what it comes to. In his work and his, well, marriage. That's the part of it that Alison might not understand – the difference between autobiography and fiction.

Peter It's frequently muddling.

Charles Well, not for you – you'll know at once – his attitude to the children, for example, his wife's pregnancies – and various things that he does or feels at work –

Peter What work does he do?

Charles He's a teacher. A public school teacher. Not very imaginative that, I know, but in his real self he's so different from myself –

Peter Anyway, *your* real self.

Charles Exactly. Yes. Look – there is *one* thing – one section that I would like to clarify – where something's said, explicitly said, about his feeling for one of the boys. His sense of torture, and the way in which the word 'desire' is used – (*Painful pause.*) Well, that *is* – (*Hesitates.*) You'll understand. You'll understand. And also about friendship – there's a passage, a meditation – he thinks about his most important relationship and the tone of the passage is – well, intended to be – acerbic.

Peter (*after a pause*) Don't worry, I'll read it as a novel.

Charles I know. But I can't help feeling a little treacherous. In the sense that you meant years ago, when you first started being, mm, unfaithful – you said that for you the real treachery wasn't what you did with another woman, it was what you said to her about your wife.

Peter Did I say that?

Charles Anyway that's the sense in which I feel treacherous. Towards Alison. As if I had betrayed a deep confidence –

Peter On that analogy, you haven't, yet. Not until I've read it – or somebody else has. Perhaps you ought to reconsider letting me see it.

Charles No, no. You must read it.

Peter But only if you're sure –

Charles The treachery is finding it out. I can't go back on that. The truth is that it's all there. It's no good my fooling myself or trying to fool you, of all people. You'll know. It's all there.

Peter (*after a pause*) Yes, well, it usually is. (*Smiles.*)

Charles How do you mean?

Peter In a first novel.

Charles If it hadn't been for you, I wouldn't have written it. You're the one –

Bring them both in camera, drawing back slightly, looking towards each other.

To whom I've always privately addressed my most private feelings. Some friendships endure as what they were even though they *are*. No longer. What they were. Isn't that true? Isn't it the same for you?

Hold on the two of them, sitting in silence, for as long as possible. Then one beat longer than that, as fade into:

INT. SHOWERS

Boy is sitting staring straight ahead. Bowler is sitting opposite, staring down. He looks at Boy.

Bowler Are you all right?

Boy remains immobile, staring blankly. Bowler gets up, goes over to him slowly, apprehensively, hesitates, sits down beside him, clears his throat.

Are you?

They sit in misery. Fade to:

INT. CHARLES'S STUDY

As before. Peter suddenly coughs, clears his throat.

Peter I'm sorry.

Charles Why?

Peter Well, I hadn't realised you were un— well, unhappy.

Charles Oh, I'm sure I'm not. Any more than anybody else, anyway. I'd be far more unhappy if Alison found out – well, aren't *you* unhappy?

Peter Mmm, well –

He coughs slightly and fade to:

INT. SHOWERS

The boys as before.

Bowler (*after a pause, in a mutter*) Well, liking me so much.

Boy (*very low*) Because you've stopped liking me?

Bowler (*in a mutter*) No, well – it's not that, it's – (*Shrugs.*)

Boy You don't like me any more.

Bowler (*embarrassed*) Yes, I do.

Boy How do you know I like you?

Bowler Well, if you don't – I mean –

Boy Why don't you go?

Bowler What will you do?

Boy Stay here.

Bowler What for?

Boy doesn't answer.

Well, for how long?

Boy Until I get up.

Bowler The Refec bell's gone. (*Pause.*) We're still on Fag. (*Pause.*) Come on! (*Pause.*) We better go.

Boy continues to sit.

Well – Well, I'm jolly well –

Gets up, stands indecisively.

Boy You're very stupid.

Bowler, still indecisive, takes Boy's arm, tries to pull Boy up. Boy resists passively, until he's hauled up, then begins to resist violently, pushing Bowler away, in a sudden, unexpected burst of violence. They stand staring at each other. Sounds off, of a door opening and closing. They swing their heads in alarm, left and cut to:

INT. CHARLES'S STUDY

Alison is standing at the door, Nindy in her arms.

Peter Ah, is she? I'll be right down. (*Getting up.*)

Alison I'll dig Jeremy out of the cellar.

Charles Aren't you staying for tea?

Alison (*who has turned away, turns back, briefly*) It's rather a long drive, Hilary feels.

Charles Oh. (*Getting up.*)

Alison goes off, as Peter drains off the rest of his drink, stubs out his cigarette

We were just beginning to talk. Naturally.

Peter It is a long drive and Jeremy gets tired –

*He moves towards the door. Charles picks up the
envelope, hands it to Peter, who has left it on the
floor.*

Ah!

*Peter takes it, slips it under his arm, Charles holds the
door open for him and, as he passes, suddenly puts his
hand on Peter's arm. Peter turns, looks at him. Charles
smiles. Peter smiles back, slightly awkwardly. They go
out, leaving the door open, and fade the open door
into:*

INT. HOUSEMASTER'S STUDY

*A light, airy, and civilised place. Fading in on the open
door, seen from Housemaster's point of view from his
desk. He is not yet seen, nor his room, just the open
door, through which Bowler and Boy enter, self-
consciously. They stand in the room, Housemaster comes
into camera, but his face out of camera, passes the two
boys, closes the door, turns, passes back. Sits down. His
face coming into camera as he does so. Cut as if to the
two boys, come in on:*

INT. CHARLES'S HALL

*Front door open. Peter and Charles standing at it. From
behind, up the stairs, the cries of children, sound of
bathwater running, Alison's voice.*

Alison *(off)* Don't turn on the tap! Leave the taps alone!

Peter I'll give you a ring –

Off, sound of car honking.

Ah, there they are – Well, I'll give you a ring.

Charles (*low*) At the school.

Peter Right.

Alison comes down, stands beside Charles as Peter moves outside.

Alison I was going to fix something up with Hilary, tell her I'll give her a ring.

Peter Right, and thanks for a lovely –

Gestures. He doesn't have the envelope in his hand.

Alison No, it was lovely –

Charles Yes.

Peter Well –

Stay on Charles and Alison staring out from the hall, saluting as off, the sound of the car honking farewells. The door closes. Cut back into the hall. Alison is going up the stairs, Charles is standing in the hall, looks down, sees in the pram the envelope. Come in on his face as he picks it up.

Alison He's certainly putting it on, isn't he?

Charles What? Who?

Alison Surely you noticed? His face is quite –

A ring at the doorbell. Charles opens the door on Peter.

Peter Christ, I nearly forgot, I thought I had it in my hand. I put it –

Looks vaguely around. Charles holds it out to him.

Alison (*over*) Forgotten something?

Peter No, got it, thanks. Bye. Bye. (*The second to Charles.*)

467

Charles closes the door.

Alison (*over*) What was it?

Charles Oh just some cigarettes or something –

Alison (*over*) Can you check in the bathroom, I'm doing Ophelia. They're meant to be washing their hands but they're mucking about with the bath taps –

Charles, during this, goes up the stairs, heavily, rather tired. Camera stays with him as he opens bathroom door, then cut to his face, as if from within the bathroom, from which splashes and shouts have been coming. Just for a second an expression of collapse, then a smile, and in pleasantly jocular tones:

Charles What do you boys think you're doing? You're supposed to be washing your hands.

Cut instantly to:

INT. HOUSEMASTER'S STUDY

In on his face, friendly and slightly satirical.

Housemaster . . . all over the school. Mr Jameson finds you in the Music Room when you should be fagging at Refec, M. Fouce wonders why you always sit in the back of the class and whisper passionately over Baudelaire, he thinks, when you ought to be translating *Le Malade Imaginaire,* and Mr James stumbles across you in Change, when you should be fagging in Refec. Mmm?

Bowler *and* **Boy** (*simultaneously, after a pause*) Sir.

Housemaster How's your chest?

Boy I've still got asthma a bit, sir.

Housemaster You're still chitted for all games then?

468

Boy Sir.

Housemaster How did the Shield match go?

Bowler Oh – oh, all right, sir.

Housemaster You won then?

Bowler No, sir.

Housemaster Really. What they call in sporting circles a bit of an upset?

Bowler (*stammeringly*) Not really, sir, I mean I didn't mind too much . . .

Housemaster Mmmm.

He looks at Bowler. See Housemaster's face from Bowler's point of view. Smiles.

Well, I've really got nothing more to say to you than this. If you're going to be caught in the wrong places at the wrong times, could you contrive to do so separately?

Bowler Sir.

Boy Sir. But it's all right to be in the Music Room together at the right time, and other places at the right time?

Housemaster (*after a short pause*) There is no school regulation to prevent boys from being friends. As you're in the same house and the same form there isn't even convention to hold you back. (*Pause.*) I'd like a word with each of you privately, if I may. Why don't you run along to Matron and get your next week's chit, and then come back . . .

Boy Sir.

Boy turns, goes out, as he closes the door, see from his point of view Housemaster and Bowler, then cut to Housemaster's face, as behind, sound of door closing.

Housemaster You *are* friends, are you?

Bowler (*after a pause*) Sir.

Housemaster What sort of friends are you?

Cut to his face, looking towards Bowler, solicitously, then cut as if to Bowler, and come in on:

INT. CAR

Hilary driving, Jeremy strapped in behind, Peter beside Hilary, leaning back, eyes closed, cigarette between lips. In on his face:

Peter I suppose so. But he's, let's face it, one of those friends –

Lets the sentence trail away.

Hilary I wish you'd finish that sentence.

Peter Oh, just that one can't bear seeing.

Hilary Then why do we go on seeing them?

Peter We scarcely do any more. Besides, *you* accepted. (*Pause.*) I was prepared for a ghastly day –

Hilary Very well prepared, with your bottles of wine and cigarettes in every pocket –

Peter But not sufficiently prepared for this? (*Beats the envelope with his hand.*) Christ, a bloody novel!

Hilary You might like it.

Peter Yes. (*Gives a half-laugh.*) That'd be a blow.

Hilary To whom?

Peter To me, of course. He had his purple passage at school, he doesn't deserve another go now I've settled him down as a successful failure.

Hilary What an appalling thing to say. (*Pause.*) Besides, you used to claim he was very talented – in those days when you wanted to make your friends sound glamorous and mysterious. At least to me.

Peter That was a long time ago, and even then I was going a long way back. When it was assumed we'd both of us go a long way.

Hilary (*after a pause*) Well then, let's hope it's terrible. You can still make appropriate noises.

Peter What are the appropriate noises for not wanting to publish it?

Hilary Oh. Is that what he's after? (*Looks at Peter.*) You poor old sod.

   Cut to:

INT. HOUSEMASTER'S STUDY

Bowler is now sitting in a chair. Housemaster on the edge of the desk, talking in a low, confidential voice.

Housemaster . . . after all be a reason for choosing him among so many. You see, your interests are very different, or so it seems to an uninvolved eye. Aren't they?

Bowler Sir.

Housemaster I mean no reflection on your academic standing, you work as hard as can be expected from someone with so many obligations, in the squash courts, the cricket fields – I gather you've developed an off-spin of some consequence. (*Smiles.*) So I'm fairly confident that your general all-roundedness will stand you in some stead when you come to think between Oxford and

Cambridge. All I mean is that I shouldn't have thought it was in the general run of your pursuits to listen to Berg or even Mozart when you should be fagging in Refec.

Bowler No, sir.

Housemaster But I'm not suggesting you give him up or anything so extreme. Just that you should reflect that too much too intense friendship can lead to too many complications for a chap who wants an uncluttered life. (*Pause.*) What do you say to that?

Pause, hold on his face then cut to:

INT. NINDY'S BEDROOM

Straight in on Alison's face.

Alison . . . that I've got a perfect right to be pregnant.

Charles (*who is scrabbling around in a drawer*) Of course you have.

Alison (*putting Nindy down on the pot*) She patronises me.

Charles I don't think she means to.

Alison Because she can't help it? Or because I make it unavoidable?

Charles I can't find any with special caps on.

Alison There's a blue tin. (*To Nindy.*) How are you doing, darling? That boy of theirs is a sly little brute.

Charles Really? In what way?

Alison He's a mixer. He likes to stir things up – quite unnatural sophistication – piggy little eyes –

Charles Darling, he's only six.

Alison (*after a pause*) If he doesn't look out, he's going to have a heart attack.

Charles At six?

Alison You know perfectly well. He boozed all through the day.

Nindy on pot, sound of her peeing.

Oh, clever girl! Look, Daddy, a wee-wee for you.

She claps. Charles claps. Alison lifts Nindy off the pot, holds out her hand for the tin with the blue top, which she receives from Charles, spreads Nindy on the bed.

Can you honestly say that you still have anything in common?

Cut as if to Charles's face, but come in, instead, on:

INT. HOUSEMASTER'S STUDY

On Boy's face. He is sitting, as Bowler was.

Boy Sir.

Housemaster Unless, that is, you've undertaken to supplement his education with some courses of your own.

Boy (*after a pause*) Sir?

Housemaster Those subjects, that is, in which you have a natural advantage.

Boy says nothing.

Is that what you're doing? (*Smiling.*)

Boy We like talking about the same things, that's all.

Housemaster Really? Cricket, squash, athletics – you have an interest?

Boy I like watching.

Master But only when he's playing. No doubt. (*Smiles.*) He listens to you on Baudelaire because it's you he's interested in, not Baudelaire. What do you think this is all about?

Boy I don't know, sir.

Housemaster Well, I'm asking you to be careful, that's all.

Boy Sir. (*Little pause.*) What of, sir?

Housemaster Of yourself, and of your feelings. It's hard for you, I know, in that your health excludes you from a great deal of companionship, although I suspect you don't much regret that. You're very highly thought of, you know, by most of us – even if we find you a little frightening. I for one wouldn't dream of dictating the proper lines for friendship, there aren't any. But do remember, won't you, that your capacity for affection – (*hesitates*) deserves various, mm, expressions. (*Pause.*) I'm not saying anything at all, it's sheer nonsense. (*Pause.*) You must find your own way. Nobody wishes you any harm. Please believe that. Do you?

> *See Housemaster from Boy's point of view. Cut as if to Boy, and in fact go to:*

INT. PETER'S STUDY

He is lighting a cigarette. A suggestion of desperation; props his hand under his chin, sits smoking.

INT. CHARLES'S STUDY

He is sitting, staring ahead. A suggestion of despair.

INT. SCHOOL CHAPEL

Bowler's face, as over the service (prayer). And cut to Boy's face, his eyes moving purposefully, as if looking for Bowler. And cut to:

INT. PETER'S STUDY

Come in on him coughing slightly, the cough goes on and on, gets out of control. He stubs out his cigarette fiercely, sits shaken.

Peter Christ!

Peter gets up, hands not visible but sound of his pouring from a bottle to a glass. He sits down, coughs once or twice to clear his throat, then sits staring ahead.

INT. MUSIC ROOM

Light on. Boy is staring out of window.

EXT. MUSIC-ROOM WINDOW

From Bowler's point of view. Boy's face visible but indistinct. Cut to Bowler's face, undecided, and cut to:

INT.

Very brief. Charles staring ahead.

INT.

Very brief. Peter staring ahead. This in fact from Hilary's point of view, although not yet established.

Hilary (*over*) Will you be long?

Peter (*turns*) No, I won't be long.

Hilary Jeremy's sound asleep. He's exhausted, poor child. Not a peep out of him.

Peter Well, I won't be long.

Hilary Thank you. What's it like?

Peter It's bloody handwritten, that's what it's like.

Hilary takes in the ashtray, which has a number of butts in it. Then the glass.

Hilary Another drink? (*Pause.*) You're smoking too much.

Peter Ah, that explains it.

Hilary What?

Peter Why I've got two hundred and fifty pages of handwritten novel to get through.

Hilary Well, not tonight, I hope.

Peter Some of it tonight.

Hilary Why, if you're tired?

Peter sighs. Hilary looks at him, turns, goes out. Peter stares at the empty door a moment, lights another cigarette. Hilary reappears at the door.

Look, I didn't ask to spend the day with your old school friend and his dull wife, and I didn't fill you full of wine all day to help you get through it, and I'm not pouring Scotch down your throat to help you get over it. I don't know what's the matter with you, but I've had enough of everything today, including you.

Peter (*with insulting courtesy*) Have you?

Hilary glares at him, slams the door. Hilary, off, calls out something.

Peter (*sits still for a moment, then bellows*) What?

Hilary (*reopens the door, glares at him*) Would you kindly remember that Jeremy is asleep?

INT. CHARLES'S STUDY

In on his face, briefly. Move back, to take in Alison, in her nightgown, holding two mugs.

Alison But you are, I can tell.

Charles No, contemplative.

Alison Then what are you contemplating?

Charles I'm not sure. I don't think I'd fixed on a subject.

Alison (*looks at him, troubled*) I wasn't trying to get at him, you know? (*Pause.*) Yes, I was.

Charles I've never minded your not liking him.

Alison You mustn't. As long as you go on liking him –

Charles Oh, I don't know. Old friends are like old habits. There comes a point when it doesn't matter any more whether you like them, they're what you've got.

Alison Is the same true of families?

Charles Well, I don't keep adding to my circle of friends. But with my family, on the other hand – (*Smiles.*)

Alison (*over*) I love you.

Stay on Charles's face, smiling and cut to:

INT. MUSIC ROOM

Boy bent over the gramophone. Then withdraw to take in Bowler, hands in pockets, turned away.

Bowler (*formally*) I can only stay for a little bit.

Boy (*formally*) I can't stay long either.

Cut to:

INT. PETER'S BEDROOM

Hilary lying asleep. On her face, then Peter bends into camera, kisses her on the forehead, his face withdraws. Hilary's eyes open slightly, slight smile.

INT. CHARLES'S BEDROOM

On his face, then cut to Alison, head on pillow, looking troubled. Charles puts out his hand, touches a lock of her hair, then moves out of camera. Alison smiles. It is an unhappy smile. Over, Mozart, and fade into:

INT. MUSIC ROOM

As Mozart continues from previous scene, Boy and Bowler sitting, listening. And over this:
    Credits.

SIMPLY DISCONNECTED

For Sarah

Simply Disconnected was first performed at the Minerva Theatre, Chichester, on 10 May 1996. The cast was as follows:

Simon Hench Alan Bates
Greg John Michie
Stephen Charles Kay
Jeff Gawn Grainger
Gwendoline Rosemary Martin
Julian Wood Benedick Bates
Mandy Nicola Duffett

Director Richard Wilson
Designer Julian McGowan
Lighting Designer Mick Hughes
Sound Designer Tom Lishman

Characters

Simon Hench
Greg
Stephen
Jeff
Gwendoline
Julian Wood
Mandy

Act One

*Simon Hench's country house, down there – wherever
that is. There are French windows stage right. A door
to kitchen upstage right. A door off to hall, stage left.
A drinks table, stage right. The room is comfortably
furnished but slightly neglected. There is a CD apparatus.
Slightly wilting flowers in a vase. Books on bookshelves,
with an unread look to them. There is also a neat desk
in a corner, a telephone on it. Several armchairs, as well
as a straight-backed chair at the desk.*

*Simon is sitting stiffly in a corner of the sofa, arms
folded. On the CD equipment, a church choir, amateurish
and not expertly recorded, is playing. Simon's concentration
is absolute, as if waiting for a particular passage. Nods
his head, smiles occasionally.*

*There is a screech of tyres off, car door slamming.
Greg, in his late twenties/early thirties, enters through
the French windows. He is wearing jeans, open-necked
checked shirt, trainers. Slightly ill-kempt.*

Greg The missus here?

Simon She was, I think. Heard her hoovering upstairs
not long ago. She must have gone.

Greg She's not at home. And I didn't see her on the
road. Oh, there she is. (*As duet begins on CD.*) And
there's your missus too.

Simon (*gets up, goes to equipment*) She has a lovely
voice. Yours, I mean.

Greg Yours isn't bad. Flatter than mine, isn't she? Not
that I'm a judge.

Simon (*turns off CD*) Together they make a beautiful sound. Well matched.

Greg Well, where is she, my Mandy? I can't keep up with her. Even though she swore she'd be up here, doing your housework.

Simon (*nodding to door, left*) Perhaps she went out through the front while you were coming in by the back. You do have a habit of missing each other, I've noticed. Perhaps she's popped down to Mrs Camboy's for some shopping.

Greg Cambad's. It's Mrs Cambad's. Gertie Cambad's. All this time – what, ten years down here, and you still can't get the name of the only shop right. (*Shakes his head.*)

Simon No, it's a problem I've always had. Even in my prime. With those closest to me. Very offensive, I'm told.

Greg What's the problem?

Simon One of identification, I assume.

Greg Well, your wife got the hang of us all in a few days. I remember as a boy, and she'd only been here for a few days, and she came up to me and asked, dunno what she asked, but she asked something. And remembered the answer, I'll bet.

Simon Well, I wish I'd got the hang of us. And you in particular, Greg. But nothing I can do about it at this stage of life, is there? So why don't you nip down to Mrs Camelwell's, -boy's, -bad's –

Greg Why? She'll come down the field, I'll go up the road, or we'll do it the other way round, just as you said, and there we'll be, missing each other again. Just as you said. Back where we started.

Simon Not quite. You'll be there and she'll be here. Different places.

Greg Best if I wait around until she comes back. That all right by you? (*Sits down impatiently.*)

Simon (*looks towards CD*) I was planning to go on listening to the choir. I tend to do that, at this hour, on a Sunday.

Greg Go ahead. I like it. Perhaps she's gone down to get our supper and a bottle for me. For the football later. Or she's – she's – (*jogs his leg*) doing something. (*Little pause.*) Go ahead. Don't mind me. But I can't help worrying. Worrying and fretting when she vanishes like this. And it always falls on me. The responsibility. And here I am, behind with the rent again. With all kinds of debts I probably don't even know about or can't remember.

Simon Ah, yes. The five hundred pounds, for instance. Which you borrowed to go to Antwerp. For a football match, wasn't it?

Greg It was Amsterdam. A cup final. I had to go.

Simon And the fine for hooliganism. And the ticket back again. Wasn't it five hundred?

Greg Something like that. That's what I mean. Debts just piling up all over the place. So where she is, where is she, is all I can think about, what's money compared to her safety – ah! (*In relief, as sound of car drawing up.*) You got a visitor, from the sound of it.

Car door slams, sound of feet on gravel.

I'll be on my way. Leave you to it.

Stephen enters through front, visibly shaken.

Stephen Simon, there you are!

Simon Stephen, you're here. Why? Oh, this is Greg, Stephen. Stephen, my brother Greg. I mean, my brother Stephen.

Stephen Yes, hello, hello, can I use your phone please? I want the police.

Simon (*gestures to it*) Help yourself.

Stephen (*picks it up, begins to dial*) There's no dialling tone.

Simon No. That's right. I've had it disconnected.

> *Stephen suddenly fixes Greg with a stare, puts down telephone.*

Stephen I believe we've already met.

Greg What? Where?

Stephen About a mile down the road. You drove me off it. That's why I want the police.

Greg I've never seen you before. Never. To my knowledge.

Stephen You came out of a side road. Completely ignored the stop sign. Cut right across my bonnet.

Greg (*bewildered*) Your bonnet?

Stephen Yes. My bonnet. At about seventy miles per hour, I clocked it at. If I'd been a fraction further on I'd be a dead man now. So would you. I was driving our Dormobile. A sixties Dormobile. Remember?

Greg A Dormobile from the sixties? (*Shakes his head.*) Didn't see anything like that. Can't have been me. (*Little pause.*) No way.

Stephen It was you all right. I'll never forget that face of yours. Grinning through the window. Shaking your fist. Were you drunk? Or what? (*To Simon.*) Haven't you got a phone that works? This is a police matter. It was *your* car. That Daimler of yours. Black. Do you let him drive it?

Simon He's my chauffeur, it's true. Not that I go anywhere –

Stephen Supposing I'd been a mother. In a car full of children. Suppose that, will you? And supposing you'd come across me in my other hat!

Greg (*bewildered*) Other hat?

Stephen I'm a magistrate. In North London. If you'd come before me I'd have thrown the book at you. Any magistrate would.

Greg Well, I don't know. Our lot down here are pretty fair.

Stephen What do you mean? What the – the – do you mean?

Simon I think what Greg means is that down here he wouldn't come before a magistrate who'd be his one and only witness before throwing the book at the man he'd both accused and was trying. As well as sentencing. He'd get a colleague to do it for him. I think that's all Greg means.

Greg Yes, that's what I mean. Without having the words to say it. Now I'd better go looking for my Mandy. She's probably stopped off at the pub in case I'm there. (*To Stephen.*) Sorry about you and this Dormobile.

> *He hurries out. There is a pause.*
> *Sound of Greg screeching off.*

Stephen Listen to him! Just listen to him! It's your car all right! Is he really the best you can do for a chauffeur, careless and homicidal – especially when you don't even need a chauffeur, you say.

Simon He happens to be living with Mandy. The girl who does my housework. So I had to find something for him to do.

Stephen Did you? Why?

Simon So that I could pay him.

Stephen Why? Why do you want to pay him, if all he does is drive about in a car you don't use, nearly killing people? Why, Simon?

Simon Because if I didn't pay him I wouldn't have been able to employ her. And Beth liked her. Took her on to dust, wash the floors, make the bed – whatever she does, when she's here.

Stephen When she's here! Another of your parasites, is she? Like that Dave you had lodging in your house in London years ago, the poly student who never sat a single exam, then moved his girlfriend in with you. And then she moved her ex-boyfriend in. Before you knew it your house was virtually taken over by layabouts. How Beth put up with it –! Well, I must say, speaking as one who's sick to death of the Daves and the Gregs and – and what's-her-name –

Simon Mandy, her name is. She means a lot to me. I need her.

Stephen And overpay her. And employ her husband. How would you feel if he – because of your odd – odd – he caused a death on the road?

Simon My odd what, Stephen?

Stephen Your odd tolerance, Simon. That you seem to have been born with. I was thinking about it on the way down here. Remembering the moment – four years ago, wasn't it? – when you told me that Beth had finally – finally – left. How calm, how relaxed you were.

Simon Left? Beth?

Stephen Beth. Yes. When she left.

Simon She didn't 'leave', Stephen. She died of a heart attack. In the middle of singing her duet. Up in the church. And I don't know how I seemed when I announced the fact. To you and others. But I trust I was seemly.

Stephen Oh, yes. You're always seemly. Whatever. Seemly and tolerant. Always.

Simon Surely you haven't driven all the way down here to have a row with me about my seemliness and tolerance. How's – how's –?

Stephen Teresa.

Simon Everything all right at home?

Stephen Teresa's fine, thank you. Revelling in the grandchildren. The children are prospering too – Tom, Harry and Henrietta – in case you've forgotten. Henrietta's just served up another one for Teresa to babysit –

Simon And you yourself? Fiddle-fit, as you used to say? You certainly look fiddle-fit.

Stephen Yes, fiddle-fit, Simon, thanks. (*Little pause.*) A few problems at school, but I think they'll be sorted out in due course. Any minute now, in fact. Does it occur to you that there's another oddness? Asking how my family is, how I am, after all this time? I've written to you and written to you, made numerous phone calls to your disconnected telephone, and I haven't received as much as a card or a phone call back.

Simon But here you are. Wonderfully are.

Stephen Thanks to Teresa. She finally said, 'Why not go down and see him? Just turn up!' Why did you cut off your phone?

Simon I didn't want to answer it.

Stephen Or answer my letters?

Simon I didn't open them.

Stephen Because of Beth? Is that why you've cut yourself off?

Simon What problems at school? That you think you've sorted out?

Stephen Oh, nothing. Nothing really. I was accused of abusing one of the boys. That's all.

Simon What sort of abuse?

Stephen Sexual abuse, naturally, these days. But there's nothing to it. If you'd had a connected phone or opened my letters, you'd know all about it. A trivial incident. Trivial. You know what really happened to you, Simon? That you can't face? Beth's miscarriage. Her baby by another man –

Simon Steve. As you're here, tell me about it. What are the facts? As that's why you're really here.

Stephen There aren't any facts. It's all gossip, speculation – the result of a thirteen-year-old's mischief-making. Toby. His name is Toby. Toby Winch.

Simon And what mischief did he make, this Toby Wench?

Stephen Winch. Winch. Not Wench. Winch. He reported me for putting my hand on his bottom. And for fondling him. What I can't bear is that he was one of my best students. The best I've ever had. I enjoyed, yes, enjoyed

and admired his essays. His flights of fantasy were
unusual. Exceptional. He has genius. That's my view.
In spite of everything he's brought on me. Genius. As a
publisher, an ex-publisher, you'd have appreciated him.

Simon As an ex-publisher, possibly. What happened
between you and young – young – thirteen-year-old –?

Stephen He won the Worthington.

Simon Really? Did he? And what is it? The Worthington?

Stephen It's the prize for the best essay of the year. The
most prized prize in the school. He'd beaten boys from
higher forms. Seventeen-year-olds even. I was so thrilled
for him. And for myself, I admit. After all, I considered
him my prodigy.

Simon Prodigy?

Stephen Yes, yes, not to boast, but I've always singled
him out for special attention.

Simon Yes. But you mean protégé, don't you?

Stephen What did I say?

Simon Prodigy. Or progeny. I can't remember which. But
it wasn't protégé.

Stephen What does it matter, what does it matter –
progeny, prodigy, protégé? But that's you again, you all
over, Simon, interrupting with an irrelevant question –
do you want to hear my story, or don't you?

Simon Of course I do.

Stephen Where was I?

There is a pause.

Simon Your satisfaction at his winning the – (*forgets
name*) most prized prize in the school.

493

Stephen When I heard the news I let out a whoop of well, sheer joy. And naturally I went off to find him. Eventually I turned him up. In the changing room. Getting ready for the Junior Colts match. Such a fine young cricketer. A natural. Left-handed. He already had his box on when he saw me. Getting into his flannels. He gave me a grin – quite unembarrassed – triumphant, in fact. I put my arms around him. Of course I did. Said a few words. Very few.

Simon What words did you say? However few?

Stephen Oh, I don't know. Nothing you wouldn't expect under the circumstances – 'Wonderful, wonderful, you wonderful boy!' – that kind of thing. Gave him a pat – an admiring pat – on the bottom. And left. That was the whole thing. The whole incident.

Simon Were there any witnesses?

Stephen Only the other boys playing cricket. The two teams.

Simon So that would be – minus the star witness himself – twenty-one other witnesses. Plus the two twelfth men. The scorers –

Stephen What does it matter who saw me? I'm not ashamed of my emotions. Never have been. I've been embracing boys and patting their rumps since I started as a Junior Master for over – what is it? Heavens, yes – thirty years ago. And for nearly fifteen of those years I've been Assistant Headmaster. I've seen young man after young man come into the headmastership over my head. And now a young woman. That's the latest trend. A woman as a headmaster. She's in her early thirties, full of the latest sociological pitter-patter, but a witch-hunter at heart. Yes. A witch-hunter. And a fascist. That's what she is, at heart. But what I can't forgive, forget, is that

494

little Toby told his parents, a morally fashionably young couple, just what you'd expect these days, and they went to Helena –

Simon That's your headmaster? Helena?

Stephen – who went to the Board of Governors. Who went all over the place. Everywhere. I can't bear to go into it. But the governors are taking it seriously. And why, Simon? I'll tell you why, Simon. So that they can cut down on my pension. Possibly deprive me of it altogether. So how will I end up? Without a job, a pension, or even a home – our house belongs to the school, remember? No, I'll end up in the filthy media – those newspapers, even the so-called respectable ones like *The Times* – we won't be able to get away from it, not Teresa, not Tom, not Harry, poor little Henrietta, and their children, my grandchildren. My face, my name, with those words they're so fond of these days – 'shamed', 'disgraced' assistant headmaster of famous public school! My whole working life, thirty years as Assistant Head-master, twelve as a practising magistrate – ending in nationwide humiliation. 'Shamed', 'disgraced', homeless, penniless. And all because Toby, Toby of all my best boys – my very best boy –

Simon Have they reached their verdict yet? The governors? In a press-release sort of way?

Stephen They convened an hour before I set off to come down here.

Simon Ah.

Stephen 'Ah'! What do you mean, 'ah'?

Simon Only that there's nothing you can do. Either of us can do. (*Little pause.*) The die is cast. Your fate is sealed. That's all I meant by 'Ah!'

Stephen And that's what you'll say at the end of it all, is it? Homeless, penniless, disgraced, shamed. A universal laughing stock. That's how you'll sum up your brother's life. With an 'Ah! Ah!'

Simon I could say, 'Woe! Woe!' But whether 'Woe!' or 'Ah!' there's nothing we can do. The verdict will be the verdict. But as you're down here, who'll receive the news?

Stephen Teresa. One of the boys. Henrietta. Probably Teresa. I hope to God somebody's around to support her. I should phone, shouldn't I? To find out. What a coward I am! I've got to phone. (*Goes to telephone.*)

Simon It doesn't work, remember?

Stephen Oh, that's right. I'll stop at a station then. The first station –

Sound of car drawing up. Feet crunching across gravel.

Jeff (*off*) Simon – Simon are you there? Is this you?

Simon I think so, yes.

Jeff enters.

Jeff It *is* you. Tracked you down at last. I bring you greetings from the world you abandoned.

Goes to Simon, embraces him.

Years ago. Years and years. Christ, a lifetime it seems. How are you? How are you, how are you? (*Shaking him.*)

Simon Oh, I'm very, really – all things considered. You've met my brother, Stephen, haven't you? Stephen, you've met Jeff, I think. Jeff Golding. One of my oldest –

Jeff Oldest. And dearest. (*Takes in Stephen.*) Oh, yes. The school pederast. How do you do again? (*To Simon.*)

I've brought Gwendoline along. Never travel without her these days. She's whipped back to a garden shop she spotted down the road. Shouldn't be long as she's taken the car. She's dying to see you.

Stephen What – what did you call me?

Jeff Mmm?

Stephen You called me 'the school pederast'.

Jeff Isn't that how you introduced yourself, the first time we met? As the school pederast. At – at Amplebums or somewhere, you taught at, wasn't it?

Stephen Sides! Amplesides! Introduced myself – introduced myself as the school – the school – what the hell do you mean?

Jeff Well, nothing insulting, I promise. (*Looks towards Simon.*) You were there, weren't you, Simon? (*To Stephen.*) Of course you were, why else would we have met? It was merely banter. A bit of banter. As I recall. You – let me think – you told me what you did, and I made some some – this was back in the – what? late sixties, early seventies – some smart-arsed remark about public schools and homosexuality, and you took it up – one thing led to another – I really don't know – but at our next meeting, that's it, our next and last meeting, you revived the whole thing by sarcastically introducing yourself, reminding me of our one previous meeting, you see, as 'the school pederast'. I've always remembered it. Don't know why. Part of the woof and weave, whatever the phrase is, the travesty – no, no, *tapestry* of human life. Human English life, anyway. Eh, Simon? In the middle classes, at least. As we were then. Twenty-five or so years ago.

Stephen So – so – you take it back then, do you?

Jeff Well, I can't take it back really, can I? As I never meant it in the first place. (*Looks at Simon in incredulity.*) I don't go around insulting people I don't give a damn about, you know. Not any more, anyway.

Simon Well then, that's all right, isn't it, Steve. An old account accounted for.

Stephen Yes, yes. Apology accepted. All forgotten and – (*gestures*) congratulations, by the way. On your many successes since then. Teresa's a great fan. And my children. And even my grandchildren. Great fans.

Jeff Thank you. Thank you and thank them on my behalf. But doesn't it take you back. Just think. There I was, a half-baked flop of a literary reviewer sneering away at public schools as anachronisms. Except as nests for perverts. And now there you are, here you are – or are you still at Ample – Ample – (*Gestures.*)

Stephen Sides. Sides. Yes, I am.

Jeff Good for you. You stuck it out, and you've turned out to be absolutely right. Your lot are right back in the mainstream, politically and socially. Although I imagine the rules and codes, and so forth, are slightly different. Given today's moral climate. Which is strictly for imbeciles.

Stephen I couldn't agree more. For imbeciles. Strictly for imbeciles, our moral climate. But what can we do but change with the times. Adapt, adapt – that's our way. Always has been.

Jeff If I'd had a child I'd have sent him to you. Count on it.

Stephen Really? To Amplesides?

Jeff Well, not Amplesides because I've never really heard of it. But certainly Eton. Somewhere like that.

Stephen At Amplesides we pride ourselves on being superior in many respects – even to Eton – but I won't sell what doesn't need selling. Especially as you haven't got a son to sell it to. (*Laughs falsely.*) But I really must be on my way, Si. Long drive back. And a phone call to make. Above all, that phone call to make.

Simon I'm so sorry, mine has stopped functioning.

Jeff Yes, the number of times I've tried to get through to you – (*To Stephen.*) I've got a mobile, if that's any use? (*Taking it out of pocket.*)

Stephen No. No, thanks. I'm not quite ready yet to make the necessary – necessary contact. Well, nice to see you again. Everybody at home will be thrilled to hear that we've met again. Si, we'll be – be – (*Goes out.*)

Jeff wags mobile in farewell as he punches buttons on it.

Jeff Ah, hello darling, there you are, where are you? (*Listens.*) Blooming. Completely and utterly blooming, from the look of him, aren't you, Simon? Yes, yes, just like the flowers in your arms. Now hurry along and join us, bringing your own bloomers with you, of course. (*Listens, laughs filthily.*) Enough said.

Turns off mobile, stands beaming at Simon.

She's on her way. Here in a minute.

Simon Good. Great. (*Gropes.*) Grand! But what about a drink?

Jeff Oh, no thanks. We don't touch the stuff any more. Though it's better if you don't offer her one.

Simon Right. But what are you doing down here, you and – and your Gwynith?

Jeff Gwendoline. Her name's Gwendoline.

Simon Ah! So you didn't marry your Welsh one?

Jeff What Welsh one?

Simon The Welsh one called Gwynith.

Jeff I've never in my life known a girl called Gwynith. And I'd never have dealings with a Welsh girl, whatever she looked like, think I'm mad?

Simon Sorry.

Jeff Don't be. I'm glad you've maintained your mastery of names. It's reassuring. It means you're still you.

Simon Thank you. And thank you for coming all the way down here to see me –

Jeff Well, to be honest, we haven't, quite. We were just passing through, the name of the village struck a chord, I asked about you at the pub – and here I am. Though actually, we're on our way to Plymouth. To do a book signing tomorrow morning.

Simon You've written a book then at last. That's marvellous, Jeff.

Jeff A book! I've written five of the buggers. No, six, counting this one. Don't you have a clue who I am these days, Simon? You heard your brother, didn't any of it register? I'm a best-seller. A household name. That's me.

Simon Well, I've been so out of touch down here, you see.

Jeff But I'm published by you! Don't you follow what goes on in your own old firm? Christ, your name is still attached. Huckle and Hench. If you took some shares when you sold out, I'll have made you a small fortune. While making myself a huge one.

Simon Well, thank you. What sort of books are they?

Jeff Travel books. With myself as comic hero. That's what turned the trick, my cottoning on to myself as sheer farce. So there I am, *Bungling Through Bombay, Toiling Around Turkey, Pootering Through Portugal* –

Simon Pottering that must be, mustn't it? Pottering through –

Jeff No, no, no. Pootering. Pootering. He's what gave me the impetus, re-reading his diary for a piece in one of the shittery reviews, dear old Pooter, my mentor, my golden goose, my inner doppelgänger – when I'm abroad I become him, you see – it's so bloody simple. I load myself up with compass, maps, binoculars, hire a bicycle – everything Pooter would do. They're sagas, you see, my books. Sagas of small catastrophes. I tumble into sewers, have rows in restaurants, mistake police cars for taxis – write up my diary every night. When I get home turn my diary into a book. On from there. Television rights, serial rights in dailies and Sundays, a film deal on the horizon –

Simon (*meditatively*) Actually. When you come to think of it –

Jeff What?

Simon Well, it's really rather brave of you. To make a living by courting misadventure.

Jeff Yes, it is. A risk a minute. But I enjoy it. And so do my fans. Like your brother and his family. They sit on their arses grinning and chortling their way through all my accidents and mishaps –

Sound of car drawing up. Car door opening, closing. Feet on gravel.

And here she is. Speaking of fans. One of your biggest,
Simon. Though I'm not sure you've ever met. But I've
told her so much about you over the years –

*Gwendoline enters. She is carrying an enormous
bouquet, seems slightly unsteady on her feet.*

Gwynith darling, here he really is. Just as I promised.
Simon, my wife Gwynith. Gwynith, my dearest and
oldest Simon.

Gwendoline Who?

Jeff Simon. This is Simon, darling.

Gwendoline Yes, hello, Simon, but – (*to Jeff*) who the
hell do you think I am?

Jeff What?

Gwendoline You just called me Gwynith. Who's
Gwynith?

Jeff I don't know. I'm sorry, darling. A Welsh invention
of Simon's –

Simon Yes, my fault, I'm afraid. I confused your name
with one of Jeff's many old mistresses. Actually one who
never existed in the first place. Being Welsh. (*Little pause.*)
Or so Jeff tells me. (*Little pause.*) Have I got that right?

Jeff Yes, obviously I couldn't get Gwynith out of my
head, once you'd planted the name, Simon. Much safer
to stick to 'darling', eh, darling, whoever one's with –
even a chap. Especially a chap. (*Laughs awkwardly.*) So.
You OK, darling?

Gwendoline No, I'm not OK. Not at all OK, darling.
I was just pulling out of the pub –

Jeff The pub? Why the pub, darling? You were going to
the gardening centre –

Gwendoline But the best place to park, as it turned out, was outside the pub. (*Lurches slightly.*) I walked to the centre from there. Then walked back. Arms full of potted shrubs, these – (*shakes bouquet*) got into the car, backed out, just as some bloody fool in one of those antiques you can sleep the babies and the cats in – haven't seen one since I was a toddler, almost – (*Lurches again.*)

Jeff A Dormobile, you mean?

Simon Oh. My brother's got one of those. Stephen.

Gwendoline There was this face, snarling out of the window. Shaking his first. Honking his bloody horn. Complete lunatic. Missed my rear end by a whisker. Last thing you'd expect down here. A loony in a dormothing driving at twenty miles an hour and nearly killing you. I could be dead.

Jeff (*watching her closely*) Oh, darling, you haven't, have you?

Gwendoline stumbles a little, backwards. Sits down on sofa.

Gwendoline No, I mean it. (*To Simon, avoiding Jeff's scrutiny.*) Dead. (*Looks down at bouquet.*) Oh, this is for you. No, no, for your Beth. I wanted to put these on her grave, Sam. Or for you to, Sam.

Jeff Simon. He's Simon, darling.

Simon takes flowers, bows slightly, puts them on table.

Simon That's very kind of you. I'll see that she gets them.

Jeff Oh Christ, forgive me, Simon. I meant to start with Beth. And apologise for not making the funeral. Actually, I didn't even know she was dead until I got it from Davina.

Gwendoline Davina? Who's Davina, darling?

Jeff Nobody, nobody. Just a piece of slag Simon and I knew once. Simon published a book of hers about some English colonialists in the Congo who stewed up a few Africans and ate them – something like that. *Boy's Own* stuff, really. She's clawed and fucked her way to the top, though, head of series at the BBC, bought the rights of Bombay, Turkey and Samoa. So I have to see her from time to time. And what a sight she is! Fat. Well, portly, anyway. Spectacles hanging around her neck. Mole on her chin. Waddles. You'd be shocked, Simon – wouldn't recognise her even if she took her top off. Probably especially if she took her top off. But Christ, what tits she had! Those were the days, eh? All that passion spent. No, wasted. Sorry to cram all this in like this, Simon, dreadfully sorry about Beth, a great lady, one of my favourites, but darling –

He's been glancing apprehensively at her through this speech, clearly not listening to himself.

We should be going, we've confirmed Simon's still alive. Time to move on. Plymouth calls. Where are the keys? I'll drive.

Gwendoline Took her top off for you, did she? No bra, I suppose.

Jeff Not then. Not that summer. The summer they stopped wearing them, which was the summer before they started burning them. You remember the summer, darling, you were around then after all. Well, Simon, thanks very much for letting us have a look at you – now darling, let's move arse.

Gwendoline I'd like a drink please, Sam.

Jeff Simon, his name's Simon, and darling if you don't mind –

Gwendoline Drink please, I said. Scotch. Another Scotch, please.

Simon hesitates, glances at Jeff.

Now, please. Without furtive looks and glances –

Simon goes to drinks table, picks up malt whisky bottle, full, and glass.

Jeff You stopped off in the pub, on the way to the gardening centre, didn't you? Then stopped off again on the way back, didn't you? The pub. The bloody pub!

Simon (*handing over her drink*) There you are.

Gwendoline (*to Simon*) So what happened with the bare-boobed Davina, before she developed her wart and waddle?

Simon I've no idea. (*To Jeff.*) What happened?

Jeff Christ, I don't know. Only what you told me. Or she told me. All I know is that it was at your place. I threw my drink over her and left, she took off her top because I'd soaked it, then strutted around negotiating a fuck or a book contract. Or both. According to you. Or according to her. Whichever one of you told me.

Gwendoline (*to Simon*) And how did the negotiations end?

Simon Well, I must have published the book. At least Jeff says I did. But then I published so many books without noticing them really, that I – cannibal stew in the Congo, was it, Jeff? (*Shakes his head.*) As for the rest of it – my place, you say it happened? Then no. I don't think there would have been a fuck. Not in my place. Beth's and my place. Not our sort of style, really.

Jeff What does it matter whether there was a fuck, there have been millions since, this was all, Christ, a quarter

505

of a century ago, when I was in my prime. Now darling, for the last time, can we please –

Gwendoline In your prime? You're always in your prime as a bloody fraud. A quarter of a century on from your prime as a drunken wreck of a fraud, you're in your prime again, and still a bloody fraud. Drunk or sober, a bloody fraud. That's you. Fraud, fraud, fraud!

Jeff (*after a pause*) We fought – we struggled and fought – to stop ourselves putting ourselves through this sort of thing ever again in our lives. We've done the lot, all the clinics from the Minnesota treatment in Arizona to Soaks in Surrey, AA, Promise, Protect, therapy here, therapy there, therapy every fucking where, until we'd overcome – until I thought we'd overcome at last.

Gwendoline Overcome? (*Laughs.*)

Jeff Yes. (*Snarling.*) Overcome.

Gwendoline holds out her glass for a refill. Simon refills.

Gwendoline Overcome what?

Jeff Overcome that! (*Then bitingly.*) Thanks, Simon.

Simon Not at all. But you, Jeff. What about you? (*Offers bottle.*)

Jeff (*glares at him*) What's the matter with you, Simon? Don't you understand –?

Gwendoline Haven't overcome *us*. *Us* is the problem, not this. (*Raises glass to her lips, savouring the smell. Gulps.*) This – is – oh, my God – bliss. That's what this is. But why did I take up my bliss in the first place? I'll tell you why. To keep up with him. He taught me about bliss in a bottle. Then I had to give it up because he was going sober, so he could Pooter, Pooter his way to a fortune. And now I'm left behind in my bliss. All alone.

Jeff You're not all alone! You're bloody well not all alone! However much I wish to Christ –! (*Stops, brings himself under control.*) Look darling, let's get in the car, open all the windows, wing our way to Plymouth, they're expecting us both. You as much as me.

Gwendoline They're expecting me to sit there maternally, maternally watching you sign your fraudlings, your little fraudlings, your babies, that's what he calls his fraudlings of books, his 'babies'. (*Laughs.*) 'With best wishes, Jeff Golding,' he writes all over his babies and they pay twelve, thirteen quid – you know how he spawns these babies of his? I'll tell you. (*Nods.*)

Jeff Remember this. This is something private. Secret. Just between the two of us. Remember that, Gwynith. (*Little pause.*) Before you speak another word, darling.

Gwendoline Like sex, eh? Except I'm not there to take part in it. Nor is Gwynith. Nor your topless from the seventies. Nobody but you. Wanking away into your computer. In your luxury suite. In the most luxurious hotel in the capital of the country you're pretending to visit. When he goes out it's on to his balcony. Then down to the restaurant for a gorge, back up to his luxury suite, consulting guidebooks, maps, making up his little comedies about himself wandering hopelessly through places he's never seen in his life, would rather be dead than have to cycle or walk to – Fraud, fraud, fraud!

Jeff (*after a little pause, calm*) So what the hell. Simon knows that all biography is fiction, all fiction biography, and what does he care anyway, he doesn't read my books, he never read books even when he was publishing them, he just said so. So what the hell?

Gwendoline The hell for me is that we haven't fucked since you went sober to begin your first baby. Not a fuck in all these years, just your five babies. *Six* babies. Separate beds. Separate beds. Is the hell for me. Did you and your Beth have separate beds? (*To Simon.*) Did you go on fucking, right to the end? Like man and wife – wife and man – did you?

Simon No. Though she did die in my arms, we weren't – (*Gestures.*)

Jeff How can you, how dare you – my oldest friend – he's my oldest and dearest and you reel in here and invade his past – Well, that's enough. I apologise, Simon. From the bottom, the very bottom –

Gwendoline Nowhere else for you to apologise from. No heart, no soul, all bottom.

Jeff I'm going. Are you coming or not?

Gwendoline Not. Bye-bye.

Jeff Can I have the car keys, please?

Gwendoline No.

Jeff Give me the keys!

Gwendoline (*shakes her head*) Go on, go and be a real explorer, fraud. Go and have lots of comic adventures on your way from down here to Portsmouth or wherever you're going, Pooter off and sign in a new baby –

She waves him away, turns to Simon.

She died in your arms. That's very moving. That's where people should die – not just in *your* arms, I mean, not all of us. But in somebody's.

Jeff lunges at her, tries to snatch the keys. There is a grotesque tussle, from which Jeff emerges, holding

508

keys. Gwendoline picks up drink, throws it in Jeff's face. Jeff reels back slightly.
Simon reaches into his pocket, takes out handkerchief, hands it to Jeff.

Jeff (*wiping his face*) Thanks, Simon. Thanks. Always there when needed, eh?

Makes to say something else, then puts his hand on Simon's shoulder, glances contemptuously at Gwendoline, goes out.
Sound of car door slamming, car driving off.
There is a pause.

Gwendoline Can I have another drink, please? I seem to have wasted the last one.

Simon pours her one.

I'm dry. Completely dry. So I haven't got an excuse for taking my clothes off. Have I?

Simon (*thinks*) I'm sure you don't need an excuse. If you have a reason. (*Little pause, then as if discovering.*) You know. I think the two may often be confused. Excuses and reasons.

Gwendoline And if I did take off my clothes, what would you do?

Simon Nothing.

Gwendoline Why not?

Simon I wouldn't have a reason for doing anything. Or even an excuse.

Gwendoline We'll see – see – if I can't give you an excuse. Or a reason even. (*Stands up, swaying.*) I've got good tits. *And* breasts. (*Fumbling at button on her blouse.*) I've got a good body all around.

Simon Still – still – you'd do better – you really would – to keep it to yourself.

Gwendoline Why? Why? Because of your Beth? We'd be defiling your place together, her memory? Is that it?

Simon No. No, no, Gwy— Gwu— (*Checks his confusion.*) My dear. My wife no longer has a memory to defile. At least as far as I understand these things. It's *my* memory that would make me behave – um – discourteously.

Gwendoline I think I'm going to cry at last. Thank God. If I can't have a good fuck then a good cry – (*Sits staring at him. Doesn't cry.*) Can't. Can't do that either.

Simon I'm very sorry.

Gwendoline (*gulps down drink*) Well – I've had my bliss. That's it then. You want me to go, don't you?

Simon Not at all. Though I was wondering how you intended to proceed. To Penzance, I mean. For the book signing. Shall I call you a cab? There's bound to be a train for somewhere. From the nearest station. Which I think is – is that way. (*Points vaguely.*)

Gwendoline I don't need a train. All I have to do is totter down to the pub and there he'll be, toying with his soda water. Or Diet Coke. Waiting for me. We'll scuffle about for a bit, he'll drag me to the car, open the windows, just as he said, and we'll be off to – to – it's Portsmouth, not Penzance. (*Little pause.*) Plymouth. For the baby signing. I love him, you know. Love him to bits.

Simon Yes. I've seen.

Gwendoline And he's the same. Loves *me* to bits.

Simon I've seen that too.

Gwendoline Sometimes in my sleep I try to kill myself. To get him over with.

Simon takes her arm, guides her to the French windows.

Simon And yet there he is. Down at the pub. Dieting off his Coke, waiting for you, not over with. I wish I could accompany you. But it seems to be one of those days. Who knows who else might turn up? I certainly don't. So I've got to stay here, haven't I? Oh, just a minute. You mustn't forget these.

He gives her her bouquet with a little bow.

Gwendoline Thank you. Thank you, kind sir.

She reels out. Simon turns away.
There is the screeching of tyres, slamming of car door. Greg enters. He is carrying two carrier bags.

Simon Oh, not you. I've already had you, surely.

Greg Who was that?

Simon Mmm?

Greg That stupid bitch. Looked pissed to me. Didn't know where she was going. I nearly ran her over. Right there, on the drive. And she didn't even notice that she'd be dead if I hadn't – (*Makes dramatic steering wheel motions with carrier bags.*) Who was she?

Simon Just a passer-through. What can I do for you – (*thinks*) Greg?

Greg What? Oh well, she wasn't up at the pub, my Mandy, I thought she might have come back down, but all there was was these – (*indicating carrier bags*) and a note saying that the small package inside is your supper, and you've got to put the rest in your fridge because ours is defrosting, it's for her and me to get us through the next few days. (*Puts bags on floor.*) She wanted me to pay up, old Gertie Cambad did, but I explained it had to go on your account until I've sorted out who owes what –

Simon Greg, isn't there a matter of five hundred we haven't settled? Pounds I think –

Greg (*crashing in*) Where, where, where, that's what I want to know, where is she, what's she up to? Is she seeing somebody, is that it? I've been driving around and around and what do I get, not a sight of her – and nothing to drink even, she always gets me a bottle when there's football, and there's football tonight, that's the one thing I've always counted on her for – a bottle of something for my football.

> *Simon picks up Gwendoline's malt, throws it casually to Greg, who catches it adroitly.*

Greg (*looks at it suspiciously*) What is it? Oh, well, I suppose I can make do with it – but I tell you the picture of my Mandy trampling through some field or other, ending up in a ditch in the rain –

Simon But it's not raining. So at least it'll be a dry ditch –

Greg I could kill her! I can't go on like this – all this worrying and fretting, fretting and worrying, I can't, it isn't human, it isn't! But how do I stop myself? What do I do?

Simon Go back to the house. Once the football's on, put your feet up and glug happily away at your bottle – by the time you've finished it you won't notice whether she's there or not.

Greg Right! – If you say so, that's what I'll do. You're the boss man around here – (*Goes towards French windows.*) Oh, don't forget to put our stuff in your fridge, or she'll kill you, Mandy will. (*Goes out.*)

> *Simon looks at shopping bags, picks them up. Voices off. Greg reappears.*

Somebody outside, asking for you – in here.

He nods to person off, goes, as:
    Wood enters. He is in his early thirties. Wears a run-down memory of a suit, Oxfamish. He is carrying two carrier bags.
    Off, sound of car door slamming, car starting up, off, as Simon and Wood size each other up, each holding their two carrier bags.

Wood Mr Hench?

Sound off, of car departing.

Simon Yes?

Wood I'm Wood. Julian Wood.

Simon starts slightly.

Does the name mean anything to you?

Simon Wood? (*After a little pause.*) How do you spell it?

Wood Usual way.

Simon That would be W-o-o-d, would it?

Wood Yes it would.

Simon Then no, it doesn't. The only Wood I knew was a long time ago, back when I was an undergraduate at Cambridge. But he spelt it V-u-l-d-t. He was German. Professor of Anglo-Saxon. Nothing memorable about him at all. Apart from the way he pronounced his name. As opposed to the way he spelt it.

Wood Nothing familiar about my face, either, eh?

Simon No. Should there be?

Wood Well, it's a matter of how you see faces. This face. That face. What's triggered off in you when you see them. (*Little pause.*) I'm here to enquire into your relationship with a seventeen-year-old woman called Joanna. You bumped into her briefly once, is my understanding.

Simon Really? When?

Wood Thirty-one years ago. To the day.

Simon (*laughs*) Really, young man! Do you think you can burst in here out of the blue, clutching a pair of carrier bags – (*suddenly aware of his own carrier bags, puts them down*) interrupting the meditations of my Sunday afternoon to ask me whether I can remember some – some – from thirty-one years ago? Really, young man!

Wood Is that your way of saying you do?

Simon No. It's my way of saying I don't.

Wood Just a minute. Just a minute. (*Puts down own carrier bags, fumbles through one of them.*) I've got something here that might help you.

Takes out pistol, points it towards Simon.

Curtain.

Act Two

Curtain up on exactly same scene, Wood and Simon in exactly the same postures. There is a pause.

Simon Help? Help? (*Looking at pistol.*) In what respect, help?

Wood Help you to remember. Help you to answer a few of my questions.

Simon Fire away.

Wood Joanna. She was an art student, seventeen and living with an older man. Much older. His name was Strapley. You and Strapley knew each other from school. The famous public school you went to. Wundale. Does that ring any bells, Mr Hench? The name Strapley?

Simon Little bells perhaps. But little bells only. Very little ones. (*Pauses as he thinks.*) Strapley, Strapley – there's an association. Masturbation. Masturbation Strapley! I seem to recall a Masturbation Strapley. Though dimly. Is that who you mean?

Wood Except that he wasn't Masturbation Strapley. He was Wanker Strapley. But still, we're getting somewhere at last, aren't we?

Simon I hope so. (*Little pause.*) But where, exactly, are we getting?

Wood To a state of calm. Calm. How about you, Mr Hench?

Simon I was perfectly calm before we began our talk, thank you. Even calmer than I am now.

Wood Joanna. This Joanna of yours wanted to do pictures for books. She went around all the publishers with her port— her port— (*Wags gun in frustration.*)

Simon Folio. Portfolio.

Wood But I know where she ended up. That's the important part of it. In your office is where Joanna ended up. Stretched over your desk. Or on your couch. Or on your carpet. While you bumped into her, Mr Hench. Bumped and bumped. Into her. And Strapley, Wanker Strapley – Strapley, the Wundale Wanker – who'd left his wife, his two sons – Rhona, she was called, Rhona, never – now she never – (*stops, attempts to find words*) never 'recovered from the blow'. Those are the words. It was cancer that got her out of it. Yes, cancer. And two sons abandoned – two – two sons! – because of your Joanna. (*Stops.*) Because of her, this seventeen-year-old. Who wouldn't even marry him. So he changed his name to hers to make them respectable in the neighbourhood where he leased a flat for her. On her account. Threw his own name, his very identity, away on *her* account. And leased a flat on his account. On her account. So that's what he was, this Wanker. Wanker Strapley, the Wundale Wanker. Just somebody for you to laugh at, Mr Hench. Sad and lonely. A sad and lonely man abandoning everybody who loved him because of a seventeen-year-old art student called Joanna! While she was doing the rounds of the likes of you with her port— port—

Simon – fol— (*Stops himself.*)

Wood Yo – yo – yo, Mr Hench. Port – fol – ee – yo – yo-yo. Is that it? Portfolio?

>   *Simon nods.*

Tracked her to your office. He knew at once what had happened. *You* had happened. Admitted it to him. Yes. You admitted it to him, Mr Hench. No shame. No – no –

at what you'd done. Nothing. Perhaps you apologised. Who knows? Do you know? Did you apologise? When he went back to his flat. Her flat. In her name. Paid for by him. What did he find? A message on the answering machine. A message from Joanna, the Joanna you'd just fucked on your sofa, your carpet, your desk, the Joanna that he adored and you'd just fucked, saying she'd never loved him, she'd only stayed with him because she was sorry for him, because of the sacrifices he'd made for her, the sacrifices of his wife, his two sons, 'hadn't known how to get out of it' was her phrase, 'out of it', but now she'd fallen in love for the first time in her life, fallen in love with you, Mr Hench, she understood – understood what 'being in love was' – he listened to it twenty times, fifty times, once. Once would be enough. Because once he'd had enough of it he shot himself. With this.

He flourishes the gun at Simon.

Simon I'm sorry. But if you can look at it from my point of view – can you try to do that? And therefore logically. I didn't kill your father. He killed himself. It was written into his stars. He can't have been called – (*slightest hesitation*) the Wundale Wanker for nothing.

Wood hurries to carrier bag, pulls out a pouch, shakes powder on to his hand, snorts frantically, shudders in painful ecstasy, relaxes visibly, blinks at Simon.

Wood She left a diary, your Joanna. A diary and some letters. I've got them here. You can have a little look. So that you know what I know is true. Old man Hench.

Holds out a carrier bag, peers into it himself, changes it for the other one, hands it to Simon.
Simon pulls out a mass of pages – pages on pages, envelopes, etc. He begins to read, with great rapidity and expertise.

That's fast. Very fast, Simon.

Simon (*still reading*) Used to be an editor. Had to read everything at high speed. Before I became a commissioning editor. Then I didn't have to read anything. (*Flicking through pages, concentrating.*) I've retained the apprentice's knack. (*As an afterthought.*) Julian.

> *Wood watches Simon as he goes on flicking the pages, suddenly screams.*

Wood That's enough, enough, you've seen enough to get the just of it.

Simon Gist of it. Yes, I have. (*Putting pages back into carrier bag.*) Julian.

> *Wood takes carrier bag from him. Puts it beside the other one. Sits down beside Simon.*
> *Simon is staring into a kind of vacancy.*

Wood Well, Simon?

> *There is a little pause.*

Well? Simon?

Simon A friend of mine, a very old friend, apparently my oldest friend, was saying just before you arrived that 'all biography is fiction. All fiction biography.' Julian.

> *Wood lets out a cry of pain. Simon looks at him.*

Wood (*muttering*) You'd better stop it with the Julians. I can't stand any more of your Julians. Makes me sound like your – your houseboy. Julian. (*Shouts.*) It's all true! You know it's all true! And the letters – the letters –

Simon I didn't read the letters. (*Reaching into bag.*) I assumed they were confi—

Wood Leave them! Leave them alone! (*Struggles with himself, then more calmly.*) One of the letters is written by you. Is that confi— confi— confi— to yourself? Or you didn't have to read it, because you remembered – eh, Hench? Mr Hench?

Simon I didn't recognise my handwriting on any of the envelopes. Most of the handwriting is flowery, affected, art-schooly –

Wood Her letters. Your Joanna's letters, you mean.

Simon She wasn't my Joanna. She's not there for me. And your wagging gun, your stuffing stuff up your nose, her diaries and letters, won't make her there for me. So, Mr Wood – Mr Strapley, to give you the name you belong to, you might as well shoot me. Or go. Or both. You won't change my memory, whatever you do.

Wood gobs, makes to spit gob into Simon's face, checks himself, swallows.

Wood You'd make a very civilised corpse, that's what you're thinking. I'd make sure you wouldn't look civilised. You'd be all over the place. (*Taps his skull with gun.*) This part of you, just like him, you'd look. Nobody could tell that part of you apart from that part of him. (*Gets up, walks around.*) Those letters she wrote to you, with the handwriting on the envelope, flowery, art-schooly, what was the other word?

Simon 'Affected', I think.

Wood You only opened the first one. The rest were returned – 'return to sender'. Unopened. Only the first one opened. And answered with a brief – a brief – (*thinks*) note from you. Ordering her to stop pestering you. What had happened on your desk, your sofa, your carpet, wherever it had happened, that was over. That was finis. Finis. Finis. The word. Finis. You enclosed a cheque for fifty pounds. 'This correspondence must close with the enclosed,' you wrote, didn't you? Finis, finis, finished, you wrote.

Simon Did I? If I did I was quite right. One always ends up paying for these things. Best to accept that and – (*little pause*) pay up. Those were different times, Jul— (*stops himself*) Mr Wood. Or Strapley. As you prefer. You must understand that those were different times. A different age. Sex happened when the mood took one. Only VD to worry about. And there were pills for that. (*Little pause.*) Before your time. Long before your time.

Wood Not long before my time. The beginning of my time, is what it was.

> *Begins to hum what becomes shortly 'Institutional Baby', stops.*

You didn't even bother to read her first letter, did you? You – you simply – scribbled out a cheque. For fifty pounds. Put your name to it. Finis. All over. Finished. Finis.

Simon I wonder if you'll understand this. Try and understand this. Sometimes, one used to find that an encounter that had been casually undertaken – as with this young art student – casually undertaken and satisfactorily concluded – (*gestures*) mutually casual, mutually concluded on one side, *my* side, wasn't thought to be concluded, wasn't thought to be casual or mutual, on the other side. *Her* side. (*Little pause.*) There were a few young women about, you see, who appeared to be the very embodiment of the times who turned out not to be in the *spirit* of the times. They had, poor souls, old-fashioned hearts. Young bodies. Strong desires. Old-fashioned hearts. She must have been one of those. In the world. Not of it.

Wood So you just cut her out. That was your system, was it?

Simon Much kinder than tears, explanations, recriminations. Surely, Julian, you understand that much?

Wood Kinder to yourself at least. I understand that much, Mr – Mr –

Simon Simon.

Wood Hench. Mr Hench. And so the fifty pounds was a – a – What was it, Mr Hench?

Simon A generous solution to a difficult case, Julian. After all, fifty pounds was quite a sum in those days.

Wood So. (*Little pause.*) That was the end of it for you, was it, Si? Fin— fin— the end? A fuck followed by an insult. You never thought, not for a second thought, there'd be further con— con— con— the word. What's the word?

Simon (*thinks*) Consequences. Could it be consequences, Julian?

Wood Like my – myself, Hench. Mr Hench. Simon. My father. I'm the con— con— con—

Simon (*automatically, dully*) – sequence. You're *my* son, then? Not Strapley's? Wanker Strapley's? Is that it? Your story? What it amounts to?

Wood (*nods*) Yes, your son. Not the Wundale Wanker's. (*Laughs.*) Yours. Finis. Finished. Because of you, because of you and her I've spent time, all my time, in instit— instit—

Simon makes to speak. Wood halts him with gun.

Wood – tutions. Institutions. Prisons. Yes. Mental bins. Yes. I wrote a song. 'Institutional Baby.' (*Begins to sing.*)

Here I am
Institutional baby!
Mama Jo!
Find a home!
For your in-stit-ution-al baby.

She put me in an orphanage, your one-fuck Joanna.
Took me back. Got me into care. Got me back. Here's
another one. Listen to this. My 'Yo-Yo Boy.' (*Croons
screechingly.*)

Yo-Yo boy.
Yo-Yo Boy!
Just another Yo-Yo?
Portofol – ee – yo –
Boy – y – y – y.

And here's another one –

Points the gun at Simon to shoot him.

Goodbye Daddy,
So Long Daddy –
Here's the end –
Here's the end for Daddy –

*Simon folds his arms, hands beneath his armpits,
waiting for shot.*
    Sound of car drawing up. Door slamming.
Footsteps on gravel.
    *Wood folds his arms, concealing gun underneath
armpit as:*
    Stephen enters.

Stephen Simon!

*Stops, seeing Simon, Wood, facing each other, arms
folded, in identical postures.*

Oh, sorry, I didn't know you had a guest.

Simon That's all right, Steve. You're not interrupting anything of – of consequence.

Wood I'd better be going. On my way.

Stephen looks at the two figures, in identical postures, to Wood.

Stephen Don't I know you? You remind me of somebody – I know! From school! Strapley! Can that be – Are you related by any – Wanker of Wundale? (*Laughs.*) Sorry. Sorry. But if you are related by any –

Wood (*cutting across him, to Simon*) Thank you very much for your time.

Shaking slightly, he goes to Simon's carrier bags, slips gun in, picks them up.

And for your help – all your help –

Walks to the door, then runs out, full tilt.

Stephen Well, then, who was he?

Simon Oh, just an itinerant. Asking for directions.

Stephen Where to?

Simon I don't know. I don't think he knew either. The world being so vague and chaotic – But what brings you back, Steve? I thought you'd gone. Weren't you – (*thinks*) on your way home? To bad news. Or – or –

Stephen (*laughs jubilantly*) That's what I thought too. But nothing could be further from the case. I stopped at the first service station to make that phone call – no, not *that* one – to the school. I told myself not to be a coward, and phoned Teresa. Took the bull by the horns, in fact.

Simon And?

Stephen The police have decided not to press charges!

Simon The police? Really? I didn't know the police –

Stephen No, no, perhaps I didn't mention the police aspect. More than I could face mentioning, even to you, Si. But anyway, now I'm in the clear, I don't mind facing up to it. I could have gone to jail, you see.

Simon Well, that's certainly something to celebrate.

Stephen The rest is really just icing on the cake. I'm not being sacked, with dishonour. I'm being pensioned off.

Simon Oh, good!

Stephen True, I'm not getting my full pension. But we can stay in the house until the end of next term – that's three months, which will give us time to look around. Adjust to circumstances. What's a bit of belt-tightening compared to the prospect I was facing an hour or so ago? And there are the children, Harry, Tom, Henrietta – the grandchildren too, to revel in. Not a cloud in the sky. Except penury. (*Laughs.*)

Simon (*after a pause*) How many miles did you drive? Before driving back again?

Stephen Why?

Simon Don't know, really. Just wondering. Trying to imagine your – your journey. So – so fraught with anxiety – How far did you get?

Stephen But I've told you. To the first service station. The first telephone.

Simon Ah! (*Nods.*)

> *There is a pause.*

Stephen Ah? You're not in the slightest bit interested, are you? I've come all the way back to share the best news of my life, and you – you couldn't care less, could you?

Simon Of course I could. I could certainly care less, Steve. Really.

Stephen If you cared less, you'd be wishing me positive harm. Yes, you would. Well, here's something else you should know. About you and your fashionable, successful, smirking friends. I saw him on the road. Coming towards me.

Simon Which one?

Stephen The one I just met again. The famous writer. Here. In this very room. His car was swerving all over the place, he had some woman with him. I just managed to swing around him. Thank God nothing was coming in the opposite direction, or I'd be a – a –

Simon Pensionless goner.

Stephen What?

Simon Who was driving, did you notice? He or some woman?

Stephen What does it matter? Why did I do it? Why did I bother to come back?

Simon I don't know. Why did you?

Stephen I don't know either. Because you're my brother. The brother I never had.

Simon And you don't know who was driving, Jeff or some woman –

Stephen To hell with you, Si. To hell with you at last.

Simon That would seem an appropriate place to –

Stephen turns, exits. Greg simultaneously enters.

Greg (*looks over his shoulder*) What's the matter with him this time? Nearly trampled all over me.

Simon (*fixes Greg with a glassy smile*) Greg, isn't it?

Greg What do you mean, Greg isn't it? Course it's Greg!

Simon Well then, Greg, what do you want?

Greg Our nosh is what I want.

Simon The football's over, the bottle finished –?

Greg (*shaking his head*) Fuck the football. She could get home any moment, she'll be hungry – She needs her food more than ever, you know that – (*Sees carrier bags.*) Not in the fridge, you didn't put them in the fridge, then? (*Picks up carrier bags.*)

Simon No. I'm sorry. I've had a stream of visitors –

Greg (*peers into carrier bags*) They'll be melting away. What's this?

Takes out Wood's gun, bits of diary.

And this, what's this?

Takes out Wood's heroin kit from other bag.

What's all this then?

Simon His paraphernalia.

Greg What? Whose what?

Simon Listen – (*Gestures.*) Listen – um –

Greg Greg. Greg's the name. Greg.

Simon Yes. Listen, Greg. All that has nothing to do with you. They're his.

Greg Whose?

Simon His. I've told you.

Greg I could go to the police with this lot. (*Drops carrier bags contemptuously.*) But they'd probably blame me for these, that's the way they are, the police. And you'd back them up – that's your type, your – your style! Pig! (*Exits.*)

Stephen (*enters, looking over his shoulder*) What a rude, aggressive young thug of a man he is, he virtually pushed me out of his way. But that's what comes out of your household these days, Simon, isn't it? Rabble.

Simon So you're back already. Before you've left, really, um – I noticed I didn't hear your car –

Stephen I've been sitting in it. Thinking. Thinking, thinking, thinking.

Simon (*after a little pause*) Have you? What about?

Stephen Oh, you mainly, I suppose, Simon.

Simon Then I'm very flattered. Given all your many problems – that you should spare a thought –

Stephen They were both driving.

Simon What?

Stephen Your fashionable friends. That's all you were interested in when I came in here a few minutes ago, teeming with good news about my future – all you wanted to know. Which of them was driving. Well, they both were. They were grappling with the steering wheel – death on the road if ever I saw it. Your friends, Simon. Just like that young man – your employee, Simon – who nearly knocked me over. Doesn't Teresa mean anything to you? My children, your nephews and niece. My grandchildren, your – your –

Simon Great nephews and nieces, they'd be, wouldn't they? Or grand. One or the other. Great or grand.

Stephen Well? Do they or don't they?

Simon (*thinks*) What should they mean?

Stephen That's not for me to say. It's for you to say.

Simon I don't really know what they mean, um – Steve. If they have a meaning it's – (*gestures*) escaped me. People are. If you see. Rather than mean. If you follow. However related they might – might –

Stephen Do you know what Beth said, just before she was taken? Sorry! *Died.*

Simon Yes. I was there. So I know exactly what she said. And as we were alone, she and I, you weren't there. So you haven't the slightest idea what she said. And I don't want to hear anything she might have –

Stephen She said – what she said to Teresa – she said, a month before we knew –

Simon Steve!

Stephen – any of us knew that she was ill. She said –

Simon I don't want to hear, Steve. I – don't – want – to – hear!

Stephen She said she wished she'd had that baby. Even if it was by another man. A man into whose arms you drove her. With your casual infidelities, your cool, predictable rationality. Your deadness of spirit. 'Yes,' she said. 'Yes. If you'd been a father, even if it wasn't your own child you were father of, you might have learnt how to live a life.' So what a tragedy – a tragedy that she lost it.

Simon She didn't 'lose' it. It died. As it was being born it died.

Stephen You've never given a thought, have you, to what you've done to other people? People who loved and needed you. Not least your Beth, whom we all loved and –

Simon Enough! That's enough, Stephen. Enough talk of babies, children, lives, unwanted deaths, unwanted lives – your mess is your mess, your muddle yours. It's nothing to do with me whether you molested a boy in the changing rooms, whether you're up before a beak, you're only my brother by some unnatural law of nature, beyond the comprehension of both of us. Go, please. Please go.

Stephen (*incredulously, after a pause*) You're throwing me out?

Simon No. No, of course not. I'm merely asking you to leave. Forthwith.

Stephen Very well. I'll go. Forthwith. Forth – I'll go. With.

Simon (*generously*) Thank you, Stephen. Thank you.

Stephen But don't expect me to forget this. Or forgive it. This is the end between us – between you and Teresa, between you and Harry, Tom, Henrietta and their children –

Simon (*moans, in a kind of relief*) Yes. If you say so. The end. Thank you.

Stephen You – you deserve everything you get.

Simon Everything I deserve, I've got.

Stephen Good! Good! I'm glad to hear it! To think I once called you brother!

> *He goes out as:*
> *Mandy enters, heavily pregnant.*

Mandy (*dully*) Yo-ho, motherfucker.

Simon (*suddenly alive*) Yo-ho, Mandy. You're not in a ditch, then? Not that I thought you were, of course.

Mandy What ditch would I be in? Spent the whole day avoiding him as he went speeding round corners in that car of yours. Swarming into the pub, the shop, picking up meals. So yo. So ho. Motherfucker. Don't know where he is. Looking for me is where he is.

Simon I gather he's up at your house. Watching the football. So I gather – (*Pause.*) You still haven't told him?

Mandy Told him what? That you used to grab me and have me while I was down on my knees swabbing your hall floor?

Simon Yes, I know. I'm sorry. I was in love with you and therefore a little – shy, you see. I didn't know how else to go about it. In the old days I would have found a different – more graceful – method, I'm sure. At least I hope so.

Mandy And now I've got a baby that could be his, could be yours. Is that what you want me to tell him, old man?

Simon Yes, tell him. I don't care whether it's mine or his. Then you come here. Live with me.

Mandy No thanks. I've made up my mind. I'm staying down there with Greg. Where I belong.

Simon Why? What is he, that I'm not?

Mandy He is. That's what he is. And you're not.

Simon I'll try, Mandy. I'll really try.

Mandy That's not enough. Trying. You don't *be*. No, you don't. You just don't *be*!

Simon (*both calmly and desperately*) I need you both. You and the baby – you're all I've got. To the end of my life.

Mandy The end of your life, that's your business. You had your missus. She was a good lady, from what I could see of her. And hear of her. I liked our duets together, even if she was a bit flat from time to time and set my teeth grating. But you didn't love her from what I could see or hear of the two of you. Or if you did you didn't make much show of it. That's not for me.

Simon Let me have him. Or her. Whatever it is. I'm not particular. I'll take you both. Or all three. If they're twins. As you sometimes say they are. I'll give you all a good home – (*Gestures around.*)

Mandy You're proposing to me, is that what this is?

Simon I'm certainly making a proposal, from the sound of me.

> *Sound of car screeching up, car door slamming, footsteps angrily crunching. Greg enters.*

Greg Not a sign of her, not a – (*Sees Mandy.*) Oh, so there you are then, I might have known I'd find you when I didn't expect you, all over the place I've been.

Mandy So what about you and your football?

Greg How could I look at football when it's you I'm after? Well, come on, then – and I've got myself a bottle, which is more than you did for me.

Mandy Go and get our supper from the fridge then and let's be gone from here.

Greg It's not there. (*Gestures to Wood's carrier bags.*) This is what we got instead. A gun and lots of rubbish –

Simon Greg, there's something you should know.

Mandy No, there isn't, no, there isn't, there's nothing he should know.

Simon It's a business transaction, Mandy. Strictly between Greg and myself. It needn't concern you. That five hundred pounds we were discussing –

Greg I told you – I told you I'd pay you back when –

Simon No, it's another five hundred pounds. I want to – to contribute it to your family. Imminent family. Every month.

Greg gapes.

All you have to do in return is let me babysit. Preferably on a regular basis. I've suddenly discovered, you see, rather late, that I'm – um – rather fond of children after all.

Greg Five hundred pounds! To be let babysit! Is that the deal?

Mandy No deal, Greg, there's no deal. Our babe's not for letting. Or hiring out. We don't take any money from him except what we earn. You understand that, Greg? Or I'm off. (*To Simon.*) As for you, when I come up to clean and clear you up, I'll bring him or her with me. You can keep an eye on it, dandle it on your lap. But that's all you'll get.

Simon Thank you.

Mandy So come along with you. You to your football, me to a snooze. And I suppose we'll have to go to the pub for our meal.

Simon Allow me – allow me to treat you. To the meal. At the pub. As it's partly my fault –

Hand goes into pocket, fishes out some money.

Greg Still, we can discuss a rise . . .

Mandy No we can't. Come on with you, I said.

Wood erupts into the room, staring around wildly, with Simon's carrier bags.

Wood Where are they, where are –?

Sees them, drops Simon's carrier bags, goes to own with a moan of relief, checks contents.

Mandy These are ours, are they?

Picks them up, hands them to Greg.

There's lamb in there, chicken, butter, biscuits, cake – so we can eat at home after all.

Wood Yes, yes, all your filthy stuff. Killer foodstuff, animals slain, eggs pilfered – so guzzle, gobble, gobble, guzzle, cigarettes too, and you're pregnant.

Greg You don't speak to my Mandy like that, no you don't!

Goes to Wood threateningly.

I've seen inside your bags, I know what's in there. City trash is what you are! Look at you, trembling, shaking –

Mandy Home, I said! (*Wheeling him out.*) Home now. We've got everything we need.

They go out.
Footsteps. Sound of car screeching, then driving sedately off.
Wood is standing, holding carrier bags at his chest, protectively.

Wood Missed your chance then. To dispose of the evidence.

Simon (*looking at him, after a pause*) Is that all you came back for?

Wood What else should I come back for?

Simon To see me. To put it right. All of it right. At last.

Wood It can never be put right. I learnt that much.

Simon Yes. Yes, it can. Look, stay with me here. Let me look after you. Be a good father to you at last.

Wood (*laughs*) I don't need a father any more. You're too late. Old man.

Simon Well then, just be my house guest. Come and go as you please. I'll keep you supplied with – with whatever I need. I promise.

Wood What you need I can get for myself. Until I don't need it any more.

Jeff enters. His clothes are in tatters. He is scratched, bruised, etc., slightly stunned.

Simon Oh hello, Jeff. Here again. This – (*indicating Wood*) is my son.

Jeff (*ignoring Wood*) Hi. Can I have a drink?

Lurches over to table, grabs bottle, opens it, swigs.

Aaagh! (*Looks at label.*) Port. Christ!

Wood (*to Simon, having flicked a contemptuous look at Jeff*) Well, that's you for a lifetime. That's what you are, Dada. A once-in-a-lifetime experience.

Simon Wait! Where are you going, Jason? What will you do?

Wood (*stares at him*) 'Jason', 'Jason', the name's Julian, Dada. Julian Strapley. Son of the Wundale Wanker. (*Jabs two fingers at him, sticks out his tongue, goes.*)

Jeff (*taking this in, vaguely*) Didn't know you had a son. Thought you and Beth couldn't – or didn't want –

Simon He's not really my son. Just a – a – figure of speech, really. (*Taking Jeff in for first time.*) Well, what – how did you –?

Jeff (*picking up another bottle*) Gin. More like it. (*Opens it, gulps.*) Terrible business in the car. She wouldn't let go of the wheel, stamped on my foot on the accelerator, singing, shouting abuses, usual nightmare. Swerved into a fence, then while she was backing up, I threw myself out. Just in time. I don't think she even noticed – I could hear the sirens coming at her from all directions, a helicopter – she's for it this time. The slammer, a year or two at the least – and where does that leave me? Pootering up to jail during visiting hours? Unless she kills herself before they get her. (*Little pause.*) Poor Gwen. Poor old Gwen. I had to hitchhike back here, you know. A truck carrying fertiliser. Excuse the smell. (*Little pause.*) Didn't know what else to do. (*Gives a little laugh.*) Just like old times, eh, Simon?

Simon Yes. Yes, indeed. Old times. Look, Jeff, if you don't mind – there's a piece of music I was playing.

Jeff Fine. Fine by me.

Pours himself a glug of gin, downs it, slams glass down on table, carries bottle to arm of sofa, sits down.

Better than Plymouth, sober at a table, signing my frauds, eh? My babies – baby frauds. Poor, poor Gwen baby too.

Simon goes to CD equipment.

Oh, fuck! It's not *Parsifal*, is it? Please?

Simon *Parsifal*?

Jeff You used to play it. All the time. My own fault. I introduced Wagner to you at Cambridge. But I couldn't take him now. Particularly haven't got the stamina for *Parsifal* any more.

Simon Nor have I. No, this is the only thing I listen to these days. It's Beth, you see. Singing in the church choir. Just up the road. Ronnie – the vicar – made a recording a few years back. Thank God. She does a duet with – with um – the mother of my – my –

Jeff I didn't know Beth could sing.

Simon lets out a terrible howl of grief and rage. Jeff looks towards him, perplexed.

You all right?

Simon Yes, fine, fine. She's a bit flat from time to time. But we won't mind that. Will we, Jeff?

Jeff Of course we won't. (*Raises bottle to lips.*) Of course not, Simon.

Simon turns switch. Church choir, Beth and Mandy singing their duet.
Simon sits, still and stiff, controlling himself. Jeff swigs contentedly from bottle as:

Curtain.